Learning in Economics

Contributions to Economics

Further volumes of this series can be found at our homepage
http://www.springer.de/cgi-bin/search_book.pl?series=1262

Frank Riedel
Imperfect Information and Investor Heterogeneity in the Bond Market
2000. ISBN 3-7908-1247-1

Kirsten Ralf
Business Cycles
2000. ISBN 3-7908-1245-5

Michele Bagella/
Leonardo Becchetti (Eds.)
The Competitive Advantage of Industrial Districts
2000. ISBN 3-7908-1254-4

Frank Bohn
Monetary Union and Fiscal Stability
2000. ISBN 3-7908-1266-8

Jaime Behar
Cooperation and Competition in a Common Market
2000. ISBN 3-7908-1280-3

Michael Malakellis
Integrated Macro-Micro-Modelling Under Rational Expectations
2000. ISBN 3-7908-1274-9

Stefan Baumgärtner
Ambivalent Joint Production and the Natural Environment
2000. ISBN 3-7908-1290-0

Henri Capron, Wim Meeusen (Eds.)
The National Innovation System of Belgium
2000. ISBN 3-7908-1308-7

Tobias Miarka
Financial Intermediation and Deregulation
2000. ISBN 3-7908-1307-9

Chisato Yoshida
Illegal Immigration and Economic Welfare
2000. ISBN 3-7908-1315-X

Nikolaus Thumm
Intellectual Property Rights
2000. ISBN 3-7908-1329-X

Max Keilbach
Spatial Knowledge Spillovers and the Dynamics of Agglomeration and Regional Growth
2000. ISBN 3-7908-1321-4

Alexander Karmann (Ed.)
Financial Structure and Stability
2000. ISBN 3-7908-1332-X

Joos P.A. van Vugt/Jan M. Peet (Eds.)
Social Security and Solidarity in the European Union
2000. ISBN 3-7908-1334-6

Johannes Bröcker/Hayo Herrmann (Eds.)
Spatial Change and Interregional Flows in the Integrating Europe
2001. ISBN 3-7908-1344-3

Kirstin Hubrich
Cointegration Analysis in a German Monetary System
2001. ISBN 3-7908-1352-4

Nico Heerink et al. (Eds.)
Economic Policy and Sustainable Land Use
2001. ISBN 3-7908-1351-6

Friedel Bolle/Michael Carlberg (Eds.)
Advances in Behavioral Economics
2001. ISBN 3-7908-1358-3

Volker Grossmann
Inequality, Economic Growth, and Technological Change
2001. ISBN 3-7908-1364-8

Thomas Riechmann
Learning in Economics
2001. ISBN 3-7908-1384-2

Nicole Pohl
Mobility in Space and Time
2001. ISBN 3-7908-1380-X

Thomas Riechmann

Learning in Economics

Analysis and Application of Genetic Algorithms

With 52 Figures and 4 Tables

Physica-Verlag
A Springer-Verlag Company

Series Editors
Werner A. Müller
Martina Bihn

Author
Thomas Riechmann
University of Hannover
Department for Economics
Königsworther Platz 1
30167 Hannover
Germany
E-mail: riechmann@vwl.uni-hannover.de

ISSN 1431-1933
ISBN 3-7908-1384-2 Physica-Verlag Heidelberg New York

Cataloging-in-Publication Data applied for
Die Deutsche Bibliothek – CIP-Einheitsaufnahme
Riechmann, Thomas: Learning in economics: analysis and application of genetic algorithms; with 4 tables / Thomas Riechmann. – Heidelberg: Physica-Verl., 2001
(Contributions to economics)
ISBN 3-7908-1384-2

Physica-Verlag Heidelberg New York
a member of BertelsmannSpringer Science+Business Media GmbH

Softcover Design: Erich Kirchner, Heidelberg

SPIN 10796530 88/2202-5 4 3 2 1 0 – Printed on acid-free paper

Preface

It took me over five years to write this book.

Finishing my research project and thus finishing this book would not have been possible without the help of many friends of mine. Thus, the first thing to do is to say 'Thanks a lot'.

This means at first place the *Evangelisches Studienwerk Haus Villigst*. They gave me a grant for my work, thus laying the important financial grounds of everything I've done.

There is such a large number of friends I worked and lived with over the last few years that I cannot possibly mention them all by name, but I'll try, anyway: So, thanks Christiane, Gilbert, Maik, Karl, and everybody else feeling that his or her name should appear in this list. And, of course, thanks Franz Haslinger, for letting me do whatever I wanted to — and for even encouraging me to stick with it.

One more thing I'd like to mention: Although this work is based on very heavy use of computer power, it is my special pride to say that not a single penny (i.e. Deutschmark) had to be spent for software in order to do this work. Instead, all that has been done has been done by free software. Thus, I would like to mention some of my most heavily used software tools in order to let you, the reader, know that nowadays you don't depend on big commercial software packages any more. Some of my favorite tools used for this book are the Linux operating system as the basic tool as well as the Emacs–Editor, the gcc compiler, Donald Knuth's and Leslie Lamport's LaTeX and friends, gnuplot and some traditional, though GNU pieces of software. Again: These tools are fabulous — and they're free.

As I know that it is the short preface which is the good preface, there is just one thing left for me to say, dear reader: Sit back, be patient with the author, and enjoy the book.

Hannover, November 2000 *Thomas Riechmann*

Contents

Part I. Introduction

Part II. General Analysis of Genetic Algorithms

Part III. Economic Applications and Technical Variations

List of Figures

List of Tables

List of Algorithms

Part I

Introduction

1. Introduction

Man is not perfect.

This – admittedly trivial – insight has up to now been applied to economics in a very limited extend. A large amount of work in theoretical economics concentrates on 'perfectly rational' subjects, who are sometimes even given the gracious gift of 'perfect foresight'. The main actors of theoretical economic models are often omniscient and omnipotent. Even more, subjects are assumed to be identical with respect to their preferences and aversions, their endowments and decisions and many things more.

These basic assumptions on theoretical economic models are in most cases justified for two reasons: First, these assumptions are said to be sufficient to explain the 'real world'. Economists mostly admit that their models are largely simplifying. Nevertheless, they claim the results of these models to be very close to what can be observed in reality. This reasoning is known as the 'as if' argument: Real people are admittedly neither fully rational nor identical to one another. But, some economists argue, in the end people behave *as if* they were. Thus, economists often focus on similarities rather than on differences.

The second justification of the severe theoretical simplifications is the following: If the simplifying assumptions were dropped, in most cases the economic models became intractable (which, in most cases means: mathematically intractable). Thus, economists *have to* introduce simplifications in order to keep the models handy.

The aim of this book is to find out if nowadays the simplifications are still necessary and if the two justifications mentioned above are still correct. This will be done by dropping the simplifying assumptions of perfect rationality and homogeneity of economic agents.

The role of perfect rationality will be taken over by learning processes: If agents do not know what to do, they must learn it. In the following, it will become obvious that this kind of learning cannot take place in a homogeneous society: Successful learning in a social context needs different kinds of behavior used by different kinds of agents. Thus, if the assumption of perfect rationality is dropped, it is inevitable to drop the assumption of homogeneity, too.

In traditional economics, the two assumptions of perfect rationality and homogeneity of agents are indeed often enough crucial for the mathematical tractability of models. In this book, though, tractability is preserved even though these assumptions are dropped. This becomes possible by the fact that this book will make use of a comparably new economic method: the modeling and analysis of economic learning processes by means of computational simulations, especially by means of genetic algorithms (GAs).

To put it in different words: The very heart of this book are genetic algorithms, or, more precise, an introduction into the structure of genetic algorithms, the analysis of their working principles, and the descriptions of modifications and applications of GAs to various economic problems.

The book consists of three parts. The first part contains a brief introduction into the central topics of the book, which are learning in economics and computational economics. The second part consists of some theoretical analysis of genetic algorithm learning. The third part shows some fields of application of economic GA learning models.

The first part is dedicated to learning and computational economics. The aim of this part is to show where in the context of current economic research the work of this book is placed. The central questions to be answered in this part of the book are 'What is the role of *learning* in an economic context?' and 'What is the role of computational economics and agent based simulation in modern economic theory?'.

A further section in the first part is a basic introduction into the economic modeling of learning processes with the help of genetic algorithms (Chap. 3). A simple economic problem is used to exemplify the basic elements needed to construct a model of economic GA learning. At this point, only a reduced version of a GA is presented, which in the further course of the book will be enhanced and extended. Nevertheless, the simple GA of this part will serve as reference GA throughout the rest of the book.

The second part of the book concentrates on general analysis of GA learning processes. GA learning will be interpreted and analyzed as a Markov process (Sect. 4.2), as an evolutionary process (Sect. 4.3), and as a process of complex social learning (Sect. 4.4). Each of these three topics reveals some *general properties* of GA learning. Each topic shows what kinds of results can be expected from economic models of GA learning and what kinds of results can never be achieved. Thus, the second part of the book develops an impression on the general capabilities as well as the limits of economic GA learning models.

The third part of the book consists of various applications of the concepts developed in the preceding parts. Different variants of GA learning models are presented, each of them applied to a different economic problem. Each section of the third part uses a technical modification of the basic GA, and each section develops a model of a specific economic problem. This allows for an impression of both, the wide range of technical variations of the basic GA and the broad field of economic questions that can be addressed. The first chapter of the third part (Chap. 6) shows a 'classical' modification of the basic GA, the election operator. In this chapter, election is contrasted with another modification, the operator of meta learning. The economic background of this chapter is a model of regional monopolies. The models of this chapter show phenomena well–known from evolutionary economics, i.e. historical lock–ins, the development of routines and inertia.

The next chapter (Chap. 7) deals with a simple cobweb model. Some modifications to the economic model and the GA learning process are shown to result in the occurrence of endogenous economic cycles and persistent heterogeneous social structures.

The third chapter of the third part (Chap. 8) presents a model of consumer choice. In order to address this problem, a GA is used to simulate decision on more than just one variable at the same time. It is found out that the quality of the behavior learned by the agents crucially depends on the learning techniques and the amount of rationality given to the agents.

The fourth chapter of Part three (Chap. 9) uses a two population GA in order to simulate learning in a model of overlapping generations with money. It is shown that the explicit introduction of heterogeneity in this model causes severe changes in the results compared to the 'classical' homogeneous overlapping generations models.

2 The Core Topics: Learning and Computational Economics

2.1 Learning

Learning in economics is one of the central topics of this book. Thus, it is necessary to explain what is meant by the term 'learning' in economics and in this book.

2.1.1 A Definition

A widely accepted definition of the term 'learning' is one by Kimble (1973, p. 116):

> 'Learning is a relatively permanent change in a behavioral potentiality that occurs as a result of reinforced practice.'

This definition contains four distinctive characteristics of learning:

Change: Learning means a *change* of the behavioral potentiality, but not necessarily an *improvement*. This means that learning alone does not always lead to a progress of behavior towards a certain goal.

Change in behavioral potentiality: Learning is no process which generally influences behavior. Learning only affects the behavioral *potentiality*, i.e. the stock of different behaviors an individual can choose to apply. The behavior actually used by an individual might, but needs not to be changed.

Relatively permanent change: Learning is a process which influences the behavioral potentiality for a comparably long time. Short term changes are not interpreted as results of learning.

Change as a result of reinforced practice: Learning causes changes in behavioral potentiality by practicing new behaviors. (This can also be done by the learning individual herself or by other persons. This can be done by practical application of the behavior or by just theoretically figuring out what consequences a certain behavior might have.) Possible 'inherited' behaviors are not considered as learned behaviors. The result of practicing behaviors is success or failure of the respective behavior. The basic principle of reinforcement is the following: Successful behaviors gain a greater importance within the pool of individually known behaviors, less successful behaviors lose importance and are practiced less often

2.1.2 The Necessity of Learning in Economic Models

In economics, there are two main reasons for the incorporation of learning processes in theoretical models: Learning as a means of equilibrium selection and learning as a consequence of bounded rationality.

Learning as a Means of Equilibrium Selection

The need for learning as a means of equilibrium selection is caused by a feature of certain economic models leading multiple solutions. Some of these models, although fully specified, cannot predict the resulting behavior of the agents, because they result in at least two outcomes equally likely, equally good, etc. An often referred to example is the model of overlapping generations with money:[1] Two generations of homogeneous agents choose their intertemporal consumption allocation. The only good in the economy is perishable. Savings can only be held in form of money. Money supply is constant over time. There are at least two stationary solutions to this macroeconomic problem: Either agents hold savings in form of money or money looses its value and there are no savings at all. Without further knowledge, modern economic theory cannot predict which one of the two solutions will be attained. The usual approach out of this dilemma is to introduce some kind of learning mechanism. This normally helps to determine a unique outcome of the model.[2] More generally, learning is often integrated in models that otherwise result in multiple equilibria, such that one of these equilibria can be clearly determined as the unique outcome of the model.

Learning as a Consequence of Bounded Rationality

The second reason for the integration of learning processes into economic models is much more far reaching. It is based on the necessity of dropping the assumption of perfect rationality, which leads to the concept of bounded rationality. An agent being only boundedly rational does by no way mean that she is irrational. In fact, being boundedly rational means behaving rational within the bound of individual skills and capabilities, and within the bounds of given behavioral possibilities. Boundedly rational agents do not generally know the optimal way of behaving in a given economic situation. This means that they have to learn a behavioral strategy performing as good as possible. Thus, the assumption of bounded rationality automatically implies the necessity of integrating learning processes into economic models.

As the concept of bounded rationality is of central importance in this book, it will be explained in greater detail. Bounded rationality of economic agents subsumes in

[1] The model can be found in e.g. McCandless and Wallace (1991), Blanchard and Fischer (1990) or Azariadis (1993).

[2] A GA learning version of the model described above can be found in Chap. 9.

fact three different types of cognitive restrictions on individual possibilities.[3] Those are:

- perceptional restrictions, i.e. restrictions on the capability of assimilating information,
- cognitive restrictions, i.e. restrictions on knowledge, and
- intellectual restrictions, i.e. restricitions on the capability and capacity of information processing.

In addition, there is a number of phenomena preventing optimal behavioral decisions that do not result from personal restriction of the deciding individual. These are mainly informational obstacles: Not every relevant information can be accessed by everybody, especially not at the same cost.[4]

According to Simon (1994), the theory of boundedly rational decisions differs from neoclassical decision theory in three respects. In neoclassical theory decision making is characterized by

- a given and unchanging space of alternatives,
- a known probability distribution for every possible alternative, and
- maximization of expected utility.

Whenever for a decision at least on of these three points is not given, it is a decision in the world of bounded rationality in the sense of Simon.[5] In an extreme case, the assumption of bounded rationality means dropping the assumption of utility maximization and thinking of agents only trying to satisfy some certain level of aspiration. This behavior is called 'satisficing'.[6]

The Concept of Minimal Rationality

Whenever in an analytical economic model the assumption of perfect rationality is dropped and bounded rationality is integrated instead, a conceptual problem arises: How much do the individuals within the model know, if they do not know *everything*? How much are they able to do, if not *everything*? The definition of bounded rationality is only a negative one. It is only known what is *not meant* by 'bounded

---

[3] Following Selten (1990) there is even a fourth restriction, the motivational restriction, which describes the phenomenon of not taking a certain action although this action has been intellectually recognized as the best one.

[4] This notion is also the basis of search theory, which apart from this point has no substantial connection to the theory of bounded rationality, see e.g. Phlips (1988).
Moreover, it is often stated, that many behaviors, routines and concepts are 'tacits', which cannot be learned by simple imitation. The ability to learn tacits requires much more sophisticate learning techniques.

[5] See Simon (1957, 1981, 1987, 1997). Other well–known supporters of this thought are Selten (1990, 1998) and Tiez (1990). A less clear concept of bounded rationality is formulated by Sargent (1993).

[6] Besides the works of Herbert Simon cited above there re many books and articles especially devoted to concepts of bounded rationality and satisficing. For recent literature, see Tisdell (1996) and Magnusson and Ottosson (1997).

rationality', but an explicit, positive general counter–concept to perfect rationality does not exist. This, of course, is a severe problem for researchers trying to integrate concepts of bounded rationality into their economic models. For this reason, this book chooses a relatively pragmatical way: As far as possible, a concept is used which can be at best described as a concept of minimal rationality. Agents are equipped with as little 'rationality' as possible. With the help of these very simple minded agents it is tried to find out if a sensible solution to the modeled economic problem can be derived. If this is the case, even very simple agents seem to be smart enough for the situation in focus. If it is not, some further 'rationality' has to be added. This procedure is repeated until a level of rationality is found, which is the minimal level of rationality necessary to solve the given economic problem.[7]

2.1.3 Methods of Describing Economic Learning

There are various types of learning techniques that can be employed in order to describe learning in economics, especially in analytical economic models. Above all, there are three different types of learning techniques: statistical learning techniques, learning modeled by game theory and learning techniques used in artificial intelligence.

Some of the statistical learning techniques are least square learning, Bayesian learning or learning by Markov processes. All of these have a common feature: Agents behave like econometricians, using econometric and statistical methods in order to make forecasts and by that, find the appropriate way of future behavior.[8]

The second group of learning techniques, namely game theoretic techniques, are essentially based on concepts from evolutionary game theory. The central feature of these group of techniques are replicator dynamics, which is a group of dynamic processes acting as the driving force of evolutionary processes. In the context of human learning rather than (biological) evolution, replicator dynamics describe the changes in frequencies of different behaviors in a population of agents. In their original form as can be found in the field of biological research, replicator dynamics are deterministic processes. This is one of the reasons why the interpretation of replicator dynamics as metaphor for economic learning processes is not undisputed among economic theorists.[9]

The set of learning techniques from artificial intelligence range from rather simple techniques like simulated annealing[10] to fairly complicated tools like neural

[7] Adding some rationality to the agents in this work mostly means improving the learning techniques used. An example is the introduction of 'meta–learning' in Chap. 6 or giving some memory to the agents like in Chap. 8.

[8] A survey of statistical learning techniques can be found in Sargent (1993). More details on Bayesian learning are given in Chao (1974).

[9] For descriptions of replicator dynamics, see e.g. Samuelson (1997) and Fudenberg and Levine (1998b) (or, in a shorter version, Fudenberg and Levine, 1998a). One of the critics is Mailath (1992).

[10] A simple 'construction manual' to this variant of hill climbing techniques can be found in Sangiovanni-Vincentelli (1991), a rigorous mathematical analysis in Rome and Sangiovanni-Vincentelli (1991).

networks[11], classifier systems[12], evolution strategies[13], genetic programming[14] and genetic algorithms.

Within this book, economic learning will mainly be modeled with the help of genetic algorithms (GAs). Nevertheless, in many of the following models, the GAs will be extended with some features of different learning techniques. An example can be found in Chap. 6. There, the concept of flexible mutation rates will be introduced, which originates from simulated annealing. Another example is the consumer choice model in Chap. 8, which integrates features of evolution strategies into a GA learning model.

The differentiation of learning techniques into three groups, as carried out above, is not very clear. In fact, to each of the groups, there are mathematical models showing some basic characteristics of the learning techniques belonging to it and the learning results gained by the techniques. So, if it is possible to show that one of the learning techniques of one group could be equally part of another group, than, for this technique, a number of additional methods for the analysis of the characteristics of this technique could be derived. By this, the respective learning technique can be analyzed and described in greater detail and with much more precision. Moreover, there is hope of getting more accurate predictions of the learning result a certain technique could be expected to produce. This, for example, has been done to neural networks, which — originally accounted for as a technique belonging to the group of artificial intelligence — have been shown to be a form of non parametric econometric estimators.[15] In the course of this work, genetic algorithm will be interpreted as a complex form of a Markov process (Sect. 4.2) as well as a special form of evolutionary game (Sect. 4.3). As a consequence, a number of analytical methods are derived, which support describing, analyzing, and predicting the behavior of genetic algorithms and GA learning processes in economics.

2.2 Computational Economics

This work is dedicated to the description and analysis of economic learning processes with the help of genetic algorithms. By the choice of GAs as learning techniques, the major part of this work can be assigned to the field of computational economics. Thus, a short description seems appropriate, of what computational economics *is* and what role this young branch of economic analysis plays in theoretical economic research.

---

[11] See, e.g. Haykin (1999).

[12] See Goldberg (1989) and Holland (1992) or a well commented economic application in Marimon et al. (1992).

[13] For a survey, refer to Bäck et al. (1991) and Chap. 8 of this book.

[14] Koza (1992) and Koza (1994).

[15] Again, see Haykin (1999).

2.2.1 Names and Definitions

Describing computational economics, the first problem comes with the name: In fact, there are currently lots of name for more or less the same field of research. In short, 'computational economics' can be seen as the generic term of all of the following terms. But, up to now, even this term has been hardly filled with a well defined meaning. Not even the editors of the 'Handbook of Computational Economics' (Amman et al., 1996) are able to deliver a precise textual definition. For the time being, computational economics seems to be the whole of scientific economic work that requires the use of a computer for more than just recording text and other data. In short: Everybody in economic research using the computer as more than just a typewriter, does computational economics. This, of course, includes a large number of activities, including statistical analysis and the solution of mathematical problems just as well as the simulation of economic processes.

As the simulation of economic processes will be a central element to this work, some more terms from this special field of computational economics will be explained. This book will particularly deal with the simulation of single agents' behavior. In the simulations, many economic units will act in parallel, influencing each other in their actions. This way of simulation of single economic agents has been coined with a number of different terms. As an example, Lane (1993a,b) calls this kind of simulations 'artificial worlds', while Tesfatsion (1997) speaks of 'ALife' (an abbreviation of 'Artificial Life'). The economic actors living in these 'artificial worlds' are called 'artificial adaptive agents' (Holland and Miller, 1991) or simply economic agents (Arthur, 1991, 1993). A general term for this group of simulation techniques, the term 'agent based computational economics' (ACE) seems to become the most commonly used phrase.[16]

In this book, the language will be the following: A single subject, acting within an economic model will be called 'economic agent'. The computational alter ego of the agent, i.e. the object implemented within the computer program, will be called 'genetic individual'. Of course, this term is a specific term for the type of simulation in use, which is the simulation by genetic algorithms.

2.2.2 The Role of Computational Economics in Economic Research

Apparently, computational economics and the technical development of computer systems are closely related with each other. The development of computers is the reason why computational economics is one of the youngest branches of economic research, but also one of the most rapidly growing ones.

There is a large number of facts indicating that computational economics is currently establishing as an important part of economic research. Some of these facts are the following:

---

[16] At the moment, there is no general literature to this field of economic research. Nevertheless, broad information can be found at the ACE–Home page at `http://www.econ.iastate.edu/faculty/tesfatsion/ace.htm`.

- In 1995, the Society for Computational Economics (SCE)[17] was founded, which, among others, holds a lively and growing annual international congress.
- The SCE publishes two important scientific journals, both dedicated to computational economics, which are the *Journal of Computational Economics* and *Section A: Computational Methods in Economics and Finance* of the *Journal of Economic Dynamics and Control.*
- There is a *Handbook of Computational Economics* (Amman et al., 1996).
- The growing importance of numerical simulation is proved by the appearance of a new textbook on this topic (Judd, 1998).

All in all, the discussion what role computational economics should play in the family of economic disciplines seems to have ceased.[18] Nowadays, the general opinion on this question seems to be that computational economics is not an economic *discipline* in its own right, but rather a new way of *formulating* economics problems and their solutions. Like other forms of description and analysis, e.g. the verbal, the mathematical, the graphical or even the game theoretic form, computational economics is not characterized by a specific question in focus, but by a specific way of finding answers. Like the other forms of description and analysis, computational economics has its own strengths and its own weaknesses. Computational economics is not a substitute to other kinds of economics, but a complementary method of economic research.

2.2.3 Agent Based Economics

The central method of this work, the simulation of economic processes by means of genetic algorithms, is a form of agent based economics. Agent based economics is based on computer aided simulations of the behavior of economic micro units, such as private households or firms. These micro units are coded as modules which are parts of larger computer programs.

Agent based economics is often seen as bringing together three formerly distinct branches of science, evolutionary economics, cognitive sciences, and computer sciences. This description is also true for large parts of this work, although some restrictions apply. First, gains from cognitive sciences are only referred to in a very intuitive way, often even without explicitly reflecting the results and meanings of their origins. Secondly, this work is not restricted to theories and results from evolutionary economics. Although returning to assumptions and insights from evolutionary economics, the main economic content of this work is based on the neoclassical tradition. This means that it is neoclassics which is the foundation of the analyzed models and it is neoclassics which represents one of the benchmarks used for the evaluation of simulation results. Third, it certainly took extensive computational work in order to prepare this book and the models in it. But this book is intended to be a primarily economic work. Consequently, computational work has

[17] The Internet Home page of the SCE can be found at `http://wuecon.wustl.edu/sce/`.

[18] Some landmark articles in this discussion are Judd (1997), Bona and Santos (1997), or — somewhat less pointed — Kydland and Prescott (1996).

only been documented in the minimal extent needed to understand the *economics*. In short: Computational work has only been documented if it seemed important to the *economist*.

It is important to stress that agent based simulations impose certain restrictions on the model builder, which are unavoidable consequences of this method. The most severe restriction lies in the fact that results gained by simulations only allow for *inductive* conclusions. More than this, there are two further restrictions which arise from the use of digital computers:[19]

- Force to discrete model building: While in analytical economic models the use of continuous representation is not unusual (e.g. models of dynamic processes in continuous time or the analysis of the behavior of a continuum of economic agents), on a computer, this is impossible. Building models of continua in an agent based model needs infinitely large computer capacities, which, of course, cannot exist.
- Force to finiteness: This second restriction is closely related to the first one: While in analytical models the time horizon (e.g. for dynamic optimization models) is often set to infinity or populations are analyzed which are infinitely large, agent based models cannot do this. The finite capacity of computers prevents the examination of infinitely large masses, the finite lifetime of researchers is a severe obstacle to the analysis of infinitely long running simulations.

2.2.4 Artificial Economic Agents

The central part of agent based economic research is the artificial economic agent. An agent of this kind is nothing more than a simple 'piece of software' intended to replicate human behavior in an appropriate way. Certainly, man as a whole is far too complicated (and too little understood) to have his behavior replicated completely and in total detail. Consequently, the aim of the construction of artificial agents is much simpler: Only behaviors important for solutions of specific economic problems shall be simulated. Thus, artificial agents, which can be very complicated 'beings', are nevertheless strongly simplified and abstract models of real life economic agents. Irrespective of the goal of its construction, every artificial agent has to be able to recognize certain events in its (artificial) environment, to analyze these events and to appropriately respond to them. An artificial agent is not an isolated being, it is usually included within a larger system consisting of more artificial agents as well as other elements, like governmental prescriptions, institutions etc. As a consequence of this description, there follows a certain structure of an artificial agent. An agent should consist of at least four elements: Receptors, effectors, a memory and a decision system.

[19] The term 'digital computer' is not a pleonasm: There are, in fact, analogue computers which, by their design, are not restricted to the digital representation of information. Some of the restrictions mentioned are no restrictions for these computers.

- *Receptors* are needed in order to receive information from the environment. This information could possibly be important for future actions of the agent. Thus, receptors are — very simplified — reproductions of the human senses.
- By their *memory*, agents are enabled to 'keep in mind' past information, the agents' evaluations of these informations as well as their own past actions and their perceived consequences. Thus, the artificial memory is a — very incomplete — reproduction of the human memory.
- The *decision system* determines the specific reaction to a the specific information an agent receives from the environment. This decision system plays the role of the human brain.
- *Effectors* are needed in order to realize the decisions formed by the decision system with the help of current and memorized information.

This type of modeling views humans primarily as information processing beings. Of course, this approach is very simplifying, but — as will turn out later — this philosophy leads to results which are very important in the context of economic research. Figure 2.1 shows the concept of an artificial agent in form of a data flow diagram, i.e. the arrows stand for the internal and external flow of information.

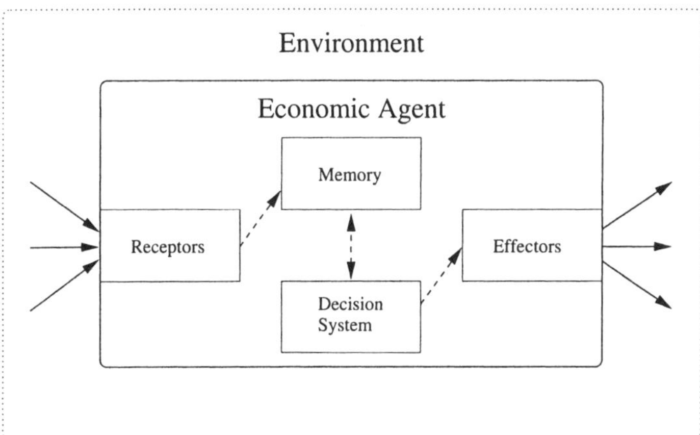

Fig. 2.1. General Structure of an Artificial Economic Agent

A simple example should help to illustrate this way of economic modeling. An economic agent who wants to buy a good is confronted with information about the availability of the good, its price, its quality etc. The agent receives this information with the help of its *receptors*. Then, the agent's problem is to buy a quantity of the good which causes the highest reachable degree of satisfaction under the restriction of the budget and the availability and desirability of other goods. The agent holds the *memory* of a similar past situation, i.e. having bought a certain amount of the good at a certain price which caused her a certain degree of satisfaction. Moreover, the agent *receives* information from some other agents about the quantity they bought as well as the price they had to pay and the amount of satisfaction they gained. Processing all this information in her *decision system*, the agent makes up her mind, what quantity to buy in the current period. The agent buys this quantities, using her *effectors*.[20]

The most important detail of the process described above, which certainly is mainly a decision process, is the decision system of the agent. This decision system can be modeled in various ways, employing very different levels of complexity and sophistication. In general, there are two different types of decision systems, static and dynamic systems. Static decision systems do not change over time. A classical example is the decision system of the agents in a standard cobweb model: Agents (in this model representing for firms) base their decision on future production levels on the price they expect to prevail in the next period. Their way of deciding on which price to expect is fairly simple. It says: 'Expect the price in the next period to be the same as the price today!'[21] In contrast to static decision systems, dynamic ones change over time. This means that the rules connecting the information received and the action resulting from it do not stay the same, but develop over time. This change of decision rules can be interpreted as 'learning'. Decision rules together with the methods of changing the rules are a dynamic decision system. Such a dynamic system is the genetic algorithm, which is the only dynamic decision system being analyzed in this work.

Helpful for the computer aided implementation of economic agents is the use of an object oriented programming (OOP) language. Object oriented computer languages differ from the usual procedural languages in at least one important respect: They integrate data and functions. In procedural languages like C, Basic or Pascal, it is necessary to separate information (data), e.g. the quantity of a good a firm plans to produce, from the functions changing the information, like the decision rule changing the planed quantity. Instead, data and functions form one common unit, which is usually called an *object*. In the economic example, every firm is an object of its own, each characterized by its own 'private' information as well as the functions the firm uses.[22] In the lingo of object oriented programming, the data part of an object is called its *qualities*, while the functions are called *methods*. With the help of OOP, the transfer of the concept of an artificial agent into a software module is straightforward: Receptors, decision system and effectors are methods of the object 'artificial agent', while the information inside the agent's memory are the object's qualities. Table 2.1 compares the concepts of 'artificial agent' and 'OOP object'.

2.2.5 Differences to Analytical Models

Obviously, analytical models and models based on agent based simulations are different. Apart from the differences concerning finiteness and infiniteness, respectively (see Sect. 2.2.3), there are some more points that deserve to be mentioned.

---

[20] This example is a simplified description of the model set up in Chap. 8.

[21] This is the simplest textbook case, as can be found in e.g. Henderson and Quandt (1986).

[22] Much more about the concept of object oriented programming languages can be found in e.g. Stroustrup (1994, 1997).

Table 2.1. Artificial Agent and OOP Object

artificial agent	OOP object
receptors	methods for information reception
memory	qualities
decision system	methods for information procession
effectors	methods for information output

The most important difference between the two types of modeling is the epistemological nature of the results. The epistemological method of analytical models is deduction. Simulations (and generally: experiments), in contrast, only allow for inductive conclusions. This means that results gained by simulations can never deliver the reason for *general* conclusions, but are only valid for the given conditions of the individual simulation they are based on. Consequently, all insights won by simulation are less 'strong' than insights gained by analytical models. In order to strengthen inductive results, there are some methods from econometrics and statistics which can at least help to find some probabilities for the case that simulation results are equal to results of analytical models or to empirical data.[23]

The fact that simulation only allows for inductive reasoning can be seen as a disadvantage of this method. At this point, analytics seems to be superior to mere simulation. On the other hand, there are a number of advantages of simulations. The main advantage is the fact, that simulation, especially in the form of agent based simulation, is able to handle problems which cannot be coped by analytics at all or can only be coped at the cost of immense mathematical efforts. Some examples are

- 'true' heterogeneity
  Analytical models of really heterogeneous cases are very rare. Even the analysis of situations with only two distinct groups of individual behavior is mostly very complicated and often leads to results of very restricted applicability. In analytical models, the fiction of a 'representative individual' is very common, a fiction which is essentially based on the concept of homogeneous behavior.[24] In agent based simulations, in contrast, the heterogeneity of agents is an essential part of the model. Further parts of this work will show that heterogeneity of the agents is not only a 'nice feature' of the models, but an indispensable prerequisite of successful social learning.

[23] Some statistical analysis will be carried out in Sect. 5. There, the hypothesis is tested, that some simulation results are similar to the results gained by the analytical formulation of the same model.

[24] See Kirman (1992) for a substantial discussion of this point.
A very different concept of the representative individual is presented by Franke (1997). This concept sees the representative individual as an individual whose behavior corresponds to the average behavior of a population, i.e. in a game theoretic sense, a mixed strategy based on the current population. This, of course, is a concept, the above criticism does not apply to.

- 'rich' dynamics
  The problems of analytical models concerning the formulation of true heterogeneity are reflected by the kind of dynamics they are able to produce. There is hardly any model showing the possibility of parallel and interdependent dynamics on the economic micro and macro level of an economy. Simulations, in contrast, can easily find these kinds of dynamics, and even special cases like strong motions of micro behavior in the absence of motions on the macro level.[25]

2.3 Summary

The starting point of this work is the sum of weaknesses and limitations of the currently prevailing economic theory and its native analytical methods. These weaknesses and limitations lead to the necessity of two changes in economic research: First, the explicit introduction of learning processes into the models instead of the assumption of perfect rationality; and second: the construction of models consequently based on heterogeneous and individual behavior. Both of these points can be reached by using the method of agent based simulations. One form of these simulations are simulations of learning per genetic algorithm.

This work has three main topics: first, a simple, cookbook–like introduction into the structure and techniques of economic genetic algorithms; second, a general analysis of the characteristics of economic processes modeled by GA learning; and third, the construction and analysis of different types of GA learning models applied to different economic problems.

[25] See Riechmann (1997) for a more rigorous characterization of possible combinations of micro and macro dynamics.

3 An Exemplary Introduction to Structure and Application of Genetic Algorithms in Economic Research

3.1 Introduction

The goal of this chapter is to provide a simple introduction into the kind of genetic algorithms applied in economic theory. The main focus will be on technical aspects, the economic example merely serves as an illustration. This means that in this chapter new economic results will hardly be found. The model shown here is very simple and, more than this, it lacks one of the most important characteristics of the models to be presented in the further course of this work: It does not include state dependency of individual economic success.[1] The large number of simplifications make the model look a little stylized. Nevertheless, the simplifications are intentionally introduced in favor of clarity of the main technical goal, the introduction into the basic techniques of modeling economic problems in form of a genetic algorithm.

3.2 The Economic Problem: A Model of Regional Monopolies

3.2.1 The General Structure of the Model

In order to provide an introduction to the general structure of genetic algorithms in economic modeling, a very simple economic problem is presented. It is a model of a chain of regional monopolists. By definition, every single monopolist is the only supplier of a certain good in her geographical region. All the monopolists have in common the same problem: They have to find the optimal, i.e. profit maximizing, production quantity q.

Every monopolist, in her region, is confronted with the same demand, the inverse of which is

$$p = p(q) \quad \text{with} \quad \frac{dp}{dq} < 0. \tag{3.1}$$

[1] The characteristic of state dependency will, later on (Sects. 4.3 and 7.2.1), become the defining characteristic of *economic* GAs as opposed to *technical* GAs. This means that the model in this chapter, although having some economic contents, is not an *economic* GA in the sense of the above definition. There are many more GAs dealing with economic questions which are not economic GAs, like e.g. the famous Traveling Salesman problem (Michalewicz, 1996).

p gives the price.

It follows that revenue E is given by

$$E = p(q)\,q\,. \tag{3.2}$$

Every monopolist employs the same technology, resulting in the cost function

$$C = C(q) \quad \text{with} \quad \frac{dC}{dq} > 0\,. \tag{3.3}$$

C stands for production costs.

Every monopolist tries to find the profit maximizing quantity q^*:

$$\max_q \Pi = E(q) - C(q)\,. \tag{3.4}$$

From the usual calculus, q^* results as the specific quantity at which marginal revenue and marginal costs are equal:

$$q^*: \quad \frac{\mathrm{d}E}{\mathrm{d}q^*} = \frac{\mathrm{d}C}{\mathrm{d}q^*}\,. \tag{3.5}$$

In the following example, the functions will be numerically specified:[2]

$$p = 100 - 4q\,, \tag{3.6}$$
$$C = 50 + 20q\,. \tag{3.7}$$

Consequently, the function to be optimized is

$$\max_q (100 - 4q) \cdot q - 50 - 20q\,. \tag{3.8}$$

The optimal quantity results as $q^* = 10$ at $p(q^*) = 60$ and $\Pi(q^*) = 350$.

Figure 3.1 shows the profit function (3.8) in the relevant interval. It can be seen that it is a simple quadratic function. All quantities between the zero points ensure positive profit. i.e.

$$\Pi \geq 0 \quad \text{for} \quad 10 - \frac{1}{2}\sqrt{350} \leq q \leq 10 + \frac{1}{2}\sqrt{350}\,. \tag{3.9}$$

It is important to see that the profit function is symmetrical to the point $q = 10$. This means that equally large deviations in the quantity in either direction causes losses in profit of the same amount.

---

[2] The example originates from Henderson and Quandt (1986).

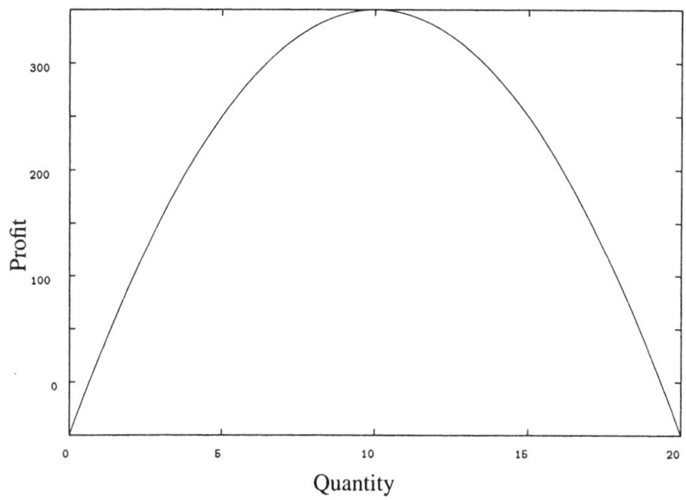

Fig. 3.1. Profit Function

3.2.2 The Consequences of Bounded Rationality

Different from the standard textbook model, the assumption of perfect rationality of the agents will be dropped. This has several consequences. It is assumed that the monopolists do not know the form of the demand function. (In fact, they do not even know, that such a thing does exist at all.) But, even if they knew about the demand function, agents are assumed not to be smart enough to derive the optimal production quantity from this knowledge.

Thus, instead of perfect rationality, some kind of learning has to be integrated into the model. This is what is done in the following.

3.3 The Genetic Algorithm

3.3.1 Introduction

Genetic Algorithms are iterative numerical optimization methods making use of some basic principles of (biological) evolution. A *population* of genetic *individuals* is submitted to some *genetic operators*, namely *recombination, mutation*, and *selection*. By *reproduction*, from one population a new generation of individuals is generated, which is submitted to the operators again, etc. This procedure of reproduction, alteration and selection is repeated until some kind of stopping criterion is met. In most cases, the last generation contains at least some individuals representing particularly good solutions of the underlying optimization problem.

The problem of monopolistic profit maximization, as described above, can be solved by a genetic algorithm. The special kind of GA used here is the most basic GA, founded by Holland (1975) (latest edition: Holland (1992)) and Goldberg

(1989). The structure of this GA, also called canonical GA or standard–GA, is shown in Algorithm 3.1. The single components of the canonical GA are described in detail below.

CAN-GA — Canonical GA

$t := 0$
Creation of First Population $\overline{m}_0$
Evaluation of $\overline{m}_0$
while Stopping Condition not Met
$t := t + 1$
Selection from $\overline{m}_{t-1}$ and Reproduction into $\overline{m}_t$
Recombination on $\overline{m}_t$
Mutation on $\overline{m}_t$
Evaluation of $\overline{m}_t$
END

Algorithm 3.1: Structure of the Canonical GA

3.3.2 Problem Definition

The first phase of the construction of a GA mainly consists of some preparatory actions.

Fixing the Optimization Problem

Genetic algorithms are optimization methods. Although they are often used as a metaphor for various forms of economic behavior, their genuine nature is that of a method for finding optimal solutions to a given problem. This means that the first step in constructing a GA is the definition of the problem to be optimized. Such a problem is usually described in form of a mathematical objective function, often accompanied by one or more restrictions.

In the given case, the optimization problem is represented by (3.4): Every regional monopolist tries to maximize her profit.

Fixing the Stopping Rule

The iterative nature of GAs demands a rule saying when to stop the iterations of the algorithm. There are different types of stopping rules:

- The GA terminates when a previously fixed number of iterations (steps, rounds) is finished. (Example: Stop the algorithm after 10 000 rounds!) This is most common stopping rule for GAs.
- The GA terminates when the individual representing the population wide best solution has remained unchanged for a fixed number of rounds.
- The GA terminates when the sum or some other aggregate of individual results has remained unchanged for a fixed number of rounds.
- The GA stops when the population is converged. The concept of convergence of genetic populations is very problematic, though. It will be shown later in this work, that economic standard GAs do actually never converge into fully uniform populations. Thus, as a weaker concept of convergence, Beasley et al. (1993a) demand the equality of 95% of the genetic material contained within the population.
- The GA terminates when a certain neighborhood of the optimal solution has been reached. This rule, of course, can only be applied if the optimum is known in advance. This means that this rule can only be used in order to test the quality of a certain algorithm with respect to a previously solved problem.

In the example of the monopolist's problem, the GA terminates after running for a fixed number of iterations.

Coding

The process of coding transfers the optimization problem into a form that can be treated by a GA. Coding gives a certain value to every genetic individual representing a concrete value of the free variable of the optimization problem.[3] It is a genuine characteristic of genetic algorithms that coding is done by a binary string, i.e. by use of the symbols '0' and '1' only.[4] The fact that coding of genetic individuals is binary does not automatically mean that *decoding* or interpreting the values of an individual is done by the *binary system*. Should this be the case, genetic individuals

[3] In more elaborate forms of GAs, a genetic individual can even represent a vector of values for a vector of variables like for instance in Chap. 8 of this book.

[4] In fact, the use of binary coding is the most important difference between genetic algorithms and 'evolution strategies' (ES), which use coding by real numbers. For some more precise characterization of evolution strategies, refer to Bäck et al. (1991), for the differences between GA and ES, see Hoffmeister and Bäck (1991).

were only capable of representing values from the set of natural numbers (including zero). Actually, the procedure used most often, is the following: A genetic individual S_i is coded as a binary bit string of length L, i.e. as a sequence of L symbols 0 and 1. Interpreted as a binary number, this string can represent a maximum value of $B^{\max} = 2^L - 1$.[5] In addition, a constant $D^{\max}$ is introduced, containing the upper bound of the range of the economic variable represented by the genetic individual. $B(S_i)$ gives the values of bit string or genetic individual S_i, won by *direct* decoding of the string by use of the dual system. The actual value $V(S_i)$ representing the value of genetic individual S_i is given by

$$V(S_i) = \frac{D^{\max}}{B^{\max}} \cdot B(S_i) . \tag{3.10}$$

In the example of the monopolist's problem, this means that every genetic individual represents the quantity decision of a monopolist. The length of the individuals' bit strings can be fixed at e.g. $L = 16$ bits. Consequently, the maximum value codebale by the dual system is $B^{\max} = 2^{16} - 1 = 65\,535$. Moreover, assume the maximum production capacity of a monopolist as $D^{\max} = 50$ units per period. Then, the bit string of genetic individual a

$$S_a = 0101011100001010$$

can be decoded as follows: The value of S_a according to the dual system (with significance decreasing from the left to right hand side of the string) is given by

$$B(S_a) = 2^{14} + 2^{12} + 2^{10} + 2^9 + 2^8 + 2^3 + 2^1 = 22\,282 .$$

Thus, the value of S_a is

$$V(S_a) = \frac{50}{65\,535} \cdot 22\,282 \approx 17 .$$

In the example, economic agent a, whose quantity decision is represented by S_a, is planning to supply a quantity of about 17 units of the good.

3.3.3 Execution of the Algorithm

Creation of the Starting Population

In genetic algorithms, a number of genetic individuals form a genetic population. A population can be interpreted as a mathematical set of individuals. At the outset of a GA, a starting population has to be created. This starting population m_0 is stochastically initialized, i.e. it is filled with individuals whose single genetic positions are determined as 0 or 1 by chance. For some purposes, however, it can be useful to set the individuals of the starting population to deterministically fixed values.[6]

[5] Some authors use decoding with the help of the so called Gray–code (see Press et al., 1992). This reduces the problem of possible large mutation steps explained below (see Sect. 3.3.3, p. 27).

[6] For an example, see Sect. 9.5.8, where a deterministic initialization of the starting population is used.

Evaluation of the Starting Population

The individuals of the starting populations are given a fitness or quality value reflecting the goodness of the individual concerning the given optimization problem. It is the fitness of an individual which in the course of the algorithm determines an individual's probability of survival or reproduction.

In economic GAs, the fitness reflects the quality of the behavioral strategy an agent chooses in a special situation.[7] In the monopoly example, the fitness of an individual is equal to the profit a firm gains with its quantity decision. Generally, genetic fitness has its economic counterpart in measures of success like profit, utility or payoffs in games. In the given example, the fitness is won by using the respective production quantity inside the objective 3.8, i.e. for individual a

$$R(S_a) = \Pi\left(\frac{50}{65\,535}\cdot 22\,282\right) \approx 154\,.$$

The identity of economic result and genetic fitness does not hold for minimization problems. In this case, the economic results have to be transformed in some useful way in order to be applicable as fitness values.

Test of the Stopping Condition

Before each iteration of the algorithm, the stopping rule has to be tested. If the rule is met, the algorithm terminates.

Selection and Reproduction

The first genetic operator to be applied in each round of the GA is the operator of selection/reproduction. By selection and reproduction, from the population of period $t-1$, $\overline{m}_{t-1}$, the population of the current period t, $\overline{m}_t$, is won. In the canonical GA, this is done by *drawing with replacement* genetic individuals from the pool of the old generation. A copy of every individual drawn is made and this copy is put into the new population. This procedure is repeated until the new population has the same number of members as the old one. The act of drawing the individual from the old population is usually called selection, while the procedure of copying the individual is called reproduction. At selection and reproduction, the probability of a certain individual to be drawn and copied is determined by its *relative fitness*.

[7] Actually, the bit string of a genetic individual does in most cases not represent a strategy in the game theoretic meaning of the term. At this point, there is a discrepancy between the use of the term 'strategy' in game theory and in the theory of economic GA learning. In game theory, the term strategy means a set of contingent actions, i.e. a compound of a condition and an action that is chosen if the condition is met. For the exact use of the term in game theory, see e.g. Fudenberg and Tirole (1991, pp. 83) or Rasmussen (1994, pp. 10). Thus, in a game theoretic sense, the above does not mean a strategy, but merely an action. In GA learning theory, though, the use of the term 'strategy' even for mere actions is very common, so that in this work, this term will be used.

Relative fitness is the fitness of the individual relative to the aggregate fitness of the whole population. The relative fitness of individual $S_{i,t}$, $F^r(S_{i,t})$ related to its population m_t is given by[8]

$$F^r(S_{i,t}) = \frac{R(S_{i,t})}{\sum_{S_{j,t} \in m_t} R(S_{j,t})}. \tag{3.11}$$

In cases like the monopoly example, where it is possible to achieve even negative fitness values, an additional problem arises: Probabilities only take values from 0 to 1. By definition, relative fitness must not be negative. Thus, there is a strong necessity of avoiding such negative values. This means that fitness values may have to be *scaled.* A possible scaling method leading to non negative values is the addition of a constant A to the fitness to each individual's fitness. A must be greater than the negative population wide minimum individual fitness value.[9] With M giving the number of members in a population, the scaled relative fitness $F^{r,s}(S_{i,t})$ is given by

$$F^{r,s}(S_{i,t}) = \frac{R(S_{i,t}) + A}{\sum_{S_{j,t} \in \overline{m}_t} [R(S_{j,t})] + MA} \quad \text{mit} \quad A > - \min_{S_{j,t} \in \overline{m}_t} R(S_{j,t}). \tag{3.12}$$

The type of selection discussed above is called 'biased roulette wheel selection' by Goldberg (1989). It is a form of *implicit* selection. Methods of implicit selection are stochastic methods. It is important to notice, that in processes of implicit selection, generally every genetic individual has a positive chance of survival, which can certainly be very small for some individuals. There is a large number of different selection methods used in economics, and even more in technical sciences. Some of those are *explicit* selection methods, which are deterministic by nature.[10]

Recombination

The second genetic operator to be used in each round of the GA is recombination. In the canonical GA, a special form of recombination is used, which is one point crossover.[11] Crossover 'crossbreeds' two genetic individual which are randomly drawn from their population. This procedure is a weak analogy to sexual reproduction in biological systems. The exact procedure is the following. The bit strings of both 'parents' are cut at a randomly chosen 'crossover point', resulting in two substrings for each individual. Then, the substrings are interchanged between the parents and united again, thus producing two new individuals. An example for this procedure is shown in Fig. 3.2. The strings shown in the upper part of the figure

[8] From this point on, genetic individuals will not only be described by their running index i but also — if necessary — by the time index of their population, t. Thus, $S_{i,t}$, is the complete 'name' of individual i of generation t.

[9] Every possible scaling method distorts the exact mathematical relation between the individual fitness values. This is the reason why there is a lively discussion about the advantages and disadvantages of various scaling methods in technical GA literature. Introductions to this discussion are given by Goldberg (1989) and Mitchell (1996).

[10] An overview of selection methods can be found in Goldberg and Deb (1991), Hoffmeister and Bäck (1991, section 5.1) and Michalewicz (1996).

[11] More variants of crossover a described in Beasley et al. (1993b).

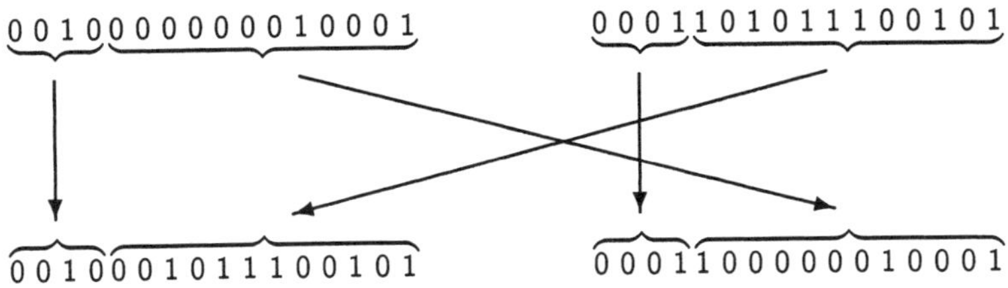

Fig. 3.2. One–Point–Crossover (Example)

represent the 'parent' individuals. From these parents, two 'children' are derived. The first child (left) consists of the left four bits of the first and the right twelve bit of the right parent. Correspondingly, the right hand child consists of the first four bits of the second and the last twelve bits of the first parent.

In the standard GA, the children replace their parents in the population. This replacement does always take place, even in cases where the children have (or are expected to have) less fitness than their parents.[12]

Mutation

The third genetic operator of the canonical GA is mutation. A genetic individual mutates by changing one or more bits of its bit string into their contrary, i.e. by 'flipping' the respective bits. Every bit at every position has the same (mostly very small) probability of being flipped. Figure 3.3 shows an example.

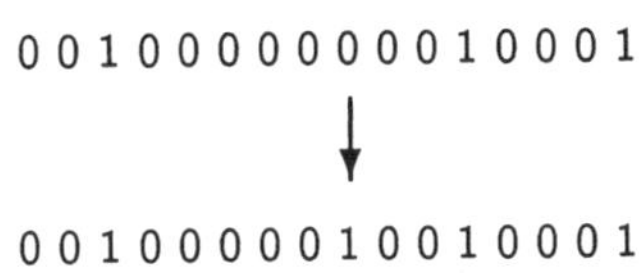

Fig. 3.3. Mutation (Example)

In the example, the 9th bit from the left is mutated. As the mutation probability for each bit of the string is the same and independent of the mutation probability of any other bit in the string, during mutation, a number of bits between 0 and L can be mutated, with L standing for the total number of bits in the bit string, i.e. the length of the string. In the canonical GA, a mutated individual replaces the original individual in the population.

A problem with this very basic type of mutation is the problem of possibly very large mutation steps. Notice, that even the flipping of only one bit can cause very large changes in the decoded value of the bit string. This change is the greater the more significant bit position is, i.e. in the notation of this work, the more to the left

[12] This leads to the fact that improvements of the fitness of individuals inside a population can only result from the working of the selection operator.

of the string the bit is located. In the example of Fig. 3.3, by flipping the 8th bit from the right, mutation changes the dual value of the bit string from 2 209 to 8 337. In contrast, flipping the very right bit, changing the upper string into 0 0 1 0 0 0 0 0 0 0 1 0 0 0 0 produces a dual value of only 8 209, whereas the mutation of the very left bit, producing 1 0 1 0 0 0 0 0 0 0 1 0 0 0 1, results in a dual value of 40 977. This problem of possibly large changes of the coded value can be weakened by using the method of Gray–coding, as described in Press et al. (1992) and Michalewicz (1996). Other than for the dual system, in Gray–coded bit strings, adjacent natural numbers differ in only one bit position. Nevertheless, the rest of this work will largely ignore the problem and stick with the standard dual coding method.

Evaluation

At the end of every iteration the newly created population is evaluated. This means that the fitness of each individual is determined. Technically, this evaluation is the same as the evaluation of the starting population described above.

Iterations

The steps selection/reproduction, recombination and mutation as described above are repeated until the stopping condition is met. At the end of the iterations the last generation or at least some individuals of this generation represent specific solutions of the underlying optimization problem.

3.4 A Simple Example

3.4.1 Coding and Running the GA

As a simple introductory example, the monopolist's problem described in Sect. 3.2 will be transferred into an economic GA.

The economic problem to be solved is fully described by (3.8). The stopping condition is introduced as terminating the algorithm after 100 iterations. The coding of the genetic individuals is done by transferring the supplied quantity into a 16 bit long bit string, using a maximum capacity of $D^{\max} = 50$ as the upper norm. A population consists of $M = 20$ genetic individuals.

The starting population is determined by chance, i.e. every bit string of every individual is set to 0 or 1 with the same probability $P(0) = P(1) = \frac{1}{2}$. Figure 3.4 shows an example of a randomly created population. For each of the individuals, the figure shows the bit string, the decoded value (i.e. the quantity), and the fitness. As evaluation has not yet taken place, the fitness of every individual is zero.

After the evaluation the population looks like Fig. 3.5. The fitness values are found by numerically computing the value of the objective function (3.8) for every

0 1 1 1 0 0 0 1 1 1 0 0 1 1 0 0	22.226291	0
1 1 1 1 0 1 1 0 1 0 1 0 0 0 1 0	48.171206	0
1 1 0 0 1 0 1 1 1 0 0 0 0 1 0 0	39.749752	0
1 0 1 0 0 0 0 1 1 0 0 1 1 1 0 1	31.565576	0
1 1 1 0 0 1 0 1 0 1 0 0 1 1 1 0	44.786755	0
1 1 0 0 0 1 1 0 1 1 1 1 1 0 1 1	38.863966	0
0 1 0 0 0 1 1 0 1 0 0 1 0 0 1 1	13.784237	0
0 0 1 0 0 1 0 1 0 0 0 0 1 1 0 0	7.2358282	0
0 1 0 1 1 0 1 0 0 0 0 1 0 0 1 1	17.592889	0
1 0 0 1 0 0 0 1 1 0 0 1 1 1 0 0	28.439765	0
1 1 0 0 1 1 0 1 0 1 0 1 1 0 1 0	40.108339	0
1 0 1 1 1 1 0 1 1 0 1 1 0 1 1 1	37.054246	0
0 0 1 1 0 1 0 0 0 1 1 0 0 1 0 0	10.2327	0
1 1 1 0 0 0 1 0 0 1 0 1 0 1 1 0	44.206912	0
0 0 0 1 1 1 0 0 1 1 1 1 0 0 1 1	5.6542306	0
1 0 0 1 0 0 0 1 0 0 0 1 1 0 1 1	28.341344	0
0 0 1 0 1 1 0 0 0 0 1 0 1 0 0 0	8.6243992	0
1 1 0 1 0 1 0 0 1 0 0 1 1 1 0 1	41.526665	0
0 1 1 0 0 1 0 1 1 1 1 1 1 0 1 0	19.917601	0
1 1 1 0 0 1 0 0 1 0 0 1 1 1 1 0	44.652476	0

Fig. 3.4. Randomly Created Starting Population

0 1 1 1 0 0 0 1 1 1 0 0 1 1 0 0	22.226291	-247.9288
1 1 1 1 0 1 1 0 1 0 1 0 0 0 1 0	48.171206	-5478.1639
1 1 0 0 1 0 1 1 1 0 0 0 0 1 0 0	39.749752	-3190.191
1 0 1 0 0 0 0 1 1 0 0 1 1 1 0 1	31.565576	-1510.2962
1 1 1 0 0 1 0 1 0 1 0 0 1 1 1 0	44.786755	-4490.4733
1 1 0 0 0 1 1 0 1 1 1 1 1 0 1 1	38.863966	-2982.5141
0 1 0 0 0 1 1 0 1 0 0 1 0 0 1 1	13.784237	292.71819
0 0 1 0 0 1 0 1 0 0 0 0 1 1 0 0	7.2358282	319.43742
0 1 0 1 1 0 1 0 0 0 0 1 0 0 1 1	17.592889	119.39213
1 0 0 1 0 0 0 1 1 0 0 1 1 1 0 0	28.439765	-1010.0997
1 1 0 0 1 1 0 1 0 1 0 1 1 0 1 0	40.108339	-3276.0483
1 0 1 1 1 1 0 1 1 0 1 1 0 1 1 1	37.054246	-2577.7289
0 0 1 1 0 1 0 0 0 1 1 0 0 1 0 0	10.2327	349.7834
1 1 1 0 0 0 1 0 0 1 0 1 0 1 1 0	44.206912	-4330.4514
0 0 0 1 1 1 0 0 1 1 1 1 0 0 1 1	5.6542306	274.45715
1 0 0 1 0 0 0 1 0 0 0 1 1 0 1 1	28.341344	-995.61965
0 0 1 0 1 1 0 0 0 0 1 0 1 0 0 0	8.6243992	342.43089
1 1 0 1 0 1 0 0 1 0 0 1 1 1 0 1	41.526665	-3625.7225
0 1 1 0 0 1 0 1 1 1 1 1 1 0 1 0	19.917601	-43.435261
1 1 1 0 0 1 0 0 1 0 0 1 1 1 1 0	44.652476	-4453.1763

Fig. 3.5. Randomly Generated Starting Population after Evaluation

genetic individual's strategy. It can be seen that the unscaled fitness is negative for a number of individuals. Thus, before selection, scaling has to be done.

Then, selection and reproduction take place. By this, a new population is produced. Figure 3.6 shows this new population before the new evaluation. This means that the last column still gives the scaled fitness computed in the period before. This new population reflects the effect of selection and reproduction: Apparently, individual number 13 (decoded value: 10.2327, unscaled fitness: 349.7834) was the most successful one. Its fitness is the highest in the starting population. Consequently, by selection (drawing *with* replacement), in the new population there are already four individuals of this type. In contrast, the worse performing individuals of the starting population (e.g. individuals number 2, 5, 14 or 20) have not made it into the new generation. It is easy to recognize, that selection and reproduction have caused some convergence in the quantities represented within the population. The interval between the highest and the lowest quantity in the population has decreased from (5.6542306; 48.171206) in the starting population to (5.6542306; 39.749752) in the second population.

```
0 1 0 0 0 1 1 0 1 0 0 1 0 0 1 1   13.784237   5771.8823
0 0 1 1 0 1 0 0 0 1 1 0 0 1 0 0     10.2327   5828.9475
1 0 0 1 0 0 0 1 0 0 0 1 1 0 1 1   28.341344   4483.5444
0 0 1 1 0 1 0 0 0 1 1 0 0 1 0 0     10.2327   5828.9475
0 0 1 0 1 1 0 0 0 0 1 0 1 0 0 0   8.6243992    5821.595
1 0 1 0 0 0 0 1 1 0 0 1 1 1 0 1   31.565576   3968.8679
0 1 1 1 0 0 0 1 1 1 0 0 1 1 0 0   22.226291   5231.2353
0 1 1 0 0 1 0 1 1 1 1 1 1 0 1 0   19.917601   5435.7288
0 0 1 1 0 1 0 0 0 1 1 0 0 1 0 0     10.2327   5828.9475
1 0 0 1 0 0 0 1 1 0 0 1 1 1 0 0   28.439765   4469.0643
0 0 1 1 0 1 0 0 0 1 1 0 0 1 0 0     10.2327   5828.9475
0 1 0 0 0 1 1 0 1 0 0 1 0 0 1 1   13.784237   5771.8823
1 0 0 1 0 0 0 1 0 0 0 1 1 0 1 1   28.341344   4483.5444
0 1 1 0 0 1 0 1 1 1 1 1 1 0 1 0   19.917601   5435.7288
1 1 0 0 1 0 1 1 1 0 0 0 0 1 0 0   39.749752   2288.9731   MAX!
0 0 0 1 1 1 0 0 1 1 1 1 0 0 1 1   5.6542306   5753.6212   MIN!
0 0 1 0 0 1 0 1 0 0 0 0 1 1 0 0   7.2358282   5798.6015
1 0 1 0 0 0 0 1 1 0 0 1 1 1 0 1   31.565576   3968.8679
1 0 0 1 0 0 0 1 0 0 0 1 1 0 1 1   28.341344   4483.5444
0 0 0 1 1 1 0 0 1 1 1 1 0 0 1 1   5.6542306   5753.6212   MIN!
```

Fig. 3.6. New Population, Derived from the Starting Population by Selection and Reproduction.

On this new generation, crossover is carried out, resulting in the population shown in Fig. 3.7. Still, no new evaluation has taken place, so that the values given in the last column are without any sensible meaning to the current population. In the population, crossover happened to the 1st and 6th individual after the 13th bit position from the right, and to the 11th and 15th individual after the 10th bit position from the right. Possibly, crossovers have also happened to some more, identical individuals (e.g. to the second and 4th individual). As crossover between identical individual does not change the individuals, such an operation cannot be recognized ex post.

```
1 0 1 0 0 1 1 0 1 0 0 1 0 0 1 1  32.534524  5771.8823
0 0 1 1 0 1 0 0 0 1 1 0 0 1 0 0    10.2327  5828.9475
1 0 0 1 0 0 0 1 0 0 0 1 1 0 1 1  28.341344  4483.5444
0 0 1 1 0 1 0 0 0 1 1 0 0 1 0 0    10.2327  5828.9475
0 0 1 0 1 1 0 0 0 0 1 0 1 0 0 0  8.6243992   5821.595
0 1 0 0 0 0 0 1 1 0 0 1 1 1 0 1   12.81529  3968.8679
0 1 1 1 0 0 0 1 1 1 0 0 1 1 0 0  22.226291  5231.2353
0 1 1 0 0 1 0 1 1 1 1 1 1 0 1 0  19.917601  5435.7288
0 0 1 1 0 1 0 0 0 1 1 0 0 1 0 0    10.2327  5828.9475
1 0 0 1 0 0 0 1 1 0 0 1 1 1 0 0  28.439765  4469.0643
1 1 0 0 1 0 0 0 0 1 1 0 0 1 0 0  39.139391  5828.9475
0 1 0 0 0 1 1 0 1 0 0 1 0 0 1 1  13.784237  5771.8823
1 0 0 1 0 0 0 1 0 0 0 1 1 0 1 1  28.341344  4483.5444
0 1 1 0 0 1 0 1 1 1 1 1 1 0 1 0  19.917601  5435.7288
0 0 1 1 0 1 1 1 1 0 0 0 0 1 0 0  10.843061  2288.9731
0 0 0 1 1 1 0 0 1 1 1 1 0 0 1 1  5.6542306  5753.6212
0 0 1 0 0 1 0 1 0 0 0 0 1 1 0 0  7.2358282  5798.6015
1 0 1 0 0 0 0 1 1 0 0 1 1 1 0 1  31.565576  3968.8679
1 0 0 1 0 0 0 1 0 0 0 1 1 0 1 1  28.341344  4483.5444
0 0 0 1 1 1 0 0 1 1 1 1 0 0 1 1  5.6542306  5753.6212
```

Fig. 3.7. New Population after Crossover

Mutation turns the population shown in Fig.3.7 into the one in Fig. 3.8. For example, mutation took place at the first individual's second bit from the right.

Now, the iteration is repeated 100 times. The last, i.e. the 100th, population (including the correct fitness values) is displayed in Fig. 3.9.

The result shows a relatively good approximation of nearly every individual to the theoretically optimal value of 10.0. From the population, some more interesting results can be seen. It seems to be one of the main characteristics of the result that the bit strings of successful individuals start (from the left) with the sequence 0 0 1 1. Actually, the first place of the bit string where agents differ is the 5th position from the left. The interpretation of this observation is the following: All the members of the last population represent values between 0 0 1 1 0 0 0 0 0 0 0 0 0 0 0 0 $= 12\,288 \cdot \frac{50}{65\,535} \approx 9.38$ (lower boundary) and the binary value 0 0 1 1 1 1 1 1 1 1 1 1 1 1 1 1 $= 16\,383 \cdot \frac{50}{65\,535} \approx 12.5$ (upper boundary).[13] This means that

$$9.38 \leq q^* \leq 12.5\,.$$

There are various reasons why the algorithm does not lead to a population solely consisting of one type of individual, e.g. the type representing the optimal number

[13] Decoding follows (3.10).

1 0 1 0 0 1 1 0 1 0 0 1 0 0 0 1	32.532998	5771.8823
0 1 1 1 0 1 0 0 0 1 1 0 0 1 0 0	22.732891	5828.9475
1 0 0 1 0 0 0 1 0 0 0 1 1 0 1 1	28.341344	4483.5444
0 0 1 1 0 1 0 0 0 1 1 0 0 1 0 0	10.2327	5828.9475
0 0 1 0 1 1 0 0 0 0 1 0 1 0 0 0	8.6243992	5821.595
0 1 0 0 0 0 0 1 1 0 0 1 1 1 0 1	12.81529	3968.8679
0 1 1 1 0 0 0 1 1 1 0 0 1 1 0 0	22.226291	5231.2353
0 1 1 0 0 1 0 1 1 1 1 1 1 0 1 0	19.917601	5435.7288
0 0 1 1 0 1 0 0 0 1 1 0 0 1 0 0	10.2327	5828.9475
1 0 0 1 0 0 0 1 1 0 1 1 1 1 0 0	28.464179	4469.0643
1 1 0 0 1 0 0 0 0 1 1 0 0 1 0 0	39.139391	5828.9475
0 1 0 0 0 1 1 0 1 0 0 1 0 0 1 1	13.784237	5771.8823
1 0 0 1 0 0 0 1 0 0 0 1 1 0 1 1	28.341344	4483.5444
0 1 1 0 0 1 0 1 1 1 1 1 1 0 1 0	19.917601	5435.7288
0 0 1 1 0 1 1 1 1 0 0 0 0 1 0 0	10.843061	2288.9731
0 0 0 1 1 1 0 0 1 1 1 1 0 0 1 1	5.6542306	5753.6212
0 0 1 0 0 1 0 1 0 0 0 0 1 1 0 0	7.2358282	5798.6015
1 0 1 0 0 0 0 1 1 0 0 1 1 1 0 1	31.565576	3968.8679
1 0 0 1 0 0 0 1 0 0 0 1 1 0 1 1	28.341344	4483.5444
0 0 0 1 1 1 0 0 1 1 1 1 0 0 1 1	5.6542306	5753.6212

Fig. 3.8. New Population after Crossover and Mutation

0 0 1 1 1 1 1 1 0 1 0 1 1 1 1 0	12.376593	327.40723
0 0 1 1 0 1 0 0 1 1 1 1 1 0 1 0	10.347143	349.51797
0 0 1 1 0 1 1 0 1 1 1 1 1 1 1 0	10.740826	347.80471
0 0 1 1 0 1 0 1 1 1 0 1 1 1 1 0	10.521096	348.91384
0 0 1 1 1 1 1 0 1 1 1 1 1 1 1 0	12.303349	328.77833
0 0 1 1 0 1 1 0 1 1 1 1 1 0 1 0	10.737774	347.82276
0 0 1 1 1 1 0 0 1 1 1 1 1 0 1 1	11.91043	335.40104
0 0 1 1 0 1 0 1 1 1 1 1 1 0 1 0	10.542458	348.82296
0 0 1 1 0 1 0 1 1 1 0 1 1 1 1 0	10.521096	348.91384
0 0 1 1 0 1 0 0 1 1 1 1 1 1 0 0	10.348669	349.51372
0 0 1 1 1 1 1 1 0 1 0 1 1 1 1 0	12.376593	327.40723
0 0 1 1 0 1 1 1 1 1 1 1 1 1 0 0	10.934615	346.50598
0 0 1 1 0 1 0 0 1 1 1 1 1 1 0 0	10.348669	349.51372
0 0 1 1 0 1 0 0 1 1 1 1 1 0 1 0	10.347143	349.51797
0 0 1 1 0 1 0 0 1 1 1 1 1 0 0 0	10.345617	349.5222
0 0 1 1 0 1 1 1 1 1 1 1 1 1 0 0	10.934615	346.50598
0 0 1 1 0 1 0 0 1 1 1 1 1 1 1 0	10.350195	349.50946
0 0 1 1 0 1 0 0 1 1 1 1 1 1 0 0	10.348669	349.51372
0 0 1 1 0 1 1 0 1 1 1 1 1 0 1 0	10.737774	347.82276
0 0 1 1 0 1 0 0 1 1 1 1 1 1 0 0	10.348669	349.51372

Fig. 3.9. Evaluated Population after 100 Iterations

q^*. Each of these reasons will be described in detail later in this work. At this point, it seems enough to say that it is *in principle* easy to achieve a uniform outcome by the introduction of some modifications to the standard GA. Nevertheless, it will be shown that the lack of total convergence into a uniform population is a *general characteristic* of the canonical genetic algorithm.

3.4.2 Representation of the Results

Apart from displaying the whole population, as has been done in the preceding section, there are many more ways of characterizing genetic populations. Some of these are important for the two following reasons: First, it is difficult to get an overview over a population, especially if it is relatively large. Secondly, in economic modeling, there are certain aggregate features of populations which are very interesting.

At this point, as an example, the development of the population wide average quantity in time (i.e. over the iterations of the GA) is displayed (Fig. 3.10).

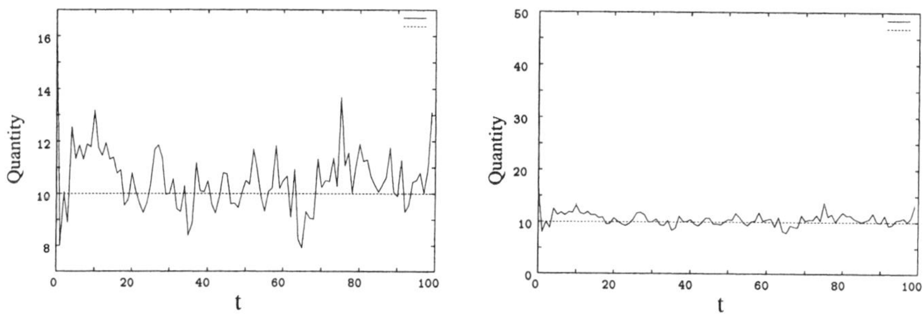

(a) Shown in the Relevant Interval (b) Shown on the Range of Quantities

Fig. 3.10. Population Average of Quantity: — av. Quantity, ··· opt. Quantity

There are some facts to be learned from the figures: The average quantity is not constant in time. Nevertheless, the right subfigure shows the oscillations to be relatively small compared to the size of the range $0 \leq q \leq 50$. But nonetheless the aggregate quantity generated by the GA oscillates and consequently cannot be the result of a converged uniform population. This result is supported by Fig. 3.11 showing the variance of the values represented by the members of the population, i.e. the population variance.

It can be seen that the variance decreases within the first few rounds of the algorithm, but then oscillates within a relatively large interval. Convergence, i.e. a clear decrease of variance, cannot be observed.

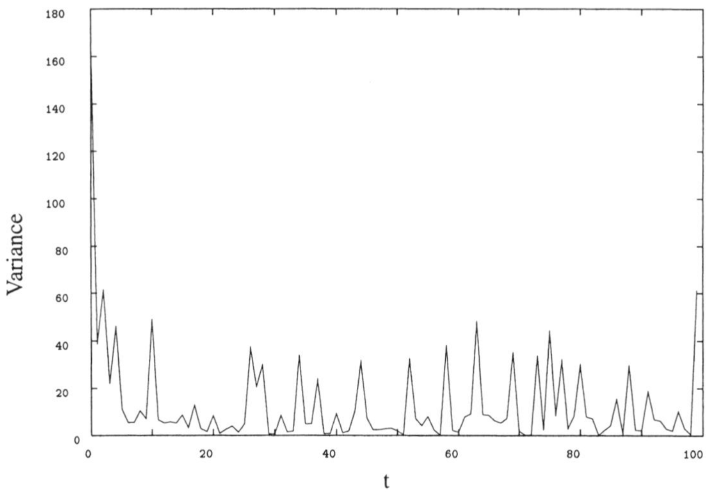

Fig. 3.11. Population Variance of Quantities

3.4.3 Interpretation

There is a clear economic interpretation to the model and its results. Following Arifovic (1994), there are two explanations, the individualistic and the social one.

Following the individualistic explanation, the genetic algorithm takes place 'inside the head' of an economic agent. In the example, every regional monopolist holds a set of ideas about different economic strategies, quantities she could produce. By using a GA, she can find the best of these strategies. The individualistic interpretation seems very questionable, which is presumably the reason why this interpretation is not used very often. The main problem of this interpretation is the following: In order to find out which strategy is the best one, the agent needs to know the exact fitness of every strategy she holds in mind. But, there is no other way of finding the fitness except of trying the strategy in practice, i.e. producing the quantity, trying to sell it and finding out the market equilibrium price and the profit connected to it. In the example, the agent would have to try all 20 different strategies of her mental population before being able to do some strategy selection. Such a kind of behavior would not only take a lot of time but would possibly require the trial of lots of bad strategies in order to find a good one. Thus, the individualistic interpretation does not seem too convincing for most economists.

The social interpretation sees the genetic algorithm as a metaphor for social learning, i.e. simultaneous learning of a whole group of economic agents.[14] This

[14] The fact that GAs are models of *social* learning is the reason for the somehow strange assumption of *a group of regional* monopolists. By definition, a monopolist is the only agent of her type in a market. This certainly means that a monopolist cannot learn from others, simply because there are not others. The construction of a number of regional monopolists, strange as it may seems, helps to overcome this problem.

interpretation is the most widely accepted one in economic GA literature and will be the foundation of this work as well. The interpretation of social learning assumes each genetic individual to represent *the economic strategy* of an agent.[15] Every agent test her personal strategy in the market, experiencing some success. If her strategy has been successful, the agent keeps it for the next period. If the strategy performed rather poorly, the agent decides to change it. Changing the strategy can be done by imitating other agents, by imitating parts of other agents' strategies (mostly as a consequence of communication) or by changing the former strategy by doing some experimentation. In the further course of this work it will be shown that these kinds of changing a strategy are very similar to the genetic operators reproduction (similar to imitation), recombination (similar to communication), and mutation (similar to experiment). These similarities allow for the analysis of GAs in form of analysis of learning processes and vice versa.

3.5 Summary

This part has shown the basic working principles of genetic algorithms applied to theoretical economic problems.

It is shown that even the most basic form of a genetic algorithm, the canonical GA, is able to find solutions which are at least close to the solutions that can be determined as optimal by traditional analytical calculus. If this is a general feature of economic GAs, still remains to be found out. The theoretical analysis of economic GAs in Chap. 4 as well as concrete applications (Chap. 6) will show, that this is not generally true.

Moreover, it is shown that GA populations do not converge into a homogeneous population. Instead, there are lasting fluctuations around the theoretical optimum which are caused in the lasting heterogeneity and structural change of the populations. This observation is one of the starting points for the general analysis in Chap. 4 and for some modifications to the canonical GA carried out in Chap. 6.

---

[15] To make this even clearer: A genetic individual does `not` represent an agent, but just the economic strategy of an agent. This has a very simple reason: Strategies may change, agents not.

Part II

General Analysis of Genetic Algorithms

4 Methods for the General Analysis of Genetic Algorithms as Economic Learning Techniques

4.1 Introduction

Economic models examining social learning with the help of GAs always come in the form of simulations. For a precisely specified economic problem, a computer program is constructed. The most important part of this program is the formulation of artificial economic agents, which are often constructed as objects. The most important part of the agents, in turn, is their decision system which, in this work, consists of a genetic algorithm or at least of parts of a GA. The core analysis of the behavior of the agents and by that the behavior of the economic model consists of running the simulation program, recording the resulting data and analyzing and interpreting the data. All the results won from this work are inductive by nature. Even if the simulation is run very many times: The results do not allow for deductive conclusions, they are never true *in general*, but only in a set of special circumstances.

Nevertheless, genetic algorithms or the process of GA learning can to some extend be analyzed for some general features. It is possible to find out some characteristics which are true for *every form* of GAs and by this for every process of GA learning. These general characteristics lead to deductive results and allow for conclusions which can be drawn even before the very first run of a GA learning simulation. In the course of this chapter it will become possible to find some results which do not only hold for some special cases but for the whole class of economic GA learning models. This is useful for two reasons: First, these results help to find out what kinds of problems are suitable for a GA learning model and which are not. Secondly, the results help to predict some general outcomes of GA learning models in advance.

In economic theory, genetic algorithms are often used as metaphors for economic learning. Agents not supplied with the gift of full information and perfect rationality must rely on learning. This means they have to continuously change their behavior to adapt to the changing environment in order to improve their economic strategies and by that their economic success.

Every form of economic learning — as long as it is described in adequate detail — can be analyzed according to its dynamics. The important question concerning the dynamics of learning processes are questions about the final learning result and the speed of the learning process. Sometimes, not even the question about the learning result ('What behavior will the agent have learned and keep using when the learning process is over?') can be answered precisely. The question about learning speed ('How fast does the agent improve her behavior?') is mostly even harder to answer. This means that even more basic questions like questions about the factors influencing learning speed are extremely important and valuable.

In this work, various methods of analysis will be used in order to examine the dynamic nature of GA learning processes. As an introduction, two methods will be presented, which have been described in greater detail in other places and the results of which are of only marginal importance to the *economic* aspects of GA processes. After that, three parts follow, which are of major importance to the understanding of dynamics of the GA learning process. These parts interpret GA learning as Markov chains, as evolutionary processes, and as compound learning processes.[1]

4.1.1 The Schema Theorem

The analysis of genetic algorithms with the help of schemata is based on the work by Holland (1975). Holland introduced the term *schema* as the set of bit strings fitting in some template. These templates can be constructed with the help of the symbols 0, 1, and $*$. Figure 4.1 shows an example.

```
1 0 * *
```

Fig. 4.1. Schema of Length 4

In order to fit into a template, a bit string must fit in bitwise with the symbols on the fixed positions, i.e. the positions marked as 0 or 1. The symbol $*$ is the 'don't care' symbol, i.e. any symbol will match the template at a position marked as $*$.

The schema in Fig. 4.1 represents the following set of bit strings:

```
1 0 0 0
1 0 0 1
1 0 1 0
1 0 1 1
```

Fig. 4.2. Strings Matching Schema 4.1

The importance of schemata lies in the fact that schemata are a means of describing common features of distinctively good (or distinctively bad) genetic individuals. As an example, reconsider the example from Sect. 3.4, Fig. 3.9. The results there was that all the successful monopolists chose quantities represented by bit strings starting (from the left) with the sequence 0 0 1 1 and having a 1 at

[1] Many of the results of the following sections are based on Riechmann (1998a) and Riechmann (1999).

the 6th, 10th 12th and 13th position. With the help of the schema concepts this can be formulated as: The successful monopolists' quantities belong to the schema `0 0 1 1 * 1 * * * 1 * 1 1 * * *`.

With the help of the schema concept, some rough predictions about the expected increase of relatively good schemata in the population can be made. These results are often called the schema theorem, which has been described by various authors, like e.g. Goldberg (1989), Mitchell (1996) or Dawid (1999). For the aim of analysis of economic GAs, the schema theorem is of only minor importance. Thus, there will not further treatment of this theorem in this work.

4.1.2 Concepts from Population Genetics

The similarity of a number of terms used in both disciplines, GA research and population genetics seems to suggest some close relationship between the disciplines themselves. Actually, this relationship is not very close. Consequently, methods from population genetics are of very limited use to the analysis of economic GA learning processes.

Nevertheless, there is at least one result from population genetics which is very useful for the analysis of GA learning: The concept of 'genetic drift' (Maynard Smith, 1989). In the absence of mutation, the phenomenon of genetic drift causes the convergence of genetic populations to a uniform state, even when there is no selective pressure.[2]

4.2 Genetic Algorithm Learning as a Markov Process

In the more technical area of GA analysis there are some pieces of work concentrating on the description and analysis of genetic algorithms with the help of Markov chains.[3] The results of this more technical field of literature can easily be transferred to economic GA models. The following section will show that this helps to find some valuable understandings about the very specific dynamics of GA learning models.

4.2.1 The Basics

Canonical genetic algorithm are, as stated above, algorithms transferring a set of genetic individuals from one generation to another. The genetic individuals are usually coded in form of bit strings. The set of individuals belonging to the same generation is called a genetic population.

A genetic individual S of length L consists of L symbols 0 or 1:

[2] For a more detailed description of genetic drift, see below (Sect. 4.2.2).

[3] To be more precise, GAs are mostly seen as, though not often called, population Markov processes. See Davis and Principe (1993), Nix and Vose (1992), Rudolph (1994), and Goldberg and Segrest (1987) for details. This work will, as far as possible in an economic context, adopt the notation of Nix and Vose (1992).

$$S \in \{0,1\}^L . \tag{4.1}$$

It follows that there are

$$|S| \equiv N = 2^L \tag{4.2}$$

different genetic individuals or genetic individuals of a different type.

The 'value' of a genetic individual results from decoding the bit string as shown above (Sect. 3.3.2). Is has been pointed out that there is a large number of different methods of coding and decoding . The common feature of all of these methods is the fact that (binary) bit strings can code only a limited number of different values. This means that the whole set of real numbers can never be encoded by a bit string of finite length.

In economic GAs, the value of a genetic individual describes a behavioral strategy of an economic agent, e.g. the quantity produced by a regional monopolist.[4] According to (4.2), there are exactly N different economic strategies that can be represented by a genetic individual of length L.

A genetic population is a set of M genetic individuals. M is often called the 'length' of the population. In economic models, the population stands for the whole of the strategies of all economic agents active at the same time and involved in the same economic situation. As an example, a population may consist of all regional monopolists' individual quantities for the same period of time.

A genetic population, consisting of M genetic individuals can be written as a vector

$$\overline{m} = (m(1), m(2), \ldots, m(N)) \tag{4.3}$$

with $\overline{m}$ giving the number of individuals of type i in the population $\overline{m}$. From this, it follows that

$$\sum_{i=1}^{N} m(i) = M . \tag{4.4}$$

The set of different *genetic populations* is S'. There are $|S'| = N'$ genetic populations of different type:[5]

$$N' = \binom{M+N-1}{M} = \binom{M+N-1}{N-1} . \tag{4.5}$$

It follows, that the whole canonical GA can be seen as a stochastic process which, by using the genetic operators, turns one genetic population into another. As can be easily shown that the canonical GA satisfies the Markov property. The Markov property is often called the 'no memory property'. GAs do not have a memory in

[4] Again, note that what is called 'strategy' may only be an 'action' in the lingo of game theory.

[5] A very intuitive derivation of equation (4.5) can be found in Nix and Vose (1992).

the following sense: The probability of reaching a specific population B starting from another specific population A only depends on the composition of the starting population A but in no way on anything else like the form of the operators or the way the process developed before reaching A, i.e. the history of the process.[6] Thus, a genetic algorithm *is* a Markov process.

4.2.2 Markov Chain Analysis

In order to gain an as simple insight into the working principles of a GA as possible without losing the appropriate precision, the GA will be analyzed piecewise. First, only a very basic algorithm will be viewed, the one operator algorithm, which only describes learning by pure imitation. After that, more genetic operators (i.e. learning methods) will be added to the algorithm, to finally result in analysis of the full canonical GA.

The One Operator Algorithm — Learning by Imitation

The heart of every genetic algorithm is the operator of selection/reproduction. Selection assigns a fitness value to each genetic individual within a population. The fitness gives information about the economic quality of the behavioral strategy encoded by the individual. Usually, the fitness equals a value given by the objective function to be optimized by the agents of the algorithm. Consider, for instance, the case of regional monopolists. Here, the fitness is given by the profit an agent experiences as a result of the quantity chosen. In the model of regional monopolists, the profit function (3.8) is the objective the fitness values are derived from.

Reproduction is the process of winning a new population from the old one. In a canonical GA, reproduction is carried out by drawing with replacement individuals from the pool of the old population and copying the chosen ones into the new population. In this process, the probability to be drawn equals the relative fitness. This means that an individual's reproduction probability is equal to the relation of the individual's fitness to the aggregate fitness of its population.[7]

Selection and reproduction can be interpreted as learning by imitation. Agents formerly equipped with relatively bad strategies, i.e. strategies leading to relatively poor results, give up this strategy and adopt a different one instead. The specific strategy they adopt is one of the strategies of a better performing agent, i.e. a genetic individual reproducing more often than the average one.

The Markov chain analysis following below shows that this simple kind of learning behavior leads to stable but not necessarily optimal behavior.

The probability of the genetic individual i to be reproduced into the next population depends on the relative fitness $P_1(i|\overline{n})$ which is the relation of the individual's

[6] More elaborate description and explanation of Markov processes can be found in many textbooks on probability theory like Goodman (1988); Feller (1968) or Isaacson and Madsen (1976).

[7] Of course, this is a slight simplification, as the possibility of scaling (see below, Sect. 3.3.3) is ignored. This does not change the quality of the results gained but simplifies the analysis.

fitness to the fitness of the whole original population $\overline{n}$. $R(\cdot)$ is the objective function, i.e. the profit function in the monopolists' model.

$$P_1(i|\overline{n}) = \frac{n(i)R(i)}{\sum_{j\in S} n(j)R(j)} . \tag{4.6}$$

It follows that the probability of population $\overline{m}$ becoming the direct successor of population $\overline{n}$ by mere selection/reproduction is

$$P_1(\overline{m}|\overline{n}) = \binom{M}{\overline{m}} \prod_{i\in S} P_1(i|\overline{n})^{m(i)} , \tag{4.7}$$

where

$$\binom{M}{\overline{m}} = \frac{M!}{\prod_{i\in S}(m(i)!)} . \tag{4.8}$$

By that, $P_1(\overline{m}|\overline{n})$ is a transition probability in a transition matrix describing the one operator algorithm as a population Markov process.

The Markov process belonging to the one operator algorithm has a number of absorbing states. Every homogeneous or uniform population, i.e. a population consisting of only one type of individual, is such an absorbing state. Thus, as there are 2^L different genetic individual, there are also 2^L absorbing states of the Markov process. Moreover, each one of the absorbing states can be reached from at least one of the remaining, heterogeneous population which are transient states of the process. This notion leads to the main result of the analysis of the one operator algorithm: As there is a number of absorbing states each of which can be reached, the Markov process *will* (at least in the long run) reach one of these states. This means that the one operator algorithm will *inevidently* end up in one of the absorbing states.

Interpreting the one operator algorithm as a process of learning per imitation, this means that the learning process will *always* end up in a situation where all individuals do the same, i.e. in a population with uniform individual strategies. In terms of stability: In the space of populations, i.e. for economic macro data, this means convergence to a state of asymptotic stability.

The drawback of this result is the following: Even if the objective function is totally flat, i.e. for $\min R(\cdot) = \max R(\cdot)$, convergence to an absorbing state will take place. This means that even in cases where the optimal solution to a given economic problem is represented by a *heterogeneous* population, the learning process ends up in a uniform population. In population genetics, it has long been known that the type of dynamics described will lead to uniformity even without selective pressure. In this branch of science, this phenomenon is called 'genetic drift'. Thus, learning by pure imitation will lead to stability, but it will not necessarily lead to a result which is optimal.

The Two Operator Algorithm — Learning by Imitation and Communication

The one operator algorithm can be enhanced by another genetic operator, recombination. The special recombination operator used in the canonical GA is one point crossover.

In crossover, two genetic individuals are drawn with replacement from the population. The bit string of these individuals are cut at a point that is determined randomly. Then the resulting parts ('substrings') are exchanged and put together again. The resulting genetic individuals are often called the 'children' of the 'parent' individuals the operator started from. Figure 4.3 shows an example of one point crossover on two 16 bit long individuals with a crossover point after the bit number $s = 4$ from the left.

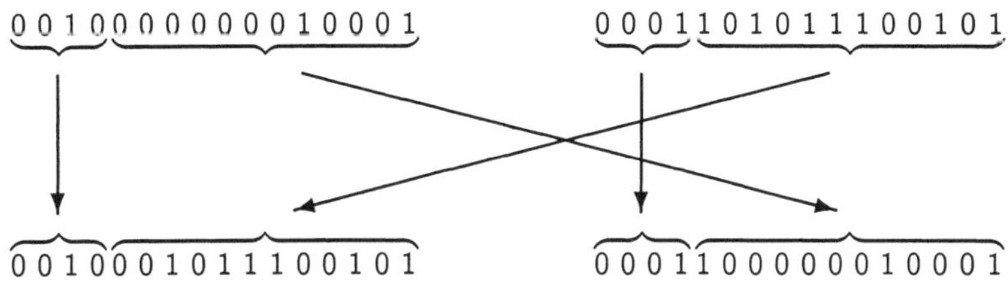

Fig. 4.3. One Point Crossover (Example)

Crossover is often interpreted as learning by communication. Two economic agents meet, talk to each other about their economic strategies and thus allow for adapting some parts of each other's strategy. This interpretation may look strange for models dealing with only one economic variable like the case of regional monopolies or the well known cobweb model by Arifovic (1994). In other models like Bullard and Duffy (1998) or the repeated prisoners' dilemma model by Axelrod (1987), this interpretation is straightforward and sensible.

Technically speaking, crossover is a mathematical function $I(\cdot)$. The function has four arguments i, j, k and s it projects on the space of boolean values:

$$I(i, j, k, s) \in \{0; 1\}; \quad i, j, k \in S; \quad s \in [1, \dots, L-1]. \tag{4.9}$$

i and j are the genetic individuals chosen to play the role of the parent individuals in crossover. k is the offspring produced by the operator. s is the crossover point, i.e. the bit position after which the parents' bit strings are cut. The function $i(\cdot)$ returns 0, if k consists of the left substring of i and the right substring of j. Otherwise, $i(\cdot)$ returns 1. In the example of Fig. 4.3, if the left parent individual is i and the right parent is j, then the specific operation can be written as $I(i, j, k, 4)$. The result of the function is $I(i, j, k, 4) = 1$.

The crossover probability χ gives the probability of an individual to be involved within crossover. This means that not every individual participates in crossover, but on the average only a share of χ of the population. Moreover, the crossover point is determined by chance. The possible points $s \in [1, 2, \dots, L-1]$ are i.i.d.

The probability of gaining genetic individual k from a population by crossover and selection/reproduction is

$$P_2(k|\overline{n}) = (1-\chi)P_1(k|\overline{n}) + \chi \sum_{i \in S} \sum_{j \in S} P_1(i|\overline{n}) P_1(j|\overline{n}) \frac{1}{L-1} \sum_{s=1}^{L-1} I(i,j,k,s). \quad (4.10)$$

Analogous to (4.7), the probability of gaining population $\overline{m}$ directly from population $\overline{n}$ by the two operator algorithm is

$$P_2(\overline{m}|\overline{n}) = \binom{M}{\overline{m}} \prod_{i \in S} P_2(i|\overline{n})^{m(i)}. \quad (4.11)$$

The stochastic process of the two operator algorithm is very similar to the one of the one operator algorithm, especially regarding the impossibility of leaving a homogeneous population. Still, the homogeneous populations represent absorbing states of the Markov process underlying the two operator algorithm. Crossover does not change the basic property of the algorithms described up to here: There is still the problem of possible lasting convergence to a homogeneous state which does not necessarily represent an optimal solution of the underlying economic problem.

The Three Operator Algorithm — Learning by Imitation, Communication and Experiment

Finally, a third operator is added, creating a three operator algorithm. This algorithm is identical to the canonical genetic algorithm (Goldberg, 1989). The third genetic operator, mutation, randomly changes single bits of the genetic individuals' bit strings. An example is given in Fig. 4.4.

0 0 1 0 0 0 0 0 0 0 0 0 1 0 0 0 1

↓

0 0 1 0 0 0 0 0 0 1 0 0 1 0 0 0 1

Fig. 4.4. Mutation (Example)

From an economic point of view, mutation can be seen as a form of learning by experiment. An economic agent slightly changes her strategy by changing little parts it.[8]

Imitation (selection/reproduction) and communication (crossover) only allow for the learning of strategies which — at least in their parts — have been member of the very first population. Learning by experiment (mutation), in contrast is capable of finding totally new strategies, i.e. strategies never used before. Experiments allow

[8] An alternative view sees mutation as a form of mistakes made in imitation. Mutation arises if agents fail to correctly imitate another agent's strategy. (See, e.g. Alchian 1950.) The main difference between the two possible interpretations is the role they give to the single agent. Learning by experiment demands an agent to actively try out something new, while learning by making mistakes just 'happens' to the agents.

the agents to develop strategies which never occurred in society before. This means the mutation is the only source of true innovation.

In a canonical GA, the main influence on mutation is the mutation probability μ. μ is the probability of each single bit of an individual's bit string to be flipped.[9] Moreover, the probability of an individual i to be turned into individual j by mutation depends on the number of bits that have to be flipped in order to turn i into j, i.e. the number of bit positions in i where the bits are not the same as in the respective positions in j. This number is called the Hamming distance between i and j, $H(i,j)$.[10] As $H(i,j)$ is a distance, it follows that

$$0 \leq H(i,j) \leq L. \tag{4.12}$$

The probability of turning individual i into j by mutation is

$$\mu^{H(i,j)}(1-\mu)^{(L-H(i,j))}. \tag{4.13}$$

Consequently, in the three operator algorithm, employing selection/reproduction, crossover and mutation, the probability of gaining individual i from population $\overline{n}$ is

$$P_3(i|\overline{n}) = \sum_{j \in S} \mu^{H(i,j)}(1-\mu)^{(L-H(i,j))} P_2(j|\overline{n}). \tag{4.14}$$

Defining $\alpha := \frac{\mu}{1-\mu}$, (4.14) can be rewritten as

$$P_3(i|\overline{n}) = \frac{1}{(1+\alpha)^L} \sum_{j \in S} \alpha^{H(i,j)} P_2(j|\overline{n}). \tag{4.15}$$

Thus, the Markov transition probability, i.e. the probability of directly turning population $\overline{n}$ into population $\overline{m}$ by use of the three operator algorithm, is

$$P_3(\overline{m}|\overline{n}) = \binom{M}{\overline{m}} \prod_{i \in S} P_3(i|\overline{n})^{m(i)}. \tag{4.16}$$

The transition matrix consisting of the probabilities (4.16) describes the three operator algorithm as a population Markov process.

Other than the one and two operator algorithm, the three operator algorithm has no absorbing states. In other words: It can be shown that $P_3(\overline{m}|\overline{n})$ is positive for every combination of $\overline{m}$ and $\overline{n}$. Every state of the Markov process can be reached directly, i.e. in one step of the process, from every state. This means that the complete Markov chain describing the canonical GA consists of one and only one transient class.

The one operator algorithm will not converge to a population consisting of uniform individuals. But, it can be shown that the algorithm reaches a situation characterized by a constant long run distribution of genetic populations.

---

[9] Usually, μ is very small, often set to a value between $1/100$ and $1/1000$.

[10] As an example, refer to Fig. 4.4. The Hamming distance between the two individual is — certainly — 1.

An outline of the proof is the following:[11] The transition matrix P characterizing one step of the canonical GA is regular. This means in this case that it is irreducible and aperiodic. For regular matrices there exists a stochastic matrix A with

$$A = \lim_{n\to\infty} P^n, \tag{4.17}$$

which consists of identical row vectors $\overline{q}_\alpha$; $\overline{q}_\alpha$ gives the constant long run distribution of the states of the underlying Markov process. This means that it characterizes a probability distribution which is left unchanged by one additional step of the process:

$$\overline{q}_\alpha = \overline{q}_\alpha P. \tag{4.18}$$

According to the definition of eigensystems, $\overline{q}_\alpha$ is the left eigenvector of P to p's eigenvalue of $\lambda = 1$.

The Perron–Frobenius theorem for regular stochastic matrices[12] ensures the existence of one unique (due to multiplication) such vector $\overline{q}_\alpha$. The stationary distribution of states is characterized by that vector $\overline{q}_\alpha$ the elements of which sum up to unity:

$$\sum_{i=1}^{N} \overline{q}_{\alpha,i} = 1. \tag{4.19}$$

From this it can be deduced that the canonical GA leads to a unique and constant distribution of *populations* in the long run. This distribution is sufficiently described by vector $\overline{q}_\alpha$.

This result looks a bit tricky. The crucial point is to keep in mind that there are two distinct distributions in focus. The first one is the genetic population, which is a distribution of *genetic individuals*. A population can be characterized by a vector of individual economic strategies. This means that a population can be interpreted as one social behavioral pattern. Secondly, and different from the first, vector $\overline{q}_\alpha$ is a distribution of *genetic populations*, i.e. a distribution of several different social behavioral patterns.

In mathematical terms, the three operator algorithm ends up in a state that can be called Ljapunov stable: There is a set of populations with a positive long run measure, and this set is a true subset of the set of all populations S'.[13]

A learning scheme consisting of the three learning techniques imitation, communication, and experiment, has some clearly defined stability properties: On the one hand, such learning behavior does never lead to asymptotic stability of individual behaviors. On the other hand, in the long run all social behavioral patterns, i.e. combinations of individual behaviors within a population, appear with constant probability. This does not mean that social behavioral patterns remain unchanged in time, but that the changes will occur due to some well defined mathematical regularities.

[11] The proof is given in length by Davis and Principe (1993).

[12] See, e.g. Isaacson and Madsen (1976, pp. 123–132).

[13] Ljapunov stability in the space of populations can alternatively be interpreted as asymptotic stability in the space of long run distributions of populations.

4.3 Genetic Algorithm Learning as an Evolutionary Process

More results concerning the dynamics of genetic algorithms can be found by interpreting GA learning as an evolutionary process.

It has already been shown that the genetic population is the most important data structure in the process of a GA. It is also known that a genetic population can be described as a distribution of the possible types of genetic individuals. This is a fact pointing to some apparent similarities between GAs on the one hand and parts of evolutionary economic theory on the other: In evolutionary economics, too, the concept of the population plays a central role.[14] This is especially true for the field of evolutionary game theory. The evolutionary branches of economics, too, populations stand for the distribution of individual behavioral strategies. Thus, it can be stated that evolutionary economics makes use of more or less the same population concept as GA learning theory does.

Starting from this conceptional parallelism, it can be found that GAs do in fact describe a special form of an evolutionary game. It can be shown that indeed GAs do meet all the three criteria Friedman (1998) uses as distinctive characterizations of evolutionary games:

1. Strategies gaining a higher payoff tend over time to displace strategies with lower payoff in the population.
2. There is some inertia.
3. Economic agents do not intentionally influence other agents' future strategies.

The adherence to the first point can even be shown at the example of the regional monopolists' case. A general proof can be gained from a look at the definition of the reproduction probabilities of GAs (4.15), which increases with an increase in fitness:

$$\frac{\partial P_3\left(i|\bar{n}\right)}{\partial R(i)} > 0. \tag{4.20}$$

A first hint toward the adherence to the second criterion (inertia) can again be gained from the introductory monopolists' case: Figure 3.10 shows that aggregate changes do not happen too abruptly. In can be shown for the general case that during reproduction GAs prefer those genetic individuals being relatively similar to those which are members of the old population. This can be shown as follows: (4.13) will be called $P_m(i|j)$. $P_m(i|j)$ is the probability of gaining genetic individual i from individual j by pure mutation. This probability depends on the mutation probability μ and the Hamming distance between i and j,

$$P_m(i|j) = \mu^{H(i,j)}(1-\mu)^{(L-H(i,j))}. \tag{4.21}$$

Differentiation yields

[14] See Witt (1993a, pp. 4–6).

$$\frac{\partial P_m(i|j)}{\partial H(i,j)} = \mu^{H(i,j)}(1-\mu)^{L-H(i,j)}[\ln\mu - (\ln 1-\mu)]\begin{cases} <0 & \text{for} \quad \mu < \frac{1}{2} \\ =0 & \text{for} \quad \mu = \frac{1}{2} \\ >0 & \text{for} \quad \mu > \frac{1}{2} \end{cases}. \tag{4.22}$$

This means that for normal parameter settings in GAs ($\mu \ll \frac{1}{2}$), the probability of small changes is much greater than the probability of big ones.

Defining $H(i|\overline{n}) := \sum_{j\in\overline{n}} \overline{n}(j)\, H(i,j)$ as the average Hamming distance between genetic individual i and the population $\overline{n}$, it results that for $\mu < \frac{1}{2}$

$$\frac{\partial P_3(i|\overline{n})}{\partial H(i|\overline{n})} < 0. \tag{4.23}$$

The greater the average Hamming distance between an individual i and a population $\overline{n}$ is, the smaller is the probability of gaining an individual i from population $\overline{n}$ in a canonical GA. This can be seen as a sign for the inertia of genetic algorithms.

The adherence to the third criterion (no intentional influence on other agents' strategies) can be proved more intuitively. Genetic algorithms model learning as adaptive learning. Agents do not have the ability to predict someone else's strategies nor can they remember what the others did in the past. This means that GA–agents simply are not smart enough to intentionally influence somebody else.

In summary, GAs can be interpreted as a form of evolutionary games. A GA making use of populations of length M and individuals consisting of L binary bits is able to describe every strategy from the set of strategies S. S contains a number of $|S| = 2^L = N$ elements. Interpreting this GA as an evolutionary game, means seeing the GA as a symmetric M person game with up to N different pure strategies. The payoffs to the agents can be calculated from the objective function R.

By definition, the main difference between games and problems analyzed by 'basic' decision theory, is the fact that in games, the situation a player is in is influenced by the actions of at least one of the other players. As mentioned above, this influence of other economic agents on the decision situation of an agent is the distinctive feature of situations with state dependent fitness. This means that for instance the monopolists' example cannot be interpreted as an economic game, because the monopolists' model does not contain any state dependency. The situation in a cobweb model[15], in contrast, contains state dependent fitness (as long as the population size is finite) and can thus be interpreted as a game.

Sometimes, there is a difference between situations which can be modeled by an economic GA and evolutionary game theoretic situations. In evolutionary game theory, there are two main ways of matching one player with another. The first form is repeated pairwise matching, the second form is playing the field. In repeated pairwise matching, from a population, two members are randomly drawn in order to let them play a two person game against each other. The process of drawing a pair of agents and letting them play is repeated several times. Playing the field, in contrast, means every member of a population playing against every other member. This is

[15] For a GA version of a cobweb model, see Arifovic (1994).

identical to every player playing against a mixed strategy reflecting the population wide distribution of pure strategies played by the individual agents.

A number of economic GAs are based on a different form of confronting the agents with each other. Mostly, every agent plays against the aggregate rest of the population.[16] Again, the introductory monopolists' model can serve as an example: Here, the profit of an agent depends on her quantity decision and on the quantity decision of all other members of the population. For the equilibrium price emerging each period and influencing the profit, it is not important how much every single agent produces, but how high the *aggregate* supply is.[17]

4.3.1 Populations as Near Nash Equilibria

The main challenge an economic agent faces is to find a strategy which, due to her economic environment, maximizes fitness relative to the fitness of the rest of the population. The environment of an agent can be completely described by two things: the objective function $R(\cdot)$ and the current population $\bar{n}$. Every agent has to cope with the problem of finding the strategy i from the given set of strategies, S, which leads to maximum relative fitness:

$$\max_{i \in S} R(i|\bar{n}) \,. \tag{4.24}$$

In a cobweb model, for example, every firm tries to find a production quantity which gains as much profit as possible in the presence of the quantity decisions of all the other agents.

This directly leads to the concept of a Nash equilibrium. A Nash strategy is a strategy which, given the strategies of all other players, maximizes payoff. This is exactly what an economic agent is trying to do: She tries to find her Nash strategy. Thus, an economic GA can be interpreted as a dynamic system consisting of a number of agents each of them trying to play Nash. In the presence of the selection/reproduction operator constantly recomposing the population in favor of better strategies, the economic GA pushes the population into a state in which most of the agents play Nash. This means, that a population cannot be completely interpreted as a state of a perfect Nash equilibrium but at least as a state which is not far from it.

4.3.2 Evolutionary Stability of Genetic Populations

As a second step in analyzing the genetic population, a look at the specific dynamics of genetic algorithms seems appropriate.

The native concept of evolutionary dynamics is the concept of replicator dynamics.[18] This kind of dynamics does not seem to be very suitable for the description of

---

16 This is, among others, true for the cobweb model in Sect. 3.5, and for the models by Arifovic (1994) and Dawid (1999, pp.111). Counterexamples can be found in Axelrod (1987) and Andreoni and Miller (1995).

17 For more details, see Franke (1997).

18 See Weibull (1995); Hofbauer and Sigmund (1988) or Hofbauer and Sigmund (1998).

economic GA learning models.[19] Mailath (1992, p. 286) even claims that 'There is nothing in economics to justify replicator dynamics'.

Instead, in this work, the concept of evolutionary stability will gain a central role. Although evolutionary stability is a concept of rest points rather than of dynamics, this concept is appropriate for the analysis of evolutionary dynamics as well.

The concept of evolutionarily stable states (ESS) can be verbalized as follows:[20] A strategy is evolutionarily stable if — relative to the population the strategy is part of — it leads to better results than a new, 'invading' strategy would gain in its place. Although this concept of an ESS is frequently used in evolutionary dynamics, this concept has two weaknesses, that make it seem to be of only limited suitability for the analysis of genetic algorithms. The first weakness stems from the fact that the concept is exclusively based on symmetric two person games. As has been said before, this is not the form of game, GA learning models can be interpreted as. Secondly, there is no explicit formulation of the exact concepts of selection and invasion, i.e. no explicit formulation of the specific kind of dynamics leading to the stability concept the ESS are based on. ESS are based on the idea of some strategies invading a population and being rejected (or not). But, there is no explicit formulation of how the processes of invasion and rejection do exactly look like. Genetic algorithms, in contrast, give a very clear definition of both, the invasion process, which is reproduction, crossover, and mutation, and the rejection process, which is selection.

Thus, in order to describe the evolutionary dynamics of GA learning, the invading processes reproduction, crossover, and mutation, and the rejection process, i.e. selection, have to be considered in greater detail.

The major importance of the fact that the invading process is a compound process in form of reproduction, crossover, and mutation, is the finding that this compound severely limits the set of possibly invading strategies in time. More to this point can be found below (Sect. 4.4).

The rejection process of selection has two important characteristics: It selects strategies due to their relative fitness, and it selects due to some amount of chance. This means that in a GA, badly performing strategies are very likely to be rejected from a population, but that they are not rejected with probability one. In other words: In the long run, there is a very high probability that a population will not contain extraordinarily bad strategies, but this is not certain.

Thus, at this point, a concept of evolutionary stability will be presented, which will, on the one hand, keep the spirit of the standard ESS concept, but will, on the other hand, open this concept for the use in GA learning theory as well. The central idea is the following: A genetic population can be called evolutionarily stable, if the GA process of selection rejects the invasion of the population by one or more strategies produced by reproduction, crossover, and mutation. Invasion can thus take

---

[19] Nevertheless, standard replicator dynamics might be interpreted as a kind of dynamics able to describe learning by imitation.

[20] More general, though highly mathematical explanations can be found in e.g. Maynard Smith (1982), Hofbauer and Sigmund (1988), Marks (1992), Mailath (1992), or Weibull (1995), to mention only a few of various sources.

place in form of a change in the frequency of the strategies already included in the population or in form of a totally new strategy entering. Thus, invasion is a term for the change of the composition of a genetic population. Knowing this, a clearer definition of evolutionary stability of genetic populations is the following: A genetic population is evolutionarily stable if it is resistant against changes of its composition.

More formally, a genetic population $\overline{n}$ is called *evolutionarily superior*[21] to population $\overline{m}$ (denoted as $\overline{n} \overset{\text{es}}{>} \overline{m}$) if it has the following two characteristics:

(a) Every strategy i contained within population $\overline{n}$ has at least the same fitness in the basic population $\overline{n}$ as it has in the invaded population $\overline{m}$, while at least one strategy has even more fitness in $\overline{n}$ than in $\overline{m}$.
(b) The invading strategies $k \in \{\overline{m} \backslash \overline{n}\}$ are the worst performing strategies contained in $\overline{m}$, so that they will be most surely rejected.

This means that a genetic population $\overline{n}$ is evolutionarily superior to genetic population $\overline{m}$, if

$$R(i|\overline{n}) \geq R(i|\overline{m}) \ \forall\, i \in \overline{n} \tag{4.25}$$

$$\wedge\ \exists\, j \text{ with } R(j|\overline{n}) > R(j|\overline{m}) \tag{4.26}$$

$$\wedge\quad R(k|\overline{m}) < R(i|\overline{m}) \ \forall\, i \in \overline{n};\ \forall k \in \{\overline{m} \backslash \overline{n}\}\,. \tag{4.27}$$

Conditions (4.25) to (4.27) induce a partial ordering on the space of genetic populations S'. A stable population in the sense of (4.25) to (4.27) is a population with no other populations being evolutionarily superior to. This means that genetic population $\overline{n}$ is evolutionarily stable if

$$\nexists \overline{m} \in S' \quad \text{with} \quad \overline{m} \overset{\text{es}}{>} \overline{n}\,. \tag{4.28}$$

Condition (4.28) is a generalization of the concept of evolutionary stability.[22]

Genetic selection is a stochastic process.[23] Thus, it is possible that invading strategies are not directly rejected even from evolutionarily stable populations, which means that they are not rejected within the course of one step of the algorithm. Nevertheless, it is sure that these strategies are rejected within a finite number of steps. This means the following: If a genetic population is evolutionarily stable it will recover from an invasion within finite time. In the long run, an evolutionarily stable population cannot be lastingly changed by the process of the GA. Nevertheless, once an evolutionarily stable population has been invaded, the emergence of a series of evolutionarily inferior[24] populations is possible. These inferior populations represent several transitory states on the way back to the evolutionarily stable population. This is the reason why the Markov chain analysis does not result in a trivial long run distribution of populations, but a non–trivial one.

---

21 evolutionary superiority

22 Note, the similarity to e.g. Weibull (1995, p.36).

23 This is true for most GAs, especially for the canonical GA (Goldberg, 1989). Nevertheless, there are also some deterministic selection methods, like e.g. in Windrum and Birchenhall (1998).

24 Take 'evolutionarily inferior' as the contrary of 'evolutionarily superior'.

4.3.3 Evolutionary Dynamics

The preceding sections show that GA dynamics can be described from an evolutionary point of view. It can be found that genetic populations tend to establish a state which is nearly an intra–population Nash equilibrium. Thus, GA learning as a process of turning one genetic population into another can be seen as an approximation of a moving Nash equilibrium process. Using the criteria of evolutionary superiority as given in (4.25) to (4.27), even more can be said about this process. Genetic algorithms perform selection in favor of evolutionarily superior populations. Thus, GA learning can be described as a process constantly dropping some populations in favor of better ones (in the sense of (4.28)). By this, the direction of the process is characterized, but not the exact path the GA takes in time. Because of the stochastic characteristics of the GA, the exact path crucially depends on the starting population. This means that, while the long run result of GA learning is independent of the starting conditions, the paths taken by the process differ between the single runs of the GA. Phenomena like historical lock–insindexlock–in, and path dependencies *can* occur, but due to the general characteristics of GAs, these are of only temporary nature.

The potential and possibility to describe phenomena like lock–ins, hysteresis and path dependencies[25] is often taken as a defining characteristic and as one of the major advantages of evolutionary economic theory in contrast to mainstream economics. Seen against this background, GAs, not able to maintain these phenomena in the long run, do not seem to be appropriate for modeling evolutionary economic processes. This objection luckily only holds for the canonical, i.e. the most basic GA. There are, instead, lots of variations to this standard GA which are free of this problem. As a detailed discussion of this point would surely exceed the framework of this book, two key words will do at this point, giving some hints to how to solve the problem: The key words are 'deceptiveness' and 'premature convergence', both meaning some technical characteristics of GAs which could provide some GA behavior that can be interpreted as genuinely evolutionary phenomena in economics. More on these points can be found at e.g. Goldberg (1989), Mitchell (1996), and Davis (1991).

What is of major importance to the evolutionary dynamics of GA learning is the way economic change takes place. Genetic operators (i.e. the different learning schemes) cause changes in the population. Again and again, new economic strategies are tested on their economic quality by being exposed to the market. The market reveals how successful a strategy is, relative to the other strategies involved in the market process. After this test, selection starts: If a strategy proved to be rather poor, the agent who used this strategy gives it up and adopts a new one (imitation) or creates a new one by communication or experiment (or, possibly, both). Relatively good strategies, in contrast, are likely to be continued by their agents. After this phase of learning, strategies are tested on the market, again. The repetition of these steps is the very heart of every economic genetic algorithm.

[25] For more information about these phenomena, see Arthur et al. (1987), Arthur (1995), and the frequently cited David (1985).

The diversity of the strategies contained within a population is of crucial importance for the dynamics and quality of the learning process. The fact that strategies within a population are different from each other is the source of economic change, i.e. the continuous alteration of the composition of populations. Under the regime of genetic algorithm learning, this alteration is mainly based on learning by imitation and communication.[26] As will be explained in greater detail below (Sect. 4.4), learning by imitation and communication can only take place in heterogeneous populations. This means that heterogeneity or social diversity of strategies is one of the main forces of economic change.

Moreover, the process of selection is an important one, too. Selection in an economic context is often interpreted as what is the role of the market.[27] While the process of economic learning is enough to explain economic *change*, economic learning cannot sufficiently explain economic *development*. Economic development can only be achieved by the combination of learning and selection. In order to turn the succession of different populations into a sequence of *constantly improving* populations (in the sense of evolutionary superiority), it needs an institution giving rise to the possibility of distinguishing good strategies from not so good ones. Having at hand such an institution, it becomes possible to decide which strategy should survive and replicate and which one should die out. In an economic context, this institution is the markets, while in the process of GA learning, it is the operator of selection. For economic change, learning is of great importance, but it is the market and only the market which turns economic change into economic development.[28]

Summarizing, the following can be said: Under the regime of the market, evolutionary dynamics of the GA learning process is mainly driven by two forces: Heterogeneity, constantly inducing economics change, and the market as a device of coordination, constantly revealing the quality of the strategies, rejecting bad ones and thus turning economic change into development.

Finally, one further point needs to be added in order to complete the analysis of GA learning as an evolutionary process. It has already been shown that GA learning and market selection lead to improvement in individual and social behavior as long as possible. This means that, once an evolutionarily stable state is reached, there simply is no room for further improvement. Nevertheless, because of the special structure of the canonical GA, economic agents do not stop changing their behavior.[29] Learning, or at least what has been called economic change above, still takes

[26] In this context, it is interesting to notice that the great importance of imitation and communication as learning techniques is recognized in population genetics and in technical optimization methods, too. In both fields, mutation is regarded as an operator of only minor importance, i.e. as a background operator (see Goldberg, 1989).

[27] As not all economic models are models of a market economy, there are certainly more interpretations than this one. An example is learning in organizations, which is a process that cannot be explained in terms of markets and market functions. See, e.g. Simon (1997, Chap. III).

[28] This argument reflects concepts like the one by Hayek (1969), more often cited as Hayek (1978).

[29] This is true for the canonical GA and most of its variants. An exception is the Meta GA (Riechmann, 1998b), which will be introduced below (Sect. 6.3).

place. Even in this phase, new strategies enter the population. Now, it is the duty of the market (i.e. selection) to drive these strategies out of the population again. As mentioned above, this process of rejecting invading strategies can take several generations, thus producing several transitory populations until the original population is regained.

In other words: Even in the second phase of a GA learning process, i.e. even after an evolutionarily stable population has been reached for the first time, this population will be challenged by invading strategies again and again. This process leads to a kind of near equilibrium dynamics resulting from the continuous interplay of invasion (learning) and rejection (work of the market).

GA learning does in fact lead to an economic process described by Witt (1993b, p. xix) as

> 'interplay of coordinating tendencies arising from competitive adaptions in the markets and de–coordinating tendencies caused by the introduction of novelty'

From the point of view of evolutionary economics, this process is seen as one of the most important characteristics of the working of the market (Witt, 1985).

The analysis of genetic algorithms or GA learning from an evolutionary point of view thus leads to results which can be understood as an addition to the results of the Markov chain analysis. Most important, it can be recognized that what has been shown to be a state of Ljapunov stability is the outcome of an evolutionary process characterized by the interplay of learning mechanisms and the role of the market.

4.4 Genetic Algorithms as Learning Processes

In the introduction, the psychological definition of 'learning' by Kimble (1973) is presented (see Sect. 2.1.1, p. 7). Thus, it seems appropriate to examine if and to what extent GA learning does reflect this definition. In the introduction, four characteristic elements of 'learning' are given:

1. Learning means changing, not necessarily improving the behavioral potentiality.
   This is especially true for economic learning per GA. Sect. 4.3 shows that learning only causes economic change. In order to move from change to improvement, i.e. economic progress, an additional process is needed, the process of selection, which is the market in models of market based economies.
2. Learning means the change of the behavioral potentiality, but not necessarily of actual behavior.
   Economic agents leaning within a framework of a canonical GA model do not have a memory of their own. This means that they do not have a private behavioral potentiality in the meaning of a stock of behaviors to chose from in each period. If, in canonical GA models, there is a stock of behavioral strategies at

all, it is a social stock, i.e. the whole of the strategies contained in the population. Thus, GA learning is a process of social rather than individual learning. Nevertheless, in the course of this work, two variants of the canonical GA will be introduced, which make a step towards a more rigorous modeling of an individual behavioral potentiality. These variants are the election operator (Sect. 6.2) and the operator of individual preselection (Sect. 8.3.4).

3. Learning causes a relatively permanent change of the behavioral potentiality. GA learning causes a relatively permanent change in the behavioral potentiality of a *population*, for the process of social learning modeled by the GA hardly ever returns to a population that has been reached before but changed thereafter. This is one of the central results of the analysis of GA learning as an evolutionary process (Sect. 4.3).
4. Learning means change as a result of reinforced practice. This of course is the core mechanism of GA learning: Behavioral strategies are tested and are kept in practice or discarded depending on the results of the practical tests.

In theoretical economics, genetic algorithms are most often used as metaphors for social learning. Some authors call this interpretation 'population learning' (See e.g. Windrum and Birchenhall 1998.), by this stressing the close relationship between evolutionary games and GA learning models. Social learning is a form of learning from one another. Different heterogeneous individuals do not only learn from their own experience, but also from the experiences and actions of others. This means that the concept of social learning is different from learning mechanisms viewing learning as a process taking place in isolation from other agents. Examples for mechanisms of individually isolated learning are statistical learning mechanisms[30] and learning with the help of neural networks (Heinemann, 1998).

It has been shown already that learning per GA can be interpreted as a form of compound social learning consisting of three different learning schemes. Only one of these three learning schemes imitation, communication, and experiments can take place in the absence of other individuals: learning by experiments. Both of the other learning techniques cannot be used without the existence of a whole society of agents.

From the analysis of GA with the help of Markov chains as described above it is possible to find some general characteristics of GAs as learning mechanisms. In the following, the three single learning schemes included in the canonical GA will be described individually before the concluding description of the characteristics of the GA as a whole.

4.4.1 Learning by Imitation

In Sect. 4.2.2, it has been shown that learning by imitation (in canonical GAs) leads to situations that can be described as asymptotically stable. The phenomenon of

[30] See Sargent (1993) for a survey and Lucas (1986) or Marcet and Sargent (1989) for some nearly classical examples.

genetic drift results in uniform populations: At the end of the learning process, all economic agents behave the same.

In addition, it can be found that only those strategies can be learned which are in use by at least one member of the current population. (You can only imitate what is already there. This is the simple but true meaning of imitation.) Because of the ongoing disappearance of strategies from the population (as a consequence of selection and reproduction) the set of different strategies grows smaller and smaller until at last there is only one strategy left.

This recognition leads to a better understanding of the concept of genetic populations as near Nash equilibria: Every economic agent tries to adopt the strategy leading to maximum possible success, relative to the rest of the population. But, caused by the learning technique of imitation, the set of strategies available for imitation, is restricted. Learning by imitation only allows for the adoption of strategies contained in the current population. This means that not the set of *all possible* strategies S can be learned by imitation, but only the much smaller set Z_I, the set of strategies *learnable by imitation*. Thus, for imitation, problem (4.24) can be formulated more precisely:

$$\max_{i \in Z_I} R\left(i|\overline{n}\right); \quad Z_I \subseteq S \tag{4.29}$$

At the start of the learning process, the set Z_I consists of all strategies contained in the historically first population. In the course of the process, the set is reduced in size by means of the selective force of the market, until at last there is only one strategy left.

The dimension of the difference between the set of all possible strategies and the set of all strategies learnable by imitation can be easily calculated. According to (4.2), a genetic individual of length L is capable of representing one of $|S| = 2^L$ different economic strategies. In order to make all these strategies available for imitation, a genetic population must consist of at least $|S| = 2^L$ individuals, i.e. $M \geq 2^L$. A population of such a large size is very unusual in normally specified genetic algorithms. An example will demonstrate this: Consider a GA with individuals coded as bit strings of length $L = 16$. This means that a number of $2^{16} = 65\,536$ different strategies can be coded ($|S| = 65\,536$). A population is assumed to contain $M = 100$ genetic individuals. Thus, the maximum number of strategies learnable by imitation is $|Z_I| = 100$. This means, that at best $\frac{100}{65\,536} \approx 0.15\%$ of all possible strategies can be learned by imitation. Correspondingly small is the probability of learning the theoretically optimal strategy by use of pure imitation.

The game theoretic results can be enhanced with respect to learning by imitation: The state resulting from learning by imitation is an ESS only with respect to the set of strategies available for imitation. An invasion of the current population can only take place by strategies contained in the same population. This means that a structural change of populations can only take place in form of a change of the frequency of strategies contained. During the learning process, the set of possible invaders is decreased. At the end of the process, i.e. after reaching a homogeneous population, invasions are no longer possible. This is another explanation of the phenomenon called above a final state of genetic drift and an absorbing state of the Markov process.

Summarizing, there are two important characteristics of learning by imitation: Learning by imitation generally leads to societies with uniform behavior, and learning per imitation does not generally lead to individually or socially optimal behavior.

4.4.2 Learning by Communication

Learning by communication, as described in Sect. 4.2.2, is very similar to learning by imitation. In fact, learning by communication in the concept of GA crossover is nothing more than learning by imitation of parts of strategies, or, following Birchenhall (1995), modular imitation.[31] Like with imitation, the results of learning by communication is decisively determined by the contents of the very first genetic population. Again, the set of strategies learnable by communication Z_C, is not necessarily identical with the set S of possible strategies. Thus, for learning by communication, (4.24) can be written as

$$\max_{i \in Z_C} R(i|\overline{n})\,; \quad Z_C \subseteq S\,. \tag{4.30}$$

In contrast to learning by pure imitation, with communication parts of strategies, i.e. parts of bit strings, can be exchanged or 'learned'. But only those parts can be exchanged which are part of strategies employed within the population. Technically, this means the following: If, for example, the bit string representing the first best strategy, requires a '1' at the second position, but the population contains only strategies with a '0' on this position, the perfect strategy cannot be learned by crossover.[32]

It can be shown, though, that by communication more strategies can be learned than by pure imitation. The maximum size of the set Z_C is normally[33] greater than the size of Z_I:

$$|Z_I| < |Z_C| \leq 2\binom{M}{2}(L-1)\,. \tag{4.31}$$

Moreover, from (4.31) it is clear that for population sizes of more than 10 individuals ($M > 10$), populations are nearly surely large enough to contain every possible strategy.

31 Technically, imitation can — apart from the reproduction operator — be formulated by use of a slight modification to the operator of crossover (see Sects. 3.3.3 and 4.2.2): Allowing the edges of the bit strings as crossover points as well, i.e. changing equation (4.9) into

$$I(i,j,k,s) \in \{0;1\}; \quad i,j,k \in S; \quad s \in [0,\ldots,L],$$

lets crossover allow for real imitation.

32 With the help of the schema concept (Sect. 4.1.1) for bit strings of length 16, the example reads: The schema # # # # # # # # # # # # # # 0 # cannot be transferred into # # # # # # # # # # # # # # 1 # by crossover.

33 Precisely: It is greater whenever the length of the individuals is greater than 1 and the population has more than 2 members.

Like at imitation, at communication the selective function of the market continuously decreases the number of strategies learnable, until at last there is only one strategy left.

Learning is often interpreted as a process of search within a highly dimensioned and thus very large search space (see Romer 1992). For this interpretation two aspects of learning are of great importance, exploration and exploitation of the search space. Exploration means searching different areas of the search space in order to find out if search results in these different ares are relatively good or bad, respectively. Exploitation means the more intensive search of areas which have been shown to contain relatively good search results during the step of exploration. More technically oriented work on GAs (e.g. Goldberg 1989 or Holland 1996) demonstrates that the operator of crossover, i.e. learning by communication,strongly accelerates the exploration of the search space. This means that learning by communication leads to a relatively faster learning process.

In learning by communication, too, the degree of heterogeneity of the society is of great importance. The more different strategies are used within the population, the more strategies can be learned. In addition, the quality of both, individual and social behavior can be expected to improve faster if the diversity of a population is greater. Thus, it seems appropriate to think of a close connection between the degree of heterogeneity of a population on the one hand and the speed of improvement in behavior and economic success on the other. In population genetics, a positive correlation between the variance of a population and the speed of improvement of quality (i.e. of fitness of the members) has been found. There, this correlation is known as the 'Fisher Principle'.[34] Birchenhall et al. (1997) show that the Fisher principle can be useful as a behavioral interpretation of economic GA learning processes as well. Following this interpretation, a strong result arises concerning the role of heterogeneity for economic progress: The diversity of economic behaviors within a society is an indispensable prerequisite of economic development.

4.4.3 Learning by Experiment

Learning by experiments is very different from the two other learning mechanisms of the canonical GA. The most important difference is the fact that learning by experiment is able to generate strategies which have not been contained in any population (including the starting population) before — not even in their parts. Learning by experiments is the only learning technique of GA learning capable of producing real innovation.[35]

An economic agent, using the technique of learning by experiment, can learn every possible strategy. This means that the set of strategies learnable by experiments, Z_E, is identical with the set of all strategies, S. Learning by experiments makes it possible to test every strategy and by this, in the long run, to find the optimal one.

[34] For a transfer of the Fisher Principle into economics, see Metcalfe (1994).

[35] For similar arguments see Blume and Easley (1993) and Hirshleifer and Martinez Coll (1992), who show the validity of this idea even for the field of evolutionary games.

In the long run, the possibility of ending up in individually suboptimal behavior does not exist in the presence of experimental learning. This, on the other hand, means that the impossibility of modeling path dependencies and similar phenomena by means of a canonical GA, can be blamed on the working of learning by experiments. Markov chain analysis has already shown (Sect. 4.2.2) that the long run learning results are independent of the starting conditions of the learning process.

In the canonical GA, the frequency of experiments is constant over time.[36] This fact in the long run leads to the near equilibrium dynamics described above (Sect. 4.3.3).

4.4.4 GA Learning as a Compound Learning Mechanism

Learning according to the rules of the canonical GA means learning according to the simultaneous use of three learning techniques: imitation, communication and experiments. Thus, in order to characterize GA learning, it is not enough to analyze each learning technique alone. It is also important to look at the co working of the three techniques. The first result of this analysis of the compound learning mechanism of the GA is the finding, that learning by experiments does to some respect dominate the process. It is learning by experiments that makes GA learning a process capable of reaching every possible behavioral strategy and by this of generating every possible social behavioral pattern. Due to the working of the selection operator, the strategy learned is optimal in the long run, at least with respect to the economic problem to cope with. On the other hand, it is learning by experiment which prevents GA learning from convergence into an asymptotically stable result. The ongoing and never decreasing application of experiments continuously disturbs the social structure, thus preventing the arise of a structurally stable social behavioral pattern. The highest degree of social stability reached is the state of Ljapunov stability of social behavior as described above (Sect. 4.2.2).

Compared to learning by experiments, imitation and communication are of minor importance. The main role of these two techniques is the role for the speed of the learning process. Imitation and communication make sure that relatively good strategies can spread throughout the society. This is a fact that remarkably increases learning speed.

4.5 Summary

Theoretical analysis of economic learning by genetic algorithms is essentially based on three methods: analysis with the help of Markov chains, with the help of evolutionary and game theoretic tools, and analysis in a way more oriented to learning.

Each of these forms of analysis leads to some results, which are the essential base of the rest of this work. These results will prove to be helpful in explaining the behavior of GA learning processes in different economic contexts.

---

[36] An extended GA with varying frequencies of experiments can be found in Riechmann (1998b).

Markov chain analysis essentially helps to find some general results concerning the stability properties of the learning process. In order to extend the understanding of the learning process it proves useful to separate the process into its parts, i.e. the three learning mechanisms learning by imitation, by communication, and by experiments. Learning by experiments or the operator of mutation turns out to be the central mechanism, crucially determining the stability characteristics of the whole learning process. Whereas learning by imitation and communication alone converges to an asymptotically stable state, the introduction of experiments dramatically changes these properties: Learning by experiments prevents the whole compound learning process from convergence, only leaving room for a much weaker state, the state of Ljapunov stability in the space of genetic populations.

The analysis of GA learning as a dynamic evolutionary game leads to Additional results. It can be shown that GA learning leads to a form of economic change which can be interpreted as economic progress along a series of populations improving in the sense of an economic partial ordering of genetic populations until an evolutionarily stable state is reached.

The analysis of GA learning as a compound of three different learning techniques is the logical extension of the two above forms of analysis. The central result of this analysis is the finding that there is an important difference between the role of social learning (imitation and communication) and individual learning (experiments). GA learning is shown to gain its characteristic stability properties from the combination of both families of learning techniques.

5 Statistical Aspects of the Analysis of Economic Genetic Algorithms

5.1 Introduction

Simulation based on economic genetic algorithms generate a large amount of data informing about the performance of the agents and the results of the model. Every analysis and interpretation of GA models is thus based on statistical examinations of these data.

Generally, the simulation results can be interpreted as time series, each period consisting of a relatively large set of data. In every period of time, data arise carrying information about the respective population. This population information consists of at least two numbers per agent, one characterizing the economic strategy and the other economic success. For the introductory example of regional monopolists these numbers are the supplied quantity and the profit gained. In relation to their population, these individual data can be interpreted as a statistical distribution (see Sects. 4.2 and 4.3). This means that one way of describing a population is looking at the statistical moments of the distribution of its data. The advantage of this method is the fact, that it leads to a very handy abbreviation and aggregation of the raw data. The disadvantage is of course the loss of information connected with every way of aggregation. Thus, aggregation of population data by statistical mechanisms makes it impossible to carry out the micro analysis of the individual behavior of the members of the populations. Statistical analysis of GA simulation results is thus useful in order to obtain macro results but it is not if the major focus of analysis lies on the micro level.

The description of the development of a complete set of genetic populations over time would require the production of a 'movie', showing the change of the distribution of strategies over time. This, of course, lies far beyond the technical possibilities of this work. Instead, two different approaches are used: In order to demonstrate the movements on the macro level, the development of the moments of the characteristic distribution of the population is plotted. (See, e.g. Fig. 5.2.) The micro structure of populations is — as a form of still in time — shown as a histogram of the distribution of population specific micro data. (See, e.g. Fig. 7.3 in Sect. 7.4.1 below.) The interpretation of the data as time series allows for more analytic methods, such as frequency analysis as carried out below (Sect. 7.4.2).

This section will be restricted to some relatively simple statistical methods. The main aim of this section is to give some statistical evidence for the validity of the theoretical insights into the working of the GA learning process derived above.

5.2 Analysis

From the theoretical analysis of genetic algorithms as Markov processes, evolutionary games, and learning techniques there result two hypothesises which can be tested empirically:

1. Out of the three learning techniques, learning by imitation, by communication, and by experiments, due to the restrictions of the sets of strategies learnable, learning by imitations leads to the relatively worst, learning by experiments to the relatively best learning results.
2. Out of the three learning techniques, learning by imitation is the fastest to converge into a homogeneous population, learning by communication the second fastest, while learning by experiments does not converge at all.

In order to test the hypothesises, the following simple experiment was carried out: For the simple example of regional monopolies from Sect. 3.2, a GA model is set up and coded as a series of computer simulations. The single computer programs only differ with respect to the genetic operator included. The first program is based on selection/reproduction only, thus representing learning by pure imitation. The second program uses selection/reproduction and crossover in order to model learning by imitation and communication. The third model includes selection/reproduction and mutation, by this standing for learning by imitation and experiments. For reference, a fourth program is included, using the whole set of GA operators, i.e. selection/reproduction, crossover and mutation. Each of these programs is run 10 000 times, each run starting with a different first population generated randomly. Each run is a simulation over 500 rounds or periods of the GA. Population size is $n = 100$ agents or genetic individuals of length $L = 16$. For each simulation, the population mean of the supplied quantity was calculated for each period from $t = 301$ to $t = 500$.[1] In addition, for these last 200 periods the population variance is computed, i.e. the variance of quantities represented by the individuals of the same population. For these data, population mean and population variance of 200 population of 10 000 simulation runs respectively, the arithmetic mean and the variance is computed across the populations of the same round. Figure 5.1 summarizes the statistical methods used. Table 5.1 shows the results.

Learning Technique	Mean Quantity			Mean Variance	
	Mean $\bar{x}$	Variance s^2	Test Stat. T	Mean	Variance
Imitation	9.99086	1.14802	−0.85	0.00652639	0.010127
Communic.	9.953	0.73984	−5.47	0.00997675	0.00837719
Experiments	9.92884	0.141672	−18.73	14.2485	1.19473
full GA	9.97426	0.231098	−5.36	14.5619	1.34209

Table 5.1. Statistical Results

[1] The first 300 periods are not analyzed in order to give the simulations time enough to develop results sufficiently independent from their respective starting populations.

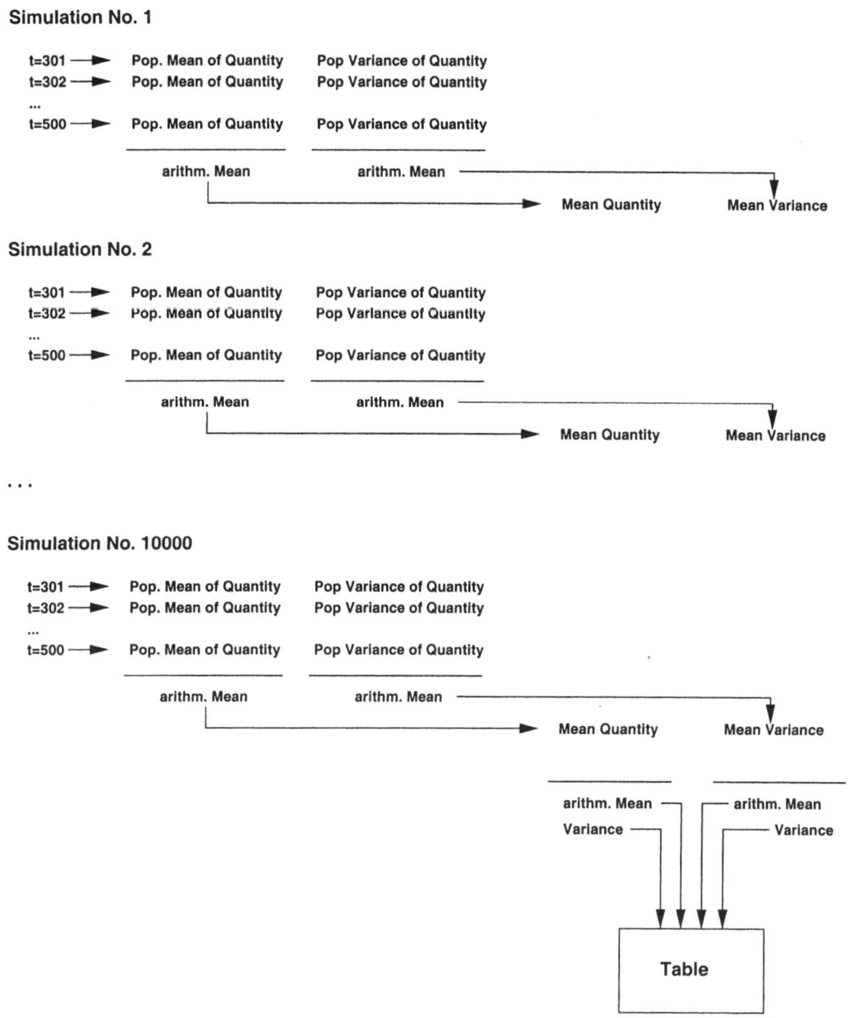

Fig. 5.1. Emergence of Data in Table 5.1

Looking at the results summarized in Table 5.1, a question becomes important: Are the quantities learned by GAs identical to the theoretically optimal quantities or are there systematic differences between these two kinds of results? In order to answer this question, the hypotheses 'The population mean of quantities learned is 10.' is tested. The mathematical form of this hypothesis is

$$\bar{x} = q^{\star} \equiv 10\,, \tag{5.1}$$

or

$$\bar{x} - q^{\star} = 0\,. \tag{5.2}$$

The hypothesis is tested using an approximate Gauss test.[2] Technically, the test requires the construction of a test statistic T. The size of T relative to a confidence interval, which is determined by the confidence level α, decides on the rejection (or not rejection) of the hypothesis. T is determined as

$$T = \frac{\overline{x} - 10}{s} \cdot \sqrt{10000}. \tag{5.3}$$

The value of the test statistic T is included in Table 5.1. According to these tests, for usual confidence levels of $\alpha = 0.01$, $\alpha = 0.1$ and $\alpha = 0.5$, only for learning by imitation the hypothesis cannot be rejected. In short, this means that due to statistical results, only learning by imitation seems to result in the learning of optimal behavior. For every other form of learning, the results learned do not seem to be the same as the theoretically optimal one. This result, at this point only valid for the case of regional monopolists, is the first hint that for other economic problems, too, GA learning does not generally produce optimum solutions. In fact, this suspicion will be substantiated in the context of other economic problems in the further course of this book: There is rarely one economic problem which is solved by GA learning in a theoretically optimal way. This does not mean that GA learning is a 'bad' learning technique. Mostly, this difference between optimal (neoclassical) theoretical solution and solution learned by GA is caused by the features of bounded rationality incorporated in the models in focus. Moreover, the result learned often display other theoretically convincing features, like being local optima or Nash equilibria.

A further look at Table 5.1 gives some evidence concerning the hypothesises 1 and 2 from the start of this section: The first hypothesis (Imitation leads the relatively worst, experiments to the relatively best results.) is hard to test. Assuming the best result learnable is $q^{\star} = 10$, the approximate Gauss test seems to defeat this hypothesis. In the mean, learning by experiments leads to a result not significantly differing from the theoretical optimum. What is problematic about this, though, is the fact that this is only true for the *mean* result of 10000 simulations. The data from Table 5.1 also show, that the single results of the 10000 simulations have a large spread around their mean, as indicated by their variance of $s^2 = 1.14802$. This means that the results of the *single* simulation runs do in fact systematically differ from the theoretical optimum. The results for learning by communication is very similar to this: Although the mean results of the 10000 simulation runs is quite close to the theoretically optimal quantity of 10, their variance indicates that this is not true for most of the single simulation results. The opposite picture results for learning by experiments: The mean quantity learned by experiments, calculated for all 10000 simulations, is relatively far from the theoretical optimum, but the spread between the single simulation results is remarkably small. Thus, the first thesis, applied to each single result of the simulations, can hardly be defeated. Proving this hypothesis, though, is hardly possible as well. The only true result of this analysis does not

[2] This is a simple t–Test for large samples that needs no further assumptions concerning the distribution of the underlying populations, which makes it very appropriate for the given problems, with sample sizes of 10000 elements.

apply to the absolute quality of the learning techniques, but rather to their reliability: It can be found that social learning, i.e. learning by imitation or communication leads to relatively good results only in the mean. In each single case, the results may be rather poor. This means, that in the individual case, social learning techniques are not very reliable. Individual learning by experiments, in contrast, does not lead to as good mean results as social learning, but in the individual case, learning by experiment turns out to be more reliable than social learning techniques. At last, it should be pointed out that the full GA, i.e. the compound of learning by imitation, communication and experiments, leads to results lying in between the results of social and individual learning techniques concerning the quality of the mean results as well as the reliability of the individual results. The full GA as the combination of individual and social learning thus produces outcomes incorporating characteristics of all the three learning techniques involved.

The second hypothesis, concerning the speed of convergence, can be tested with the help of population variances. The variance of a genetic population or the variance of the quantities symbolized by the genetic individuals of a population can be used as a measure of the convergence of populations. The lower the variance is, the more 'converged' is the population. The results of the theoretic analysis imply that the convergence speed of populations is fastest for learning by imitation, slower for learning by communication and slowest for learning by experiments.[3] The theoretical results are confirmed by the results of the simulations. It is obvious that the mean variance of the populations is smaller for learning by experiments than for learning by communication. This variance, in turn, is still much smaller than for learning by experiments. This result is confirmed by the variance of the population variances. Thus, the second hypothesis cannot be defeated: Learning by imitation leads to faster convergence than learning by communication, while learning by experiment does not converge at all.

As a further illustration, the following figures show the results of individual simulation of the different learning techniques applied to the case of regional monopolies. For this case, each simulation is based on the same starting population, which will help to keep the results comparable. Figures 5.2 to 5.5 confirm the results given above. Learning by imitation (Fig. 5.2) leads to an early convergence of the population. Less than 50 periods are enough to stop the changes of the population mean of the quantity, the population variance becomes zero. Moreover, it is interesting to notice, that the quantity learned is not very close to the optimal quantity.

Learning by communication, too, leads to full convergence of the population (Fig. 5.3). In contrast to learning by imitation, convergence takes a bit longer, i.e. about 300 periods.

Learning by experiments (Fig. 5.4) leads to continuous oscillations in the quantities as well as in population variance. There are no tendencies to converge to some fixed quantity or into a uniform population with a population variance of zero. The same is true for learning according to the full GA as shown in Fig. 5.4.

[3] In fact, due to the Markov chain analysis, learning by experiments does not lead to total convergence, i.e. population variance of 0, at all.

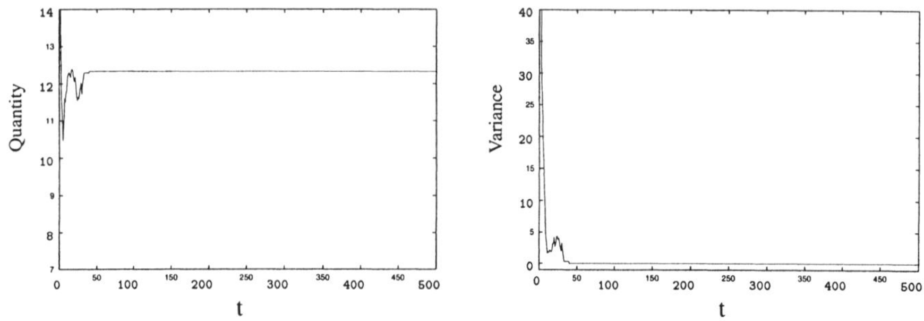

(a) Population Mean Quantity (b) Population Variance

Fig. 5.2. Learning by Imitation. Example

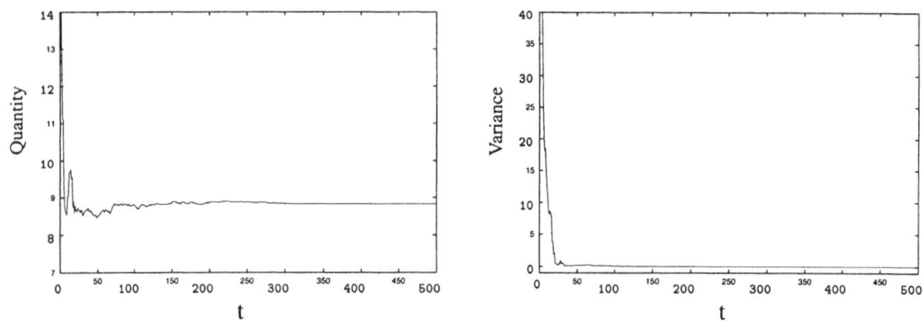

(a) Population Mean Quantity (b) Population Variance

Fig. 5.3. Learning by Communication. Example

5.3 Summary

Statistical analysis of a number of simulations of different learning techniques in the case of regional monopolists confirm the theoretical result derived above. Social learning, i.e. learning by imitation and communication leads to strong convergence of individual behaviors. Convergence in the individual case rakes place on different, often suboptimal levels. Nevertheless, in the mean of many simulation runs, the results learned are close to the theoretically optimal result. In contrast to social learning techniques, learning by experiments, which is a form of individual learning, leads to relatively bad results compared to the theoretical optimum. This result, on the other hand, is reached with great reliability: The differences between results of many simulation runs are very small. With learning by experiments, populations do not converge to uniformity.

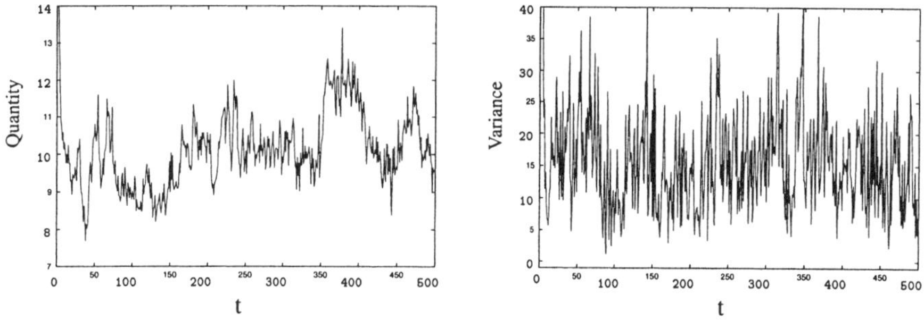

(a) Population Mean Quantity (b) Population Variance

Fig. 5.4. Learning by Experiments. Example

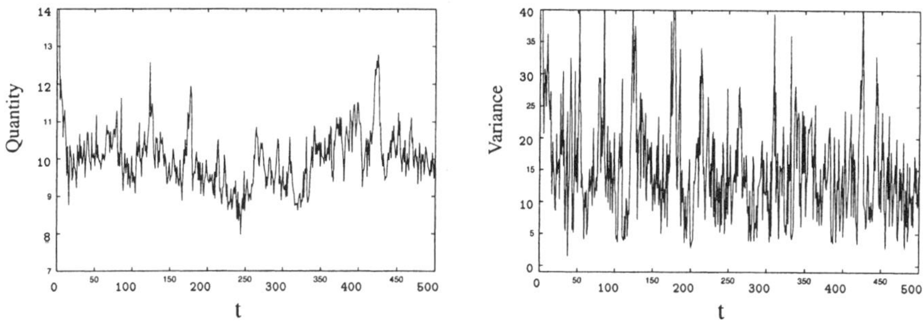

(a) Population Mean Quantity (b) Population Variance

Fig. 5.5. GA Learning. Example

A second important result is the following: Only learning by imitation is capable of producing results resembling the theoretically optimal outcomes of learning processes. This finding seems to arise the suspicion that GA learning may not systematically reproduce the results of main stream economic models. This suspicion will return in more or less every following section of this book.

Part III

Economic Applications and Technical Variations

6 Modifications: Election and Meta–Learning

6.1 Introduction

Up to this point, the main focus of the book was on the behavior of the canonical GA (Goldberg, 1989) used as a metaphor for learning in economic models. Originally, the canonical GA has been developed as a tool for optimization of non economic, static problems. The canonical GA is not a genuine tool for economic, agent based modeling. If a genetic algorithm is to be used as a true metaphor for economic learning, modifications to the canonical form of the algorithm are needed.

Mainstream economists often complain about the fact that the results of GA simulations do not fully converge but continuously maintain a certain degree of oscillations. It has already been shown that these oscillations are caused by the use of mutation or learning by experiments. On the other hand, mutation is the operator needed to reach an optimal solution regardless of the composition of the starting population. With mutation, there are oscillations, without it, there is no possibility of reaching every possible solution. Thus, if oscillations should be reduced or even eliminated, it is not a good idea to simply leave mutation out of the algorithm. Instead, there is a modification to the canonical GA, which considerably smoothes simulation results without abandoning mutation. This modification is the operator of election (Arifovic, 1994). In the following, it will be shown that election in fact smoothes oscillations without reaching worse results than a canonical GA reaches. Unfortunately, there is hardly any sensible behavioral interpretation of this operator. If used in an agent based economic context, it should be possible to tell what people do when learning according to election. An answer to this question is hard to find. Building up on this weakness of election, another operator is developed, which has a straightforward behavioral interpretation and which results in relatively smooth simulation results. This operator is the operator of meta mutation or the concept of meta learning (Riechmann, 1998b). This operator, too, will be described, analyzed and discussed in length. After this, there follows a confrontation of both operators. It will turn out that meta learning leads to results very different from results of the canonical GA. Above all, it can be shown that meta learning is capable of modeling temporary lock–ins and the phenomenon of inertia.

In order to make clear that the results of this chapter are caused by the technical modifications of the GA and not by the economic problem in focus, the economic model underlying this chapter is still the introductory model of regional monopolies as in Chap. 3.

6.2 Election

A modification to the canonical GA frequently used is the operator of election, introduced by Arifovic (1994). Arifovic focuses the results of GA learning processes in a cobweb model and confronts the results with results of economic experiments for the same model. Her main finding is the fact that a canonical GA in its basic form is not capable of reproducing the results of economic experiments. One of the main problems stressed in the paper is the fact that learning as modeled by a canonical GA does not converge to an asymptotically stable state. This finding can be theoretically confirmed by the results of the Markov chain analysis carried out in Sect. 4.2. In order to solve the problem of non convergence, Arifovic develops the operator of election. Election takes the place of crossover and mutation in the run of the GA. Election acts as a form of preliminary selection of strategies which can be used by an economic agent.[1]

During the operator of election — similar to the procedure in crossover — the first step consists of selecting pairs of genetic individuals or economic agents by chance. Both members of such a pair develop one new strategy each by communication (one point crossover) and experiments (mutation). Then, the agents decide which strategy to use: One of the original strategies the agents used the period before or one of the new strategies developed during the first step of election. In order to decide, some measure of fitness is needed. The original strategies already have a fitness, the fitness gained at the market in the previous period. The new strategies still need a measure of fitness. The agents' problem is to find such a fitness without exposing the new strategies to the market. Thus, they create a *potential fitness* instead. Potential fitness is computed using the best information the agents have, which, for the example of regional monopolies, is the market price of the preceding period. In this example, where fitness equals profit, the potential fitness of a new strategy is calculated as the mathematical product of the quantity represented by the strategy and the market price of the last period. As market prices change from period to period, this potential fitness can only by chance be the same as the actual fitness the strategy would gain when exposed to the market. Potential fitness is only a hypothetical fitness. After calculating potential fitness, the agents choose which strategy to use in reality, i.e. which quantity to produce in the current period. They choose from the four strategies they know, two old and two new ones. They choose according to fitness or potential fitness, respectively. According to the original rules of the election operator, one of the agents uses the 'best' strategy, i.e. the one with the highest fitness or potential fitness, respectively. The second agent chooses the 'second best' strategy.

Algorithm 6.1 shows the structure of the election operator. The strategies of agent i and j are turned into strategies $\tilde{k}$ and $\tilde{l}$ by crossover and mutation. Then, the potential fitness of the new strategies, $\tilde{k}$ and $\tilde{l}$, is calculated. This is done by exposing the strategies to the optimization problem in its latest known form, i.e. in the form

[1] Election is in fact very similar to the operator of preselection used by Goldberg (1989, pp. 190).

of the previous period, $t-1$. After that, there exists a measure of fitness for all of the four strategies. The strategies are compared and ranked due to this fitness value. The two strategies with the highest and second highest such fitness value replace the original strategies i and j in the current population $\overline{m}_t$.

ELECTION — Election Operator

Choose two Individuals i and j from Population $\overline{m_t}$
Crossover on Strategies S_i and $S_j \Rightarrow S_k$ und S_l
Mutation on S_k and $S_l \Rightarrow S_{\tilde{k}}$ und $S_{\tilde{l}}$
Calculate *potential* Fitness $R\left(S_{\tilde{k}}\|\overline{m}_{t-1}\right)$ und $R\left(S_{\tilde{l}}\|\overline{m}_{t-1}\right)$
Replace S_i and S_j by the two 'best' Strategies from $\left\{S_i, S_j, S_{\tilde{k}}, S_{\tilde{l}}\right\}$

Algorithm 6.1: Structure of the Election Operator

There are two problems to the operator of election, the first one concerning the concept of potential fitness, the second one concerning the assumptions about the behavior of the agents involved.

The problem concerning the concept of potential fitness is the following. It is absolutely clear that there is only one way of determining the true fitness of a strategy: Try it in reality, i.e. at the market. This, of course, is not possible with an operator serving as a means of preselecting a strategy. Election is used to find out which strategy to use *before* entering the market. Thus, as true market results cannot be used, potential fitness is only a virtual value reflecting the outcome of a fictitious market.

Forecasting the fitness of a strategy without using it at the market requires the knowledge of every possible detail influencing the quality of a strategy. For the example of regional monopolies, this means that the market price of the next period must be known in advance. The pure existence of thousands of analysts, brokers, fond managers and others gives an idea of how complicated it is to acquire this knowledge.[2] For models more complex than the one for regional monopolies, the problem of determining a potential fitness which is close to real fitness becomes even harder. Assuming agents to be able to forecast fitness seems to be rather unrealistic in models of bounded rational learning behavior. Moreover, potential fitness, as used

[2] See Plott (2000) for some results about the problem of gathering the information needed to determine the quality of a market strategy.

by Arifovic (1994), is a kind of ceteris–paribus fitness: Letting the agents assume next period's market price to be the same as the current one means letting each agent assume all influences on the price to remain unchanged. This leads to two wrong assumptions of each agent. First, the agent believes that she is the only one to change her plans while all others do nothing, and secondly, it means that the agent believes that her influence on the market price is small enough not to change it. The second assumption might be true for large populations, but the first assumption, in a model of social learning and, more than this, inside a procedure where two agents meet in order to change their plans, does not look very plausible at all.

On the other hand, the inability of forecasting future influences on economic success can be seen as a sign of the boundedness of individual knowledge. There is a number of economic models assuming that it is a symptom of bounded rationality that agents form simplified auxiliary models of their economic environments in order to help them find a solution to economic problems.

A second problem to the operator of election lies in the way the agents select their strategies. Following Arifovic (1994), two agents meet, create two new strategies from two old ones, form believes about the future fitness of the strategies and then select which strategy to use at the market. Selection works as follows: One of the agents chooses the presumably first best strategy, the second agents selects the presumably second best one. But, why should anyone do this? If the second agent believes that the strategy she selects is only the second best one, why does she not select the first best one? In models of learning, with strategies having the character of non rival public goods, what should prevent two agents from selecting the same strategy? The assumption, an agent could select a strategy which she believes is not the best one available, seems very implausible.

Franke (1997, 1998) shows a variant of the election operator, which he calls 'weak election'.[3] Weak election does not suffer from the problems of the original election operator. During weak election, too, two agents meet and generate a new strategy each, using a the method of crossover. What is different from ordinary election is the fact that each agent keeps her result by herself, i.e. neither of the agents tells her partner about her learning result. Thus, after further modifications of the two new strategies by use of mutation and the calculation of potential fitness, the selection of the strategy to use at the market is a choice between only two strategies: The original strategy of the agent and her newly generated one. This procedure has a more logical interpretation than the original election operator. Nevertheless, a still more logical version could let the partners chose between *three* different strategies: the two original strategies of the partners and, as the third strategy, the individually generated new strategy of each of the partners. The set of strategies available should include both of the original strategies, because during the process of generating a new strategy, each of the partners knows both of the original ones. But, even if the problem of strategy selection can be solved, the problem concerning the computation of potential fitness without referring to the market still remains.

[3] Similar suggestions can be found in Birchenhall et al. (1997).

Algorithms based on the election operator show a remarkably different behavior from the canonical GA. It can be recognized that during the run of the algorithm, the usually never ending heterogeneity of populations does not occur. Instead, algorithms based on election lead to convergence to uniform populations. This, of course should not be interpreted as a sign of good quality of the economic result generated by election. Uniformity of populations does not necessarily mean optimality of behavior. In fact, later in this book (Chap. 8), a case will be shown where simulations using election result in states of the population which are uniform but are totally nonsensical in their economic interpretation.

Figure 6.1 shows the behavior of an algorithm based on election. The economic background of the algorithm, again, is the model of regional monopolies. The data originate from the same experiments as the ones leading to the results shown in Sect. 5, which makes the new results perfectly comparable to the results from that section.

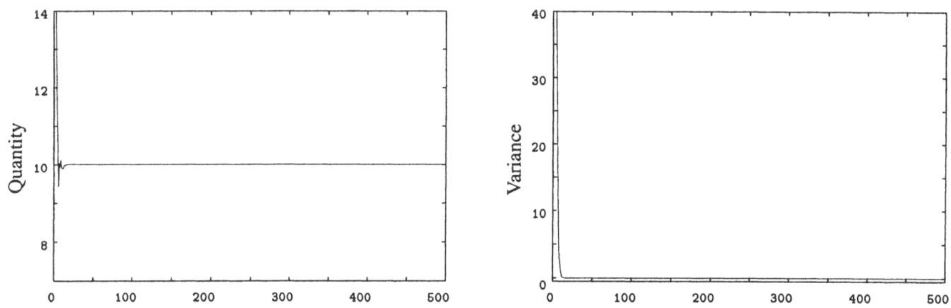

(a) Population Mean Quantity (b) Population Variance

Fig. 6.1. Election

What is most striking at Fig. 6.1 is not only the fact that convergence of the population happens, but that it happens extremely fast. In fact, populations converge even faster than in the case of genetic drift (see Figs. 5.2 and 5.3). In addition to the simulations leading to Fig. 6.1, an analysis of 10 000 runs of the simulation was run, resembling the procedure leading to the results shown in Tab. 5.1. The results are shown in Table 6.1.[4] Altogether, the result seem to confirm the result shown in the exemplary case which leads to the figure above.

The simulations based on election reach the mean quantity with a much smaller variance than any other GA variant does. This could be seen as sign that the best economic strategy is reached very exactly. But this is not the case, as can be shown

[4] The results for imitation, communication, experiments and the full GA originate from Table 5.1 and are included for reference.

Learning Technique	Mean $\bar{x}$	Mean Quantity Variance s^2	Test Stat. T	Mean Variance Mean	Variance
Election	9.95729	0.0673331	−16.43	$4.17907e-8$	$1.73602e-11$
Imitation	9.99086	1.14802	−0.85	0.00652639	0.010127
Communic.	9.953	0.73984	−5.47	0.00997675	0.00837719
Experiments	9.92884	0.141672	−18.73	14.2485	1.19473
full GA	9.97426	0.231098	−5.36	14.5619	1.34209

Table 6.1. Statistical Results

by an approximate Gauss test, which has been applied analogously to the tests in Sect. 5.2. The hypothesis tested is that election leads to the theoretically optimal outcome of the learning process. The test statistic of $T = -16.43$ shows that for the usual significance levels of $\alpha = 0.01$, $\alpha = 0.1$, and $\alpha = 0.5$ this hypothesis must be rejected.

The results concerning variance and convergence of populations, on the other hand, are very clear cut. Mean population variance is very small, populations are almost always completely uniform.

Summarizing these results, it can be stated that election is perfectly suitable if it is the aim of a simulation to achieve behavioral uniformity and stability. But election is not generally capable of reproducing a learning process leading to optimal behavior in the mainstream economic meaning of the term.

The results indicate that the question is important which is the role of individual behavioral uniformity in economic theory. In fact, behavioral uniformity is a characteristic of most of the results of modern mainstream economic models. This fact is mostly a consequence of the assumptions these models are based on. Often, the focus of these models is directed to the behavior of a 'representative individual', such that nothing else than uniformity can be observed due to the mere nature of the model.[5]

Evolutionary economists, in contrast, often stress the fact that heterogeneous behavior which is continuing over time is a basic feature of economic dynamics, and even more: Heterogeneity can be seen as the main force behind economic dynamics.[6]

Seen at this background, it is a question of purpose when to use or not to use election for the simulation of economic learning processes. If the purpose is to reproduce some results of mainstream economics, election can help to reach the characteristic uniform results. If, on the other hand, the purpose is to reproduce economic processes which can well be interpreted as processes of social and individual learning, election should better not be used.

[5] For some critique on the concept of representative individual, see Kirman (1992).

[6] The list of authors supporting this point of view is long. Some of the more important works on this topic are Hayek (1969) (or Hayek 1978) and Witt (1993a).

6.3 Meta Learning

Another modification to the canonical GA is the concept of meta learning or the operator of meta mutation.[7]

Theoretical analysis of genetic algorithms shows the particular role of the mutation operator or of learning by experiment. Learning by experiment is the driving force of true innovation. Only learning by experiment is capable of generating truly new strategies or to rediscover forgotten strategies. On the other hand, it is mutation, or, more exact, the ongoing appearance of behavioral experiments, that leads to continuous fluctuations and prevents the process of GA learning from converging into a state of asymptotical stability. There is always at least one agent in the population that behaves different from the others, thus inducing new sources of social behavioral instability. This is even worse in models with state dependent quality of individual strategies, like most economic models. In these models, one destabilizing strategy can be the course of a chain reaction, leading a large number of other agents to change their behavior as well. This, in turn, will lead to strong fluctuations of social and individual behavior over time.

Arifovic (1994) solves this problem by increasing the selective pressure (election). The concept of meta learning is another possible solution. But, different to election, meta learning does not affect selection, but mutation or the process of learning by experiment.

For the canonical GA, the working of the mutation operator can easily be described: Every single bit of the bit string of a genetic individual is flipped with a certain mutation probability μ. This probability, μ, is constant, it is the same for every bit of the bit string of every genetic individual of every population. In the interpretation of mutation as a change of individual behavior caused by experiments, this means the following: Every economic agent changes her strategy in every period of her life with the same probability. This assumption seems implausible in two aspects. First: Why should all agents conduct experiments with the same probability? Looking at heterogeneous agents, one should expect to find heterogeneous propensities to experiment. Second: Why should an economic agent behave the same in every period of time? Why should she not change her behavior, especially concerning her propensity to experiment? Focusing on the process of learning, one should expect to find agents determining the adequate frequency of experiments by themselves. Summarizing these two arguments, it can be found that the canonical operator of mutation seems to be too simple as to provide a satisfying metaphor for learning by experiment.

The concept of meta learning is based on this idea. Meta learning endogenizes the individual propensity to experiment. The classical operator of mutation is replaced by an enhanced operator. Every genetic individual (within every generation) gets its own — private — mutation rate. Thus, the representation of a genetic individual, $S_{i,t}$, has to be expanded: In addition to the usual bit string of length L, every individual's representation contains a real valued variable $\mu_{i,t}$, which can have values

[7] An early version of this concept can be found in Riechmann (1998b).

from 0 to 1:

$$S \in \{0,1\}^L \times]0,1[\tag{6.1}$$

$\mu_{i,t}$ stands for the individual's private mutation rate in period t.[8]

The endogenization and privatization of the propensity to experiment changes the definition of the economic strategy of an agent. Now, the economic strategy consists of two parts, the specific choice of the economic control variables and the individual propensity to experiment. The values of the control variables are of course the economic core strategy, i.e. the part of the strategy determining behavior in a specific economic situation. Thus, in meta learning, too, the core strategy is represented by the individual bit string.[9] The private propensity to experiment of agent i in period t is given by the variable $\mu_{i,t}$. The propensity to experiment does not give any information about the agent's planned behavior for specific economic situations. The propensity to experiment characterizes the *individual* process of learning by experiment. It does not tell how an agent will behave, but how she will *change* her behavior. It is no core economic strategy, but a learning strategy. Thus, an economic strategy is now characterized by two things, the economic core strategy and the learning strategy. 'Good' economic behavior, i.e. behavior leading to high economic success, does not only originate from good behavior during the economic periods, but also from the way this behavior is changed over time. This means that economic learning takes place on two different stages: On the one hand, it is necessary to learn good economic core strategies. On the other hand, the optimal learning behavior must be learned as well. The enhanced operator of meta mutation thus describes a form of meta learning — learning how to learn.

Genetic algorithms building up on the idea of endogenization and privatization of the mutation probability will be called *meta GAs*. While privatization of the propensity to experiment has already been described above, the endogenization still has to be explained. For this, it is important to keep in mind that now the mutation probability $\mu_{i,t}$ is an integral part of the genetic individual and its representation as shown in 6.1. This means that the mutation probability (or propensity to experiment) $\mu_{i,t}$ is also subject to the operators of crossover and reproduction. In crossover, the mutation probability of each of the parents becomes the mutation probability of one of the offsprings, respectively. During reproduction, a complete genetic individual is transferred into the next generation. Reproduction now concerns the bit string and the private mutation probability. In addition, mutation probability is subject to a mutation process of its own. This process of meta mutation, i.e. mutation of the mutation rate, is the actual motor of the process of meta learning. For the special form of this process, some behavioral assumptions will be made:[10]

[8] The alternative of coding the mutation probability within a binary bit string has turned out not to be too successful, see Bäck (1992a,b).

[9] In most of the economic GA learning models, there is only one control variable, like e.g. the supplied quantity in the model of regional monopolies. There are some models using more than one control variable like Axelrod (1987). In Chap. 8 of this book, there is also a model employing more than just one control variable.

[10] Some of the following assumptions are derived from Bäck and Schütz (1996).

1. The propensity to experiment cannot be learned by communication. This means that there will be no development of the mutation rate due to recombination (crossover).[11]
2. Experiments aiming to find better values of the propensity to experiment, form a process without a trend. This means two things:
   a) *Systematic* changes in the propensity to experiment do not result from mutation, but from selection.
   b) Changes in the mutation rate at factor c are equally likely as changes at factor $\frac{1}{c}$.
3. Small changes in the propensity to experiment are more likely than big ones.
4. Experiments regarding the propensity to experiment $\mu_{i,t}$ take place at the same probability as experiments regarding the core economic strategy. The mutation probability $\mu_{i,t}$ is the mutation probability of both processes, the first stage learning of core economic behavior and the meta stage of learning how to conduct experiments.[12] This means that $\mu_{i,t}$ is the mutation probability for both processes, the process of learning the core economic strategy (mutation of the bit string) and the process of meta learning, i.e. the process $M(\mu_{i,t})$.

A simple stochastic process, meeting all the above assumptions can be described by the following stochastic differential equation:

$$\mu_{i,t+1} = \left(1 + \frac{1-\mu_{i,t}}{\mu_{i,t}} exp(-\nu)\right)^{-1} \quad \text{mit} \quad \nu \sim N(0,1) \tag{6.2}$$

In the context of the genetic algorithm, it is important to know that the process of meta mutation does not replace mutation but works as an additional process preceding mutation in the order of genetic operators within one round of every simulation. In every round, first the new mutation probabilities are computed by meta mutation. Than, based on these new mutation probabilities, mutation of the bit strings takes place. Algorithm 6.2 shows the algorithm.

The resulting tendency to learn 'better' propensities to experiment is caused by the fact that selection prefers better propensities over worse ones. This is identical to assumption 2 above. As has been introduced above, a strategy now consists of two parts, the core economic strategy and the learning strategy. Both parts decide on the long run economic quality of an agent and by that on reproduction probability or the long run survival of a strategy. This is the way the value of the propensity to experiment gains importance for the performance of an agent.

Using the operator of meta mutation in an economic GA leads to some surprising results. To demonstrate this, the model of regional monopolies is used again, this time employing simulations with meta mutation. The simulations were run 10 000 times. The results of these runs are analyzed analogously to the analysis in Sect. 5, as described in Fig. 5.1. The results are displayed in the first line of Table 6.2.

[11] This assumption is enforced by a technical requirement: As mutation probability is coded as a real valued number, crossover in the usual form cannot be applied.

[12] By this assumption, an infinite regression in mutation probabilities is avoided.

META GA — Meta GA

$t := 0$

Creation of First Population $\overline{m}_0$

Evaluation of $\overline{m}_0$

while Stopping Condition not Met

- $t := t + 1$
- Selection from $\overline{m}_{t-1}$ and Reproduction into $\overline{m}_t$
- Recombination on $\overline{m}_t$
- **Meta Mutation** on $\overline{m}_t$:
  - for Each Individual $i \in \overline{m}_t$
    - Mutation of Mutation Probability: $\mu_{i,t} = M\left(\mu_{i,t-1}\right)$
- Mutation on $\overline{m}_t$ with Probability $\mu_{i,t}$
- Evaluation of $\overline{m}_t$

END

Algorithm 6.2: Structure of the Meta GA

An approximate Gauss test, run like the one in Sect. 5.2, results in a test statistic of $T = 0.31$, indicating that the hypothesis, meta learning leads to theoretically optimal results, cannot be rejected for the usual significance levels of $\alpha = 0.01$, $\alpha = 0.1$, and $\alpha = 0.5$. In this sense, meta learning is the first learning technique leading to optimal results in the mainstream economic meaning. The drawback is revealed by the variance: In the individual simulation run, the simulation results have a large spread, meaning that meta learning is not a very reliable learning technique.

The relatively high variance is a hint that during a single run of the simulation as well as during different runs highly differing quantities are 'learned'. Moreover, the high mean population variance and its dispersion is very striking. The high value of the mean population variance is a sign that at least some simulation runs maintain a high degree of heterogeneous population structures throughout the whole run of a simulation, i.e. over 500 periods. The high dispersion of mean population variances, on the other hand, shows that for other runs of the simulations, the contrary is true: Some simulation runs seem to end up in homogeneous population structures.

Learning	Mean Quantity			Mean Variance	
Technique	Mean $\bar{x}$	Variance s^2	Test Stat. T	Mean	Variance
Meta–GA	10.0022	0.50007	0.31	1.23965	2.94332
Election	9.95729	0.0673331	−16.43	$4.17907e-8$	$1.73602e-11$
Imitation	9.99086	1.14802	−0.85	0.00652639	0.010127
Communic.	9.953	0.73984	−5.47	0.00997675	0.00837719
Experiments	9.92884	0.141672	−18.73	14.2485	1.19473
full GA	9.97426	0.231098	−5.36	14.5619	1.34209

Table 6.2. Statistical Results

The results of the analysis shall be made more explicit by showing some examples. The ideal type of a run of the meta GA can be seen at Fig. 6.2. The economic base of the simulation leading to these results is still the model of regional monopolies. Subfigures (a) and (b) show the development of the population mean quantity and the population mean variance of these quantities in time. These figures are perfectly comparable to Figs. 5.2 to 5.5 and 6.1 showing similar results for different forms of GA learning simulations. In addition, subfigures (c) and (d) show the development of the population mean propensity to experiment (or mutation probability). This is shown in a linear scale (subfigure (c)) as well as in a semi logarithmic scale in subfigure (d).

The plots of quantities and population variances shows a remarkable difference compared to the results of the canonical GA (Fig. 5.5) as well as to the results of the pure mutation algorithm (Fig. 5.4) and the algorithm based on election (Fig. 6.1). Compared to the canonical GA and the pure mutation algorithms, it can be found that with meta learning there is a process of stabilization of the quantities. The oscillations decrease in time. This impression can be confirmed by a look at the population variances, which are also decreasing. As the population variance is used as a measure of behavioral heterogeneity, it can be stated, that in the meta learning algorithms, the degree of of behavioral heterogeneity decreases in time and behavioral homogeneity increases. Still, and unlike the case of election, meta learning does not lead to a total stop of oscillations. There is still an ongoing process of individual experiments and the populations do not become purely uniform. This means that, compared to the canonical GA, the frequency of individual behavioral experiments and their effects on behavioral stability are weakened but not fully removed.

In contrast to the variants of genetic algorithms discussed before, the meta GA contains the concept of endogenized mutation probabilities or propensities to exper-

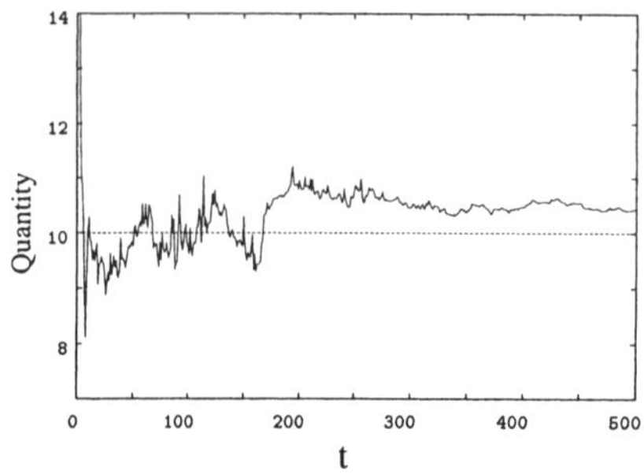

(a) Population Mean Quantity

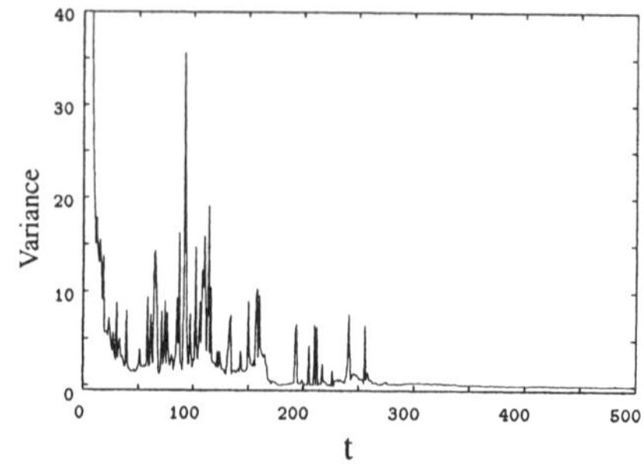

(b) Population Variance of Quantities

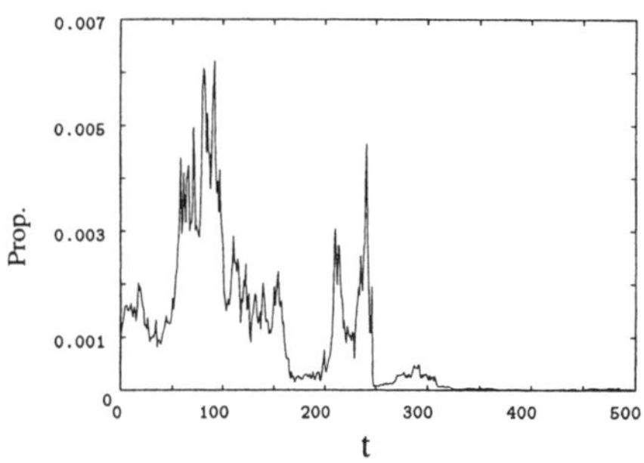

(c) Population Mean Propensity to Experiment (linear Plot)

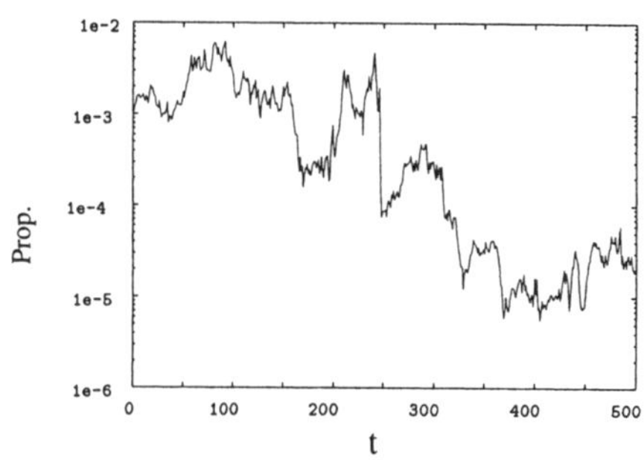

(d) Population Mean Propensity to Experiment (semi log. Plot)

Fig. 6.2. Meta GA

iment. Subfigures (c) and (d) of Fig. 6.2 display the development of this variable in time. For this, Subfigure (d) is of particular use, because it shows the development of the *level* of the population mean propensity to experiment. With the help of this figure, it is possible to explain the process of meta learning in greater detail. Generally, for the interpretation of the meta learning process, three phases can be distinguished. All of these phases, each of which has a particular economic meaning, can be characterized by the special behavior of the propensity to experiment. Its is important to mention that the time span of the phases differs from one simulation run to another. Nevertheless, the phases themselves can be recognized at every meta learning process, where they might even appear several times during one and the same simulation run. The process shown in Fig. 6.2 is thus only an example, though it contains all the general characteristics of a meta learning process. In order to make things more clear, subfigures (a), (b), and (d) of Fig. 6.2 have been rearranged in Fig. 6.3. There, two vertical lines have been added to roughly indicate the borders between the three phases of the process. Moreover, there are three additional lines in the third subfigure, indicating the trend of the development of the propensity to experiment within each phase of the learning process.[13]

The 'pre–first' phase of the process is a phase without any economic content, but is only a technical necessity. In the example of Fig. 6.3, this technical starting phase lasts to about the 50th period and can be seen as the time the algorithm needs to initialize and start up. Due to the initial setting of the private mutation probabilities of $\mu_{i,t=0} := 0.001\ \forall\, i$, the propensities to experiment of the next few generations stay on this initial level. Moreover, at the outset of the simulation the individual quantity decisions are initialized randomly with values from the range of $0 \leq V\,(S_{i,t=0}) \leq 50$, with each value being equally probable. Consequently, for the first generations, the quantities of the agents are relatively high and relatively diverse, as can be seen from the relatively high population variances.

The first phase of the learning process is the 'exploration phase'. In the example, exploration lasts from the 50th to approximately the 170th period. During this phase, a rough delimitation of the set of relatively good supplied quantities takes place. It can be recognized that this phase is characterized by relatively high oscillations of the population mean quantity. Populations are very heterogeneous, they contain many different behavioral strategies. The population mean propensity to experiment is high, i.e. ranges from about $\frac{1}{1000}$ to about $\frac{1}{100}$.

The second phase of the learning process is the phase of 'concentration'. In the example, concentration roughly lasts from the 170th to the 300th period. During concentration, there is a closer delimitation of the set of successful strategies. The oscillations of the mean quantities decrease, populations become less heterogeneous. The level of the propensities to experiment becomes lower, which is a sign that further experiments become less attractive for the agents.

The third phase is the phase of 'convergence', which in the example starts around the 300th period. Now, the oscillations of the quantities get even less than before, populations are nearly uniform. In this phase, experiments seem unattractive to the agents, thus the propensities to experiment remain at a very low level.

It has already been mentioned that the simulation run leading to the results shown in Figs. 6.2 and 6.3 is an example which displays the different phases of the learning process very clearly. Sadly, this is not the case for every simulation run. The results of the statistical analysis of 10 000 runs of the simulation (Table 6.2) are in fact severely influenced by the fact that the length of the phases differs from one simulation run to another and that the phases sometimes show up more than once during a simulation run.

Figure 6.4 shows why the analysis leading to Table 6.2 results in such a remarkably high population variance: Many of the simulation runs did not reach the third phase of the learning process within the first 500 periods. The simulation run displayed in Fig. 6.4 did not even reach the second phase.

Figure 6.4 clearly shows that during the whole 500 periods covered by the statistical analysis, the population mean propensity to experiment remains within the range between $\frac{1}{1000}$ and $\frac{1}{100}$. This is the level of propensities to experiment charac-

[13] These lines are no plots of regressions, but only slightly vague indications of the trend.

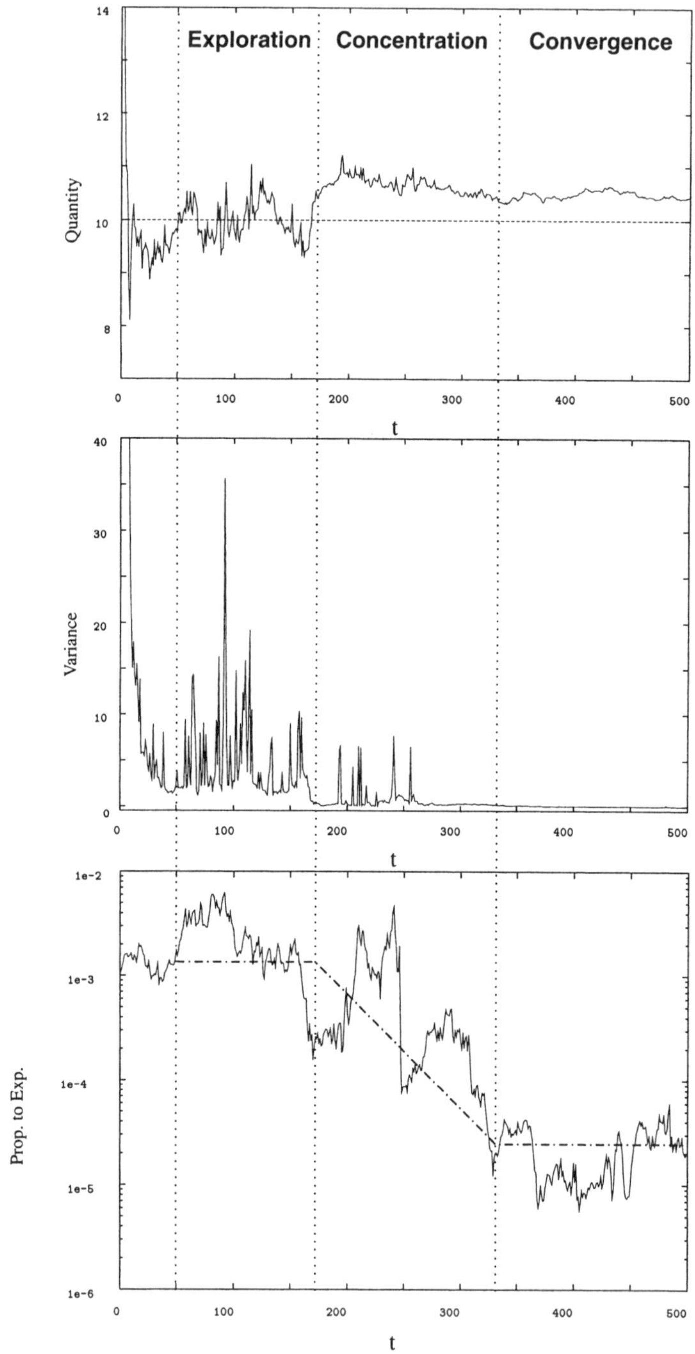

Fig. 6.3. Sketch of Learning Phases

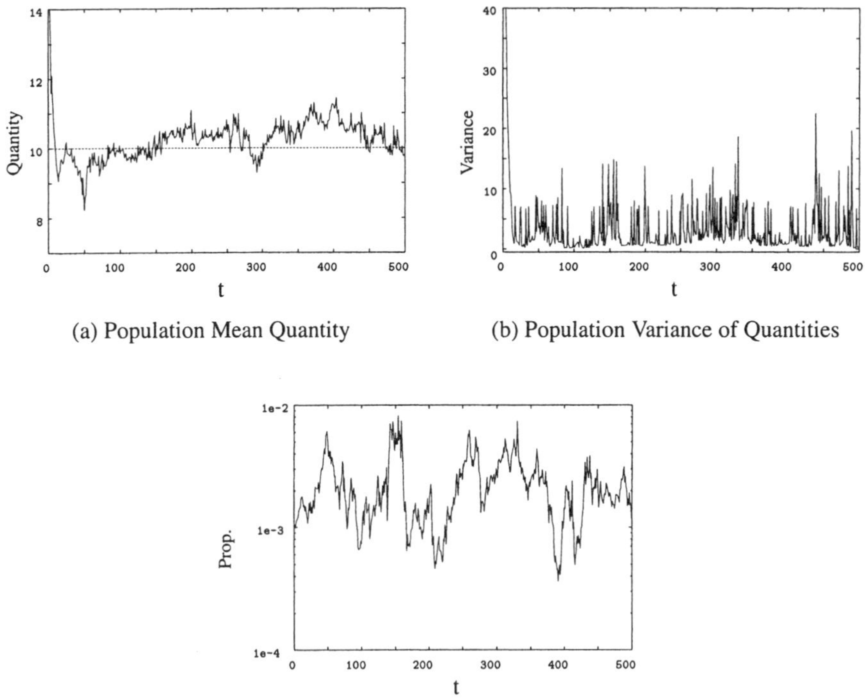

(a) Population Mean Quantity

(b) Population Variance of Quantities

(c) Population Mean Propensity to Experiment (semi log. Plot)

Fig. 6.4. Meta GA

terizing the first learning phase, the phase of exploration. This notion is confirmed by the other two variable: The population mean quantities show heavy oscillations, the populations are relatively heterogeneous.

A third type of meta learning process, which can be observed quite often, is shown in Fig. 6.5.

To begin with, there is a clear distinction between the three phases: Exploration runs from about the 50th to about the 140th period, concentration from the 140th to the 220th period, and convergence starts roughly at period 220. What is different from the results displayed above is the fact that approximately at period 300 the level of the population mean propensity to experiment rises again, while the population mean quantity and the population variance remain unchanged. Then, around period 370, the change in the level of propensities to experiment are followed by changes in the economic core strategies. Population mean quantities start oscillating again, populations become more heterogeneous. The learning process enters a new phase which can be interpreted of a new, weaker phase of concentration. Then, from about

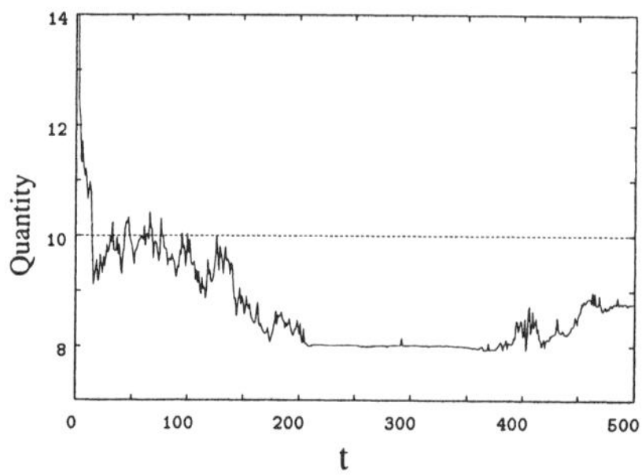

(a) Population Mean Quantity

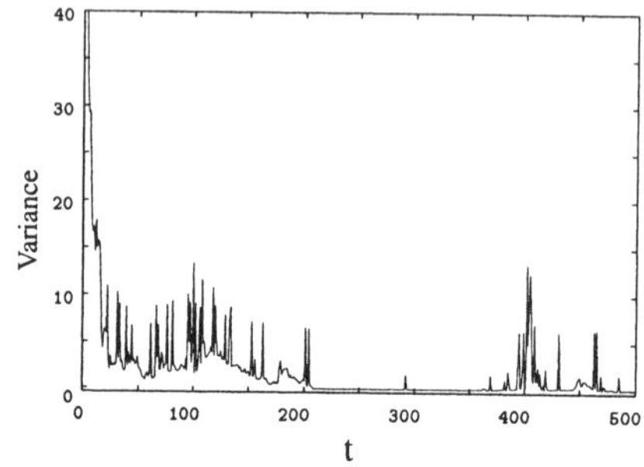

(b) Population Variance of Quantities

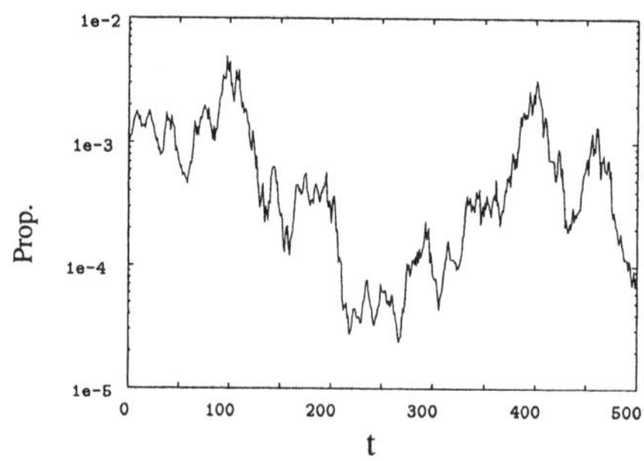

(c) Population Mean Propensity to Experiment (semi log. Plot)

Fig. 6.5. Meta GA

period 470 on, there follows a new phase of convergence. Oscillations of the quantities decrease, populations become more homogeneous again. Thus, Fig. 6.5 can be seen as a proof that learning phases can occur more than once during a GA meta learning process.

The learning process shown in Fig. 6.5 has another interesting feature. The strategies remain unchanged from period 220 to 370. Most of the populations in these periods are uniform. This observation is important, because, as has been shown above (Sect. 4.2), such a state of uniformity can not be achieved by a canonical GA. Only GAs without mutation, standing for learning processes without learning by experiments, can reach such a state. The introduction of election (Sect. 6.2), however, leads to a comparable behavior of the observed learning dynamics. In both cases, GAs without mutation and GAs with election, the nature of the uniform, asymptotically stable state of the learning process is of a different nature than the uniform state observed in the meta learning process above. The canonical GA without mutation leads to uniformity and asymptotical stability because of genetic drift. This process is irreversible: Once such a state is reached, it cannot be left any more. Not even in the case of a change in the economic environment of the learning agents (e.g. the occurrence of higher fixed costs) can cause a further change in their behavior. The absence of the possibility to conduct individual experiments prevents agents from adjusting their behavior to new circumstances. In the case of GAs with election, asymptotical stability is caused by very high selective pressure due to the interaction of two selection operators, standard GA selection and individual preselection in form of the election operator. Agents still conduct experiments, but, due to the process of election, as long as their original strategies seem to perform better than the results of their experiments, agents do not use the resulting strategies. Thus, once the economic environment changes, election algorithms do allow for the adjustment of individual behavior. Meta learning, too, allows for the adaption of behavior to a changed environment, even after populations have converged. In a meta GA, convergence to asymptotic stability takes place, because agents *choose* not to conduct experiments any longer. Agents simply decrease their propensity to experiment. They do so, because conducting experiments does not seem to be fruitful any more. If their environment changes, and different strategies perform better than the one currently used, experiments are valuable again. This will lead the agents to conduct more experiments again and thus to change their behavior. It is a characteristic of meta learning processes, though, that convergence often takes places at suboptimal levels of economic behavior. In the example of Fig. 6.5, the quantities converge to a common quantity of approximate 8. This quantity is relatively far away from the optimal individual quantity of 10.[14] The suboptimal convergence in focus is only of temporary nature. After some time of low propensities to experiment, experiments increase again and the phase of convergence ends. After this, the learning process converges again at some other levels, which might be better than the one before.

The phenomenon of remaining in suboptimal economic strategies like in the process described above has been described in economic literature before. According to (Arthur, 1989, 1995), it is called a (historical) lock in. An example frequently cited is the development of the 'QWERTY' layout of typewriter keyboards, as described by (David, 1985). Genetic algorithms using the operator of meta mutation are capable of modeling the phenomenon of lock ins. However, the kinds of lock ins GAs can reproduce are only temporary ones. And, more than this, the statement that in the long run, GAs lead to optimal behavior, still remains true even for GAs incorporating meta mutation.[15]

14 The difference in profit is in fact remarkable high. At a quantity of 8, the individual profit is 94, whereas the individual profit at the optimal quantity of 10 is 266. This means that the individual strategies converge at a level where only 27% of the maximum profit is achieved.

15 During the analysis of meta learning, there were several simulation runs which did not converge into the global optimum, even if the experiments were run for more than 10 000 periods. Apart from stating that the 'long run' might of course last very much longer than this, there are some technical characteristics of the process of meta learning (6.2), which may have caused these results. For more technical details on this problem, refer to Sect. 6.5.

6.4 Comparison of Learning Techniques

In order to get even more information about the behavior of different types of economic genetic algorithms, in this section, different variants of GAs will be compared. Again, the economic background is the model of regional monopolies. As the main focus will be on the ability of the algorithms to adapt to a change in the economic environment, there will be a slight modification to the original economic model introduced in Sect. 3.2: After 500 periods, the amount of variable production costs will change. The main question of the analysis is then, how the agents behaving to different GA variants will adopt their behavior to this external shock of the model. In detail, this means the following. Up to period 500, the cost function is the same as usual (3.7):

$$C_1 = 50 + 20q\,, \tag{6.3}$$

so that the optimal individual supply is $q^{\star} = 10$. Then, starting at period 501, the variable costs are doubled, resulting in the new cost function

$$C_2 = 50 + 40q\,. \tag{6.4}$$

For this cost function, the optimal quantity changes to $q^{\star} = 7.5$.

There are four variants of genetic algorithms that will be analyzed due to their behavior in the situation described above, namely the two operator algorithm introduced in Sect. 4.2.2, the canonical GA, the GA with election and the meta GA.

The two operator algorithm, using the operators of selection/reproduction and recombination (one point crossover) only, is known to converge to a uniform population because of genetic drift. The learning methods incorporated, imitation and communication, leave not possibility to get out of such a uniform population again. Thus, it can be found even without running a simulation, that the two operator algorithm, once converged, will not lead to any form of adaption to the change in the variable costs.

The theoretical results are confirmed by the outcome of the simulation. Fig. 6.6 shows an example. The population converges to a uniform state. The change in variable costs in period 500 has not effect at all: The population does not change.

In contrast to the two operator algorithm, the canonical GA using selection/reproduction, crossover, and mutation shows a different behavior. Figure 6.7 displays the results of an exemplary run of the simulation. It is easy to see that the canonical GA does react: After the change in variable costs in period 500, quantities decrease and move towards the new optimum. (Old and new optimum are indicated by horizontal lines.) There is no effect on the amount of the population variance, though. Because of the strong effect of experimental learning, population variances are always very high, so that the external shock in the variable costs does not cause even more heterogeneity in the population.

Still clearer is the effect of an external shock for the election GA as displayed in Fig. 6.8.

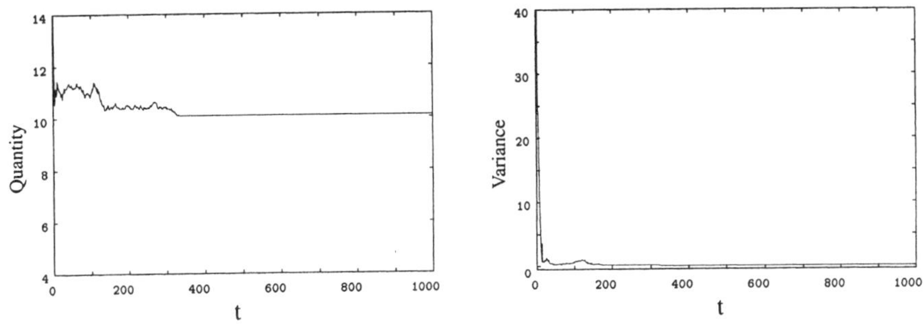

(a) Population Mean Quantity (b) Population Variance of Quantities

Fig. 6.6. Two Operator Algorithm

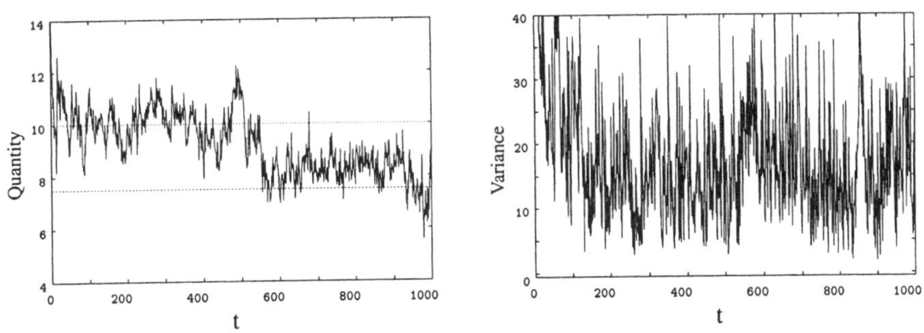

(a) Population Mean Quantity (b) Population Variance of Quantities

Fig. 6.7. Canonical GA

As usual for election, there is a very early convergence into a uniform population with quantities very close to the theoretical optimum. But, as mentioned above, even after convergence experimental learning does not stop, but the results are not used in practice. Thus, the adoption after the shock is still possible. After period 500, the results of the ongoing though further on fruitless experiments are now more promising, which means that agents use these experimental results. The consequence is a very quick process of adjustment of behavior to the new circumstances. This process is reflected by the population structures: During the phase of adoption, i.e. shortly after period 500, the population variance shortly increases, showing a temporarily heterogeneous state of the population. After the new optimal quantity is found, the population variance drops to zero, showing that the population is uniform again. Thus it can be seen that election indeed leads to a quick and effective adoption of agents' behavior to new economic circumstances.

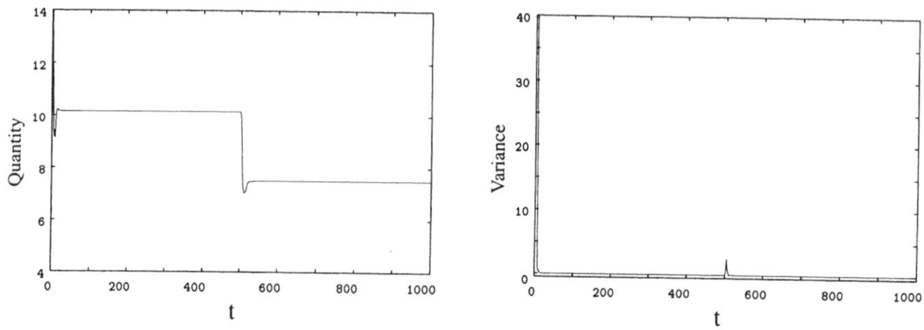

(a) Population Mean Quantity (b) Population Variance of Quantities

Fig. 6.8. Election GA

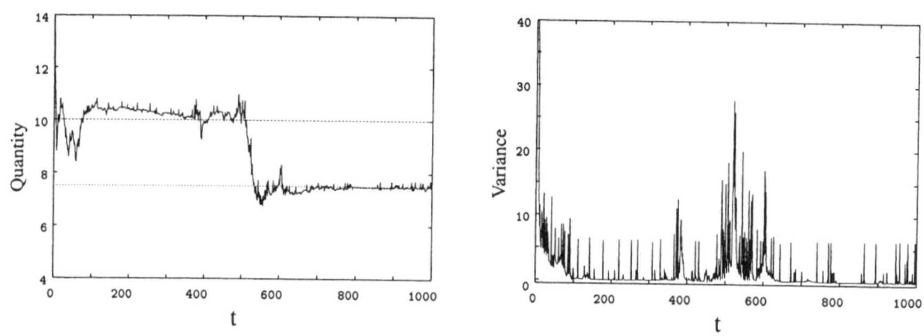

(a) Population Mean Quantity (b) Population Variance of Quantities

Fig. 6.9. Meta GA — Instantaneous Adoption

With meta learning, too, a clear adoption process can be recognized (see Fig. 6.9).

After the shock in period 500 a process of new learning starts. This means that the usual three phases of learning described above (Sec. 6.3) are repeated. This notion is confirmed by the levels of the population variances. The variance rises in the periods after the shock, i.e. during the process of new learning. After relatively good strategies have been learned, the level of heterogeneity decreases again.

A remarkable observation in the context of meta learning is the fact that the adoption to changed circumstances sometimes happens with some delay, i.e. not directly after the shock has happened. An example can be seen at Fig. 6.10.

The reason for this delay in adoption is the following. If the population has converged into a state with high homogeneity and very low propensities to experiments, experiments take place very rarely. Thus, it takes some time, until the agents

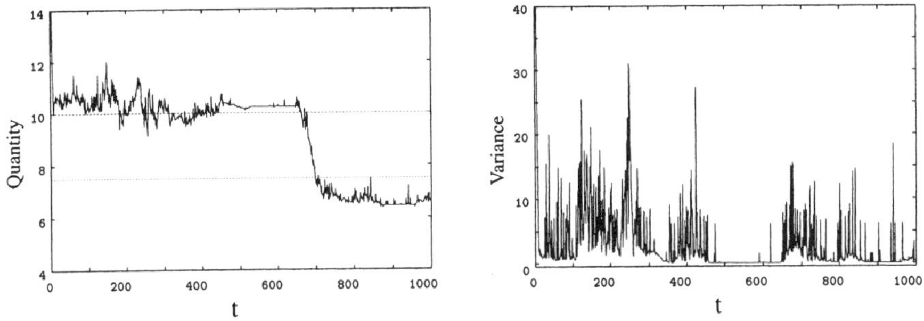

(a) Population Mean Quantity (b) Population Variance of Quantities

Fig. 6.10. Meta GA — Delayed Adoption

even recognize that experiments are more successful than before. This, at least, is the main principle of meta learning: Agents conduct experiments only if they are promising. If experiments did not lead to more successful behavior, agents give up experimenting. Because of the change in the economic environment, experiments are more promising again, but the agents do not recognize this. Thus, it takes at least one agent to conduct an experiment to induce a change in behavior, which may take some time to happen. It can be seen that in the example of Fig. 6.10, it takes until approximately period 650 — about 150 periods after the shock — to start the adoption process. After this process has started, however, the adoption runs as usual, leading to a new near optimal state of the population.

In the world of the theory of economic policy, there is a similar concept of delays in adoption to changes in the economic environment, the theory of time lags. In this branch of economics, a time lag is the time span between the occurrence of the necessity of some measure of political regulation and the point in time when this measure shows some effect. Usually, time lags are divided into three phases:

1. Recognition lag: the time between the occurrence of the necessity of a political correction and the time of recognition of this necessity
2. Action and administrative lag: the time it takes to plan a political measure and put it into practice
3. Policy effect lag: the time it takes for the political measure to show some effect

The delay that can be seen in the GA simulation can be interpreted in these terms. Most of the delay can be seen as a true recognition lag. It has been shown above that due to very low propensities to experiment it is often hard for the agents to recognize that a change in behavior could improve their performance. There is no action and administrative lag, though. If agents recognize that they should change their behavior, they do it instantaneously. Third, there is something like a policy effect lag, because it takes some time for the whole population to settle into a new state of near optimal, homogeneous behavior. Thus, it can be seen that parts of the theory of political economics can be usefully transferred to GA learning theory, even if this is not the original purpose of political economics.

Another way of explaining the delay in adoption stems from evolutionary and institutional economics. There is a concept of 'routines', i.e. individual ways of behavior which have been learned and are kept in spite of changes in the environment. As a reason why agents do not change their behavior as a reaction to a change in their environment, it is often said that people do not try to maximize their economic success but only perform 'satisficing'. Due to evolutionary economics, this means that agents are content with a relatively 'good' level of success, even if it is possible to achieve even more. From the existence of these behavioral routines there follows the existence of 'inertia'. Behavioral inertia is often said to be the reason that people (or even institutions) need some time until they adopt their behavior to changed economic environments.[16]

These two explanations of delayed adoption to changes in the environment, i.e. the theory of lags and the theory of routines and inertia, differ in an important point. The first explanation provides that agents do not recognize changes in the environment and the chance of improving their economic success accompanying these changes. This is a reason for not changing their behavior. The second explanation says that agents might even recognize the changes and chances. The reasons for not changing behavior are different ones like difficulties in the reorganization of the firm or simply because they do not like to change their behavior.

A more technical observation shows that the adoption to changes in the environment is the more delayed, the more homogeneous a population is before the changes. This is another good point for the theory of routines: The wider a routine is spread throughout a society, the longer it takes to break this routine.

6.5 Summary

There are some complaints saying the canonical GA is not suitable as a model of economic learning, because it produces to much noise and does not converge to a long run asymptotically stable state. These complaints can be weakened by constructing some variants of the canonical GA which show different stability properties, namely GAs with election and meta GAs, i.e. GAs with meta mutation.

Election models a way of individual preselection of economic strategies. Election turns out to be very successful in achieving asymptotically stable states of learning processes. Moreover the stable states are often very close to states representing some form of optimal individual behavior. The drawback of election GAs is the fact that they can hardly be interpreted as sensible metaphors for economic learning processes.

The alternative to election GAs are GAs incorporating the idea of meta learning, i.e. learning how to learn. The core idea of meta learning is the privatization

[16] See Magnusson and Ottosson (1997, pp. 110), Nelson and Winter (1982, pp. 14–21), or Heiner (1988) for more explanations on routines and inertia. A short survey is Nelson (1994).

and endogenization of the individual propensity to experiment. Deeper analysis of meta learning processes shows that they are processes which show complicated but well interpretable results over time. Meta learning processes can even produce results which can be interpreted as signs of phenomena like lock ins, inertia and path dependencies. This means that, apart from its better economic interpretability, the concept of meta learning leads to richer results, results which can often be observed in the economic reality.

Appendix: Technical Characteristics of the Meta Learning Process

In the simulations, the process of meta learning is described by the stochastic difference equation (6.2):

$$\mu_{i,t+1} = \left(1 + \frac{1-\mu_{i,t}}{\mu_{i,t}} exp\left(-\nu\right)\right)^{-1} \quad \text{mit} \quad \nu \sim N\left(0,1\right).$$

This process is a Markov process with two absorbing states. The absorbing states are $\mu_{i,t} = 0$ and $\mu_{i,t} = 1$:

$$\lim_{\mu_{i,t} \to 0} \mu_{i,t+1} = 0 \tag{6.5}$$

$$\mu_{i,t+1}\left(\mu_{i,t} = 1\right) = 1 \tag{6.6}$$

During the simulations (including a number of simulations over more than the usual 500 periods and simulations using economic problems other than the problem of local monopolies), there were only very few cases leading to absorptions at $\mu_{i,t} = 0$ and not a single case leading to absorption at $\mu_{i,t} = 1$. This phenomenon is very likely to result from the following two causes: The first cause is the fact that a full absorption of the population wide process of meta learning provides the absorption of every single process of individual meta mutation. This might take place due to genetic drift: Mutation probabilities or propensities to experiment are learned by imitation, too. The more important cause for absorption to be so rare seems to be the second one, which refers to the role of selection: Absorption at $\mu_{i,t} = 1$ is prevented by selection, because large probabilities of mutation lead to very bad economic strategies.[17] It is the role of selection to prevent these badly performing strategies. On the other hand, absorption at $\mu_{i,t} = 0$ is prevented by selection as well, because on the long run, the total disappearing of experiments is not too sensible economically, either.

These observations of the meta learning process thus confirm assumption 2a (p. 81) stating that changes (or not–changes) of the propensity to experiment only result from the work of the selection operator.

[17] Refer to Sect. 4.3 (particularly Equation 4.22) for an analytical proof of this, showing that for $\mu_{i,t} > 1/2$ the process of experimental learning degenerates to something like a random walk.

7 Extensions: Variable Time Horizon of Selection

7.1 Introduction

The model of regional monopolies discussed up to now, is too simple in at least one point: It is no satisfactory model of economic learning via GAs, because there is no state dependency. It has been mentioned above that the state dependency of individual economic success is an important characteristic of almost every economic problem. Even more, it is a major characteristic of models of economic GA learning. For example, the profit of a supplier in a market (except of a monopolistic market) does not only depend on the quantity of the good the supplier offers, but also on the market price. The market price, in turn, depends on the aggregate supply on the market, i.e. on the quantities all suppliers offer. This means that the profit of every single supplier is inseparably connected to each action of every member of the market and by that, to the state of the whole economy.[1]

In this chapter a new economic model will be discussed in order to shed some additional light on the role of state dependency.

In addition to the economic aspect of state dependency, a new technical topic will be introduced, which is another extension to the canonical GA. It will allow a long run definition of economic success other than the usual measure of one period profit. The extended definition of the time horizon of economic success and by that of the time horizon of genetic selection will lead to interesting economic effects, particularly to the appearance of business cycle like movements within the simulations.

7.2 The Economic Problem: A Cobweb Model with Declining Average Production Costs

7.2.1 The General Structure of the Model

The model in focus is mainly based on the model by Dawid (1999, pp. 121), which itself is a variant of the model by Arifovic (1994). The model is a simple cobweb

[1] A technical analysis of the effect of state dependency can be found in Dawid (1994) and Riechmann (2000).

model of the supply side of a market. The good traded on the market is homogeneous and perishable. Every supplier tries to find the best, i.e. individually profit maximizing quantity of supply. The learning techniques are modeled by means of a genetic algorithm.

The aggregate demand on the market is given by

$$d_t = \max\left[\gamma - \delta p_t, 0\right]. \tag{7.1}$$

Assume $\gamma > 0$ and $\delta > 0$. p_t is the equilibrium price in the market in period t.

There are $n > 1$ firms on the market, using the same production technology in order to produce a uniform good. Thus, firms are characterized the identical cost function $C(\cdot)$ with fixed costs α and linear variable costs depending on the individual production quantity $S_{i,t}$. Fixed costs only occur in case of production.

$$C(S_{i,t}) = \begin{cases} 0 & \text{for} \quad S_{i,t} = 0 \\ \alpha + \beta S_{i,t} & \text{for} \quad S_{i,t} > 0 \end{cases}. \tag{7.2}$$

It will be assumed that $\alpha > 0$ and $\beta > 0$. This cost function leads to declining average costs. This special form of the cost function is the only difference to the standard textbook model of the cobweb case. It will turn out, though, that this difference is the source of some very interesting economic observations.

Each period, firms decide on their supply for the next period. Every firm tries to maximize the profit of every single period. The profit of firm i in period t is defined as the difference between revenues and costs:

$$\pi_{i,t} = \begin{cases} 0 & \text{for} \quad S_{i,t} = 0 \\ p_t S_{i,t} - \alpha - \beta S_{i,t} & \text{for} \quad S_{i,t} > 0 \end{cases}. \tag{7.3}$$

The decision problem of every firm is based on the fact that the market equilibrium price in each period depends on aggregate demand in that period as well as on the supply decision of *every other* firm. As already mentioned above, this is the decisive difference to the introductory example of regional monopolies. Now, individual economic success depends on the behavior of the whole society. This case of strong interdependence of all the agents involved is an example of an economic problem with state dependent individual fitness: The fitness of every single agent depends on the state of the whole population. This state can be fully characterized by two things: first, the set of individual objective functions to be optimized, and second, the set of all economic strategies of all agents involved.

In the economic problem of this chapter, the success of every firm depends on the supply decisions of all the firms on the market. Aggregate supply in period t for n firms is given as

$$S_t = \sum_{i=1}^{n} S_{i,t}. \tag{7.4}$$

The uniform good cannot be stored, which means that the every firm has to sell everything it produces the same period, if necessary even for a price of zero. This means that individual and aggregate supply is totally price inelastic in every period: The quantity of goods sold in a single period does not depend on the price in the same period.

Consequently, the equilibrium price in every period t results from (7.1), (7.4) and the fact the goods are non storable, to

$$p_t = \max\left[\frac{\gamma}{\delta} - \frac{1}{\delta}\sum_{i=1}^{n} S_{i,t}, 0\right]. \tag{7.5}$$

For further simplification, (7.5) will be written as

$$p_t = \max\left[a - \frac{b}{n}\sum_{i=1}^{n} S_{i,t}, 0\right]. \tag{7.6}$$

The parameters result as $a > 0$ and $b > 0$.

7.2.2 Theoretical Results

According to the standard textbook analysis for price taking homogeneous firms, the goal of profit maximization leads to the rule 'Stop extending productions when the market price equals marginal costs of production.' in the example, this rule leads to the following

$$p_t = \beta, \tag{7.7}$$

and results in an individually optimal production quantity of

$$S^*_{i,t} = \frac{a-\beta}{b}. \tag{7.8}$$

The (maximum) profit for this quantity is

$$\pi\left(S^*_{i,t}\right) = -\alpha. \tag{7.9}$$

From (7.9), it can be seen that — strikingly — the maximum profit of a profit maximizing homogeneous firm is negative! Considering the fact, that fix costs do only arise in case of production, the first best decision for such a firm should be not to produce anything at all: No production induces no cost (and, of course, no revenue) and thus leads to a profit of zero, which is the best profit a firm can gain. Considering the entire problem, the first best decision is to produce a quantity of $S_{i,t} = 0$.

In mainstream economics, this case is known as the case of a natural monopoly. In order to model this case appropriately, the assumption of homogeneous behavior of all firms must be dropped. Firms must be allowed to behave heterogeneously. Let us assume that all firms i, $i \in [1, n-1]$ produce nothing, while only firm n produces a positive quantity. This is the exact picture of a pure natural monopoly. Assuming further, that the natural monopolist knows the exact functional form of aggregate demand[2], the optimal supply of the only active firm in the market can be computed as

$$S^*_{n,t} = \frac{n}{2}\frac{a-\beta}{b}. \tag{7.10}$$

This optimal supply equals exactly half of the saturation quantity of the market.

It can be found that the profit of the natural monopolist is positive, as long as her supply is less than half of the saturation quantity:

$$S_{n,t} < \frac{n}{b}(a-\beta) \quad \Leftrightarrow \quad \pi(S_{n,t}) > \pi(S^*_{i,t}). \tag{7.11}$$

The profit of a natural monopolist is positive as long as the share of fixed costs in the whole costs is sufficiently small:

$$\pi\left(S^*_{n,t}\right) > 0 \quad \Leftrightarrow \quad \alpha < \frac{1}{4}(a-\beta)^2. \tag{7.12}$$

As long as at least one firm can earn positive profits while all the other firms leave the market, it can be expected that a natural monopoly 'arises'. Depending on the structure of production costs, other cases are likely, too. For example, it could turn out that more than one firm stays on the market and makes positive profits. All in all, a kind of Bertrand game can be expected: As soon as a firm observes at least one other firm making profit, it will enter the market. As a consequence, aggregate supply rises, leading to a decrease in the price and thus to diminishing profits. When profits become negative, at the latest, most firms will leave the market again. For the remaining firms, this will mean another rise in the price and in profits. Consequently, this will be watched by other firms, leading them to enter the market again, *et cetera*. All in all, it can be expected that cycles occur, resulting from waves of firms entering the market and leaving it again. In the average over time, aggregate profits should be expected to oscillate around zero. The average number of firms staying in the market can be found to depend on the structure of production costs and the maximum production capacity of the firms.

7.3 The Genetic Algorithm

The GA used to model the problem is a simple canonical GA. There is a population of n genetic individuals in each round of the simulation. Every member of the population represents the one period supply strategy of an economic agent, i.e. of a firm. The genetic operators are the operators of one point crossover, mutation, selection, and reproduction in its simplest form. Genetic fitness of an agent is given as a positive function of the economic success of the period, i.e. by the profit:

[2] This is the usual textbook assumption for this case.

$$R(S_{i,t}) = \pi_{i,t}\,. \tag{7.13}$$

In addition, a second algorithm will be considered, which is a variation to the canonical GA. In contrast to the GA variants from Chap. 6, the learning mechanisms will remain unchanged. Instead, the changes will concern the criteria of selection. Up to now, the economic success of *one period* in time was used as the basis of selection and reproduction. Genetic fitness was a function of the economic success of the last period. In the introductory example of regional monopolies as well as in the canonical GA in this chapter, fitness equals last period's individual profit. This might in fact be a little myopic. In reality, a firm cannot be seen as very successful just because its performance was relatively good in the last period. A firm, in contrast, that used to earn high profits in every period of the past except of the last period, cannot be labeled as ineffective. Although this is the point of view of economic canonical GAs, it seems to be the wrong approach. Of course, shortsightedness is based on the myopic definition of an economic strategy. Up to this point, an economic strategy of an agent was defined as her economic action in the current period. In the case of regional monopolies, the economic strategy was fully characterized by the supply an agent plans for the current period, i.e. for one single period of time.

For the current GA variant, the definition of an economic strategy will be extended. Now, an economic strategy is a series of supply decisions over several periods of time.[3] In connection with the extended intertemporal definition of a strategy, the criterion of selection changes, too. Now, fitness, which decides whether or not a certain strategy remains in the pool of socially available strategies, is the fitness of a whole series of one period decisions.

The modified GA will change the selection criterion in the following way: Fitness will be defined as the discounted sum of all one period profits of an agent:

$$R(S_{i,t}) = \sum_{\tau=1}^{t} \rho^{t-\tau}\pi_{i,\tau}\,. \tag{7.14}$$

During the GA simulations, this term can also be computed recursively in each period t:

$$R(S_{i,t}) = \rho\, R(S_{i,t-1}) + \pi_{i,t}\,. \tag{7.15}$$

By assumption, $0 \leq \rho \leq 1$. Discounting past profits means that in the judgment of the current performance of an agent, profits are the more important, the more recent they are. This assumption means that e.g. the profit of last period is a better signal of an agent's current fitness than the profit ten periods ago, but that even the profit of the very first period still matters. Of course, this definition of fitness is general enough to even include the way the canonical GA computes fitness: For $\rho = 0$, the fitness according to (7.13) is identical to the fitness resulting from (7.14) or (7.15).

[3] In mainstream theory of economic dynamics, agents often optimize their economic success over their entire, in the extreme case even infinitely long, time horizon. This means that in mainstream economics, there is a implicit definition of an economic strategy as one decision concerning *every* period of time in one.

For both variants of fitness, normal one period fitness (7.13) and extended intertemporal fitness (7.14), simulations are performed. They are identical to the canonical GA with respect to all other characteristics.

7.4 Simulation Results

From the economic point of view, the most interesting question to be answered with the help of the simulations is the question of the structure of the results. As the alternative of producing nothing, i.e. a quantity of zero, does explicitly belong to the set of possible solutions, there are at least three possible outcomes for the simulations. The first possible outcome is a situation where all agents are homogeneously producing the quantity of $S^{\star}_{i,t}$ from (7.8). This is the solution of the textbook cobweb model and the best solution homogeneous agents can find in case of economic activity. Nevertheless, this solution represents a situation of minimized losses, but not of real profit maximization. Even the best result still represents a state of negative profits for every agent. From an economic point of view, this solution is not very sensible. If this situation turned out to be the result of the simulation, GA simulations should be doubted to be useful for the simulation of economic learning.

A second possible outcome is a homogeneous solution with all agents producing nothing at all, i.e. a situation of economic inactivity. This solution, too, is not satisfactory from the economic point of view. It has been argued in Sect. 7.2.2 that at least for some agents it is very well possible to make positive profits, at least as long as there are not too many active firms in the market. For homogeneous agents, the situation is not incentive compatible. All in all, there is no homogeneous solution which is economically convincing.

Thus, the third possible solution is a heterogeneous state: Some firms are economically active while others do not produce anything. This solution is a solution near the state of a natural monopoly described above.

The above considerations make clear that it is necessary not only to look at the macro results of the simulation, but that there must also be an analysis of the micro structure of the resulting populations.

As mentioned above, there are two different simulation models for the problem. One model is a simple canonical GA, while the other model is a canonical GA based on the concept of intertemporal fitness. The values of the parameters for the simulations are the following: The economic parameters are $\alpha = 0.75$, $\beta = 1.0$ (parameters of the cost function), $a = 5$, $b = 5$ (parameters of aggregate demand). Technical parameters: $L = 16$ (length of an individual), $n = 500$ (population size), $D^{max} = 3 \cdot \frac{a}{b}$ (maximum value of a genetic individual and thus maximum production capacity of an economic agent), $\rho = 0.98$ (discount factor for the intertemporal fitness).

Using these parameter values, the two extreme theoretical results can be computed. The individually profit maximizing production quantity for homogeneous behavior and economic activity $S^{\star}_{i,t}$ from (7.8) results as

$$S_{i,t}^{\star} = \frac{5-0.75}{5} = 0.85\,. \tag{7.16}$$

Accordingly, the respective aggregate supply $S_t^{\star}$ is

$$S_t^{\star} = 500 \cdot S_{i,t}^{\star} = 500 \cdot 0.85 = 425\,. \tag{7.17}$$

The second extreme optimal quantity is the optimal supply of one single supplier, i.e for a true natural monopolist. Assuming that only firm n is active on the market while all other do not produce, n's optimal production $S_{n,t}^{\star}$, following (7.10), is

$$S_{n,t}^{\star} = 250 \cdot 0.85 = 212.5\,. \tag{7.18}$$

It should be explicitly mentioned that for technical reasons the maximum capacity of the agents, D^{max}, has been kept at a level which is too low to allow for one single firm to reach the monopolist's quantity $S_{n,t}^{\star}$ from (7.18).[4] Because of this technical restriction, the simulations are not capable of reaching a bipolar solution as strong as a pure natural monopoly. Nevertheless, it will be shown that the solutions are still interior points for the given range of capacities, which means that within the given range there are solutions representing at least local optima to the given problem.

7.4.1 Heterogeneities

First, the development of aggregate supply will be displayed. Figure 7.1 shows these data for an exemplary run of the canonical GA (left subfigure) and for the GA with intertemporal selection (modified GA, right subfigure).

Both subfigures show that the average quantity over time is much lower than the optimal quantity for homogeneous active behavior, which, according to (7.17), is given as $S_t^{\star} = 425$. On the other hand, the average supply seems to be much higher than the optimal quantity for a natural monopolist, which is given by (7.18) as $S_{n,t}^{\star} = 212.5$. The true simulation results are an average aggregate supply of $S_t = 383.174$ for the canonical GA and $s_t = 374.772$ for the modified algorithm. These results give a first hint that neither of the two extreme homogeneous results is achieved.

[4] The reduction of the individual capacity to a level which is relatively small compared to aggregate demand has the following reason. If the capacity is high enough for every single firm to satisfy the whole aggregate demand, often the following scenario arises: From one period to the next, many firms extend their supply by a large amount. This leads to such a large aggregate supply that the market price falls to zero. A price of zero means that the quality of different (short run) strategies are hard to discriminate. Selection fails. This means that sensible economic learning becomes impossible. The model breaks down.
One possible way out of this dilemma is the introduction of costs of the expansion of capacities. Firms can expand their supply, but they need time and money to do that. A model with such an extension is not too complicated to construct, but it would nevertheless be beyond the scope of this book. Even more: The results of such a model would not have much to add to the core result of this chapter, which is — bravely shortened — GAs are even capable over producing stable and economically sensible heterogeneous solutions if the economic model implies them.

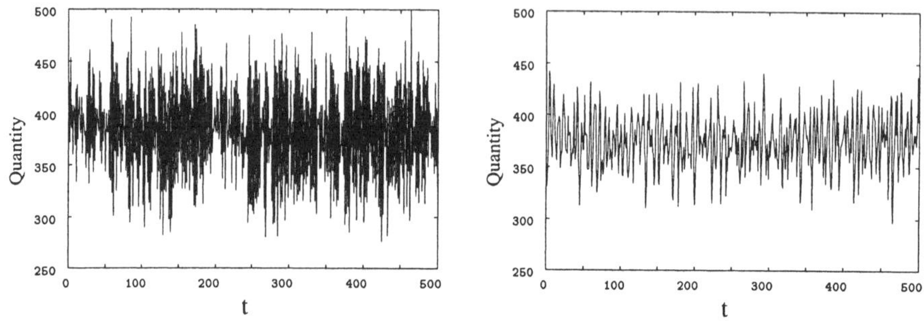

(a) Canonical GA

(b) Modified GA

Fig. 7.1. Aggregate Supply (Quantity)

The true quality of the results becomes more clear by a look at Fig. 7.2. This figure shows the number of active firms in the market, i.e. the number of firms producing more than zero. It can be seen that the number of active firms is less than the total number of firms, which is $n = 500$. Out of these 500 total firms, the average number of active ones is about 384 in the canonical GA (left subfigure) and about 364 in the modified algorithm (right subfigure).[5]

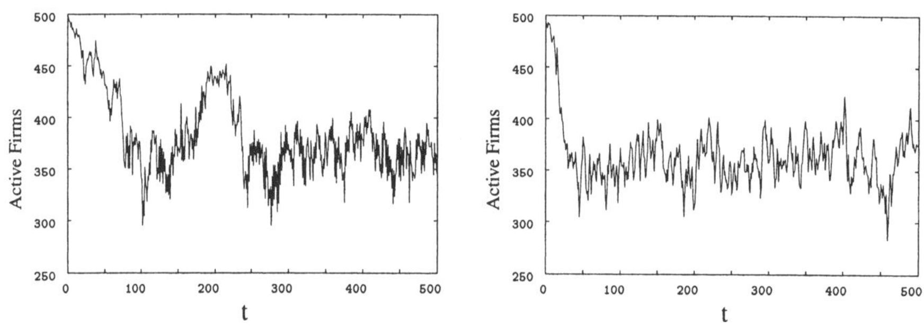

(a) Canonical GA

(b) Modified GA

Fig. 7.2. Number of Active Firms

Apparently, the simulations lead to a *heterogeneous* outcome. In both of the exemplary cases, there is a persistent share of agents not economically active. Ac-

[5] The exact data are: canonical GA, mean number of active firms: 384.002, variance: 1610.08; modified GA, mean number of active firms: 363.87, variance: 904.321.

cording to the exact nature of heterogeneity, the macro data shown in Fig. 7.3 have not enough to offer. A more elaborate analysis of the micro data is needed. A look 'into' the populations is necessary, which will offer the chance of gaining more results about the structure of the populations and of the population wide distribution of strategies. This look into some populations is offered by Fig. 7.3. The figure contains histograms showing the distribution of supply strategies for one genetic population each. The populations shown here are the populations after 50, 100, 250, and 500 periods of a simulation using the canonical GA (left row) and the modified GA (right row), respectively.[6] It can be clearly seen that in every population, a big part of the firms uses a strategy near zero.[7] This fact alone is no satisfying characterization of the state of the population. In fact, a second part of the population chooses a strategy clearly higher than zero. The pure existence of this part of the population producing more than zero, i.e. the part of the population which is economically active, is a proof that the results are clearly heterogeneous.

7.4.2 Cycles

Observations

From Fig. 7.1 it can be seen that for both of the simulations, there are oscillations much bigger than the usual oscillations caused by mutation. Comparing the form of these oscillations, they seem to have a smaller frequency and a smaller amplitude in the modified GA. Both observations can be confirmed statistically.

The average amplitudes of the oscillations can be compared as follows. The average supply in the simulation based on the canonical GA over the 500 periods of the simulation is $\mu_{CGA} = 383.174$, the variance of this mean quantity is $\sigma^2_{CGA} = 2756.29$, which implies a variance coefficient of $V_{CGA} = 0.14$.[8] For the modified GA, the respective data are: $\mu_{MGA} = 374.772$, $\sigma^2_{MGA} = 710.624$, and $V_{MGA} = 0.0711$. This means that the results of both simulation have a mean of more or less the same order of magnitude, while the level of oscillations is much lower in the modified GA than in the canonical GA. This gives strong incidence that in the modified algorithm, the amplitude of the oscillations are much smaller than in the canonical GA.

This result confirms the observation that from period to period, aggregate supply changes much less in the modified GA than in the canonical GA. One possible reason for this could be smaller changes in *individual* supply in the modified rather than in the canonical GA.[9]

---

[6] As a guide to understanding the figure, take the following example: The exemplary simulation of a canonical GA leads to a population in period 50 which consists of about 40% of all firms supplying a quantity between 0 and 0.25. About 10% of the firms in the same population supply a quantity between 0.25 and 0.5, etc.

[7] In fact, nearly all of the firms represented in the outer left column of every histogram use the zero–strategy. This, of course, cannot be seen from the picture.

[8] The variance coefficient V is defined as the ratio of the standard deviation to the arithmetic mean: $V = \frac{\sigma}{\mu}$.

[9] This is only one of many possible reasons. Macro oscillations might as well decrease because of individual changes in supply work against one another.

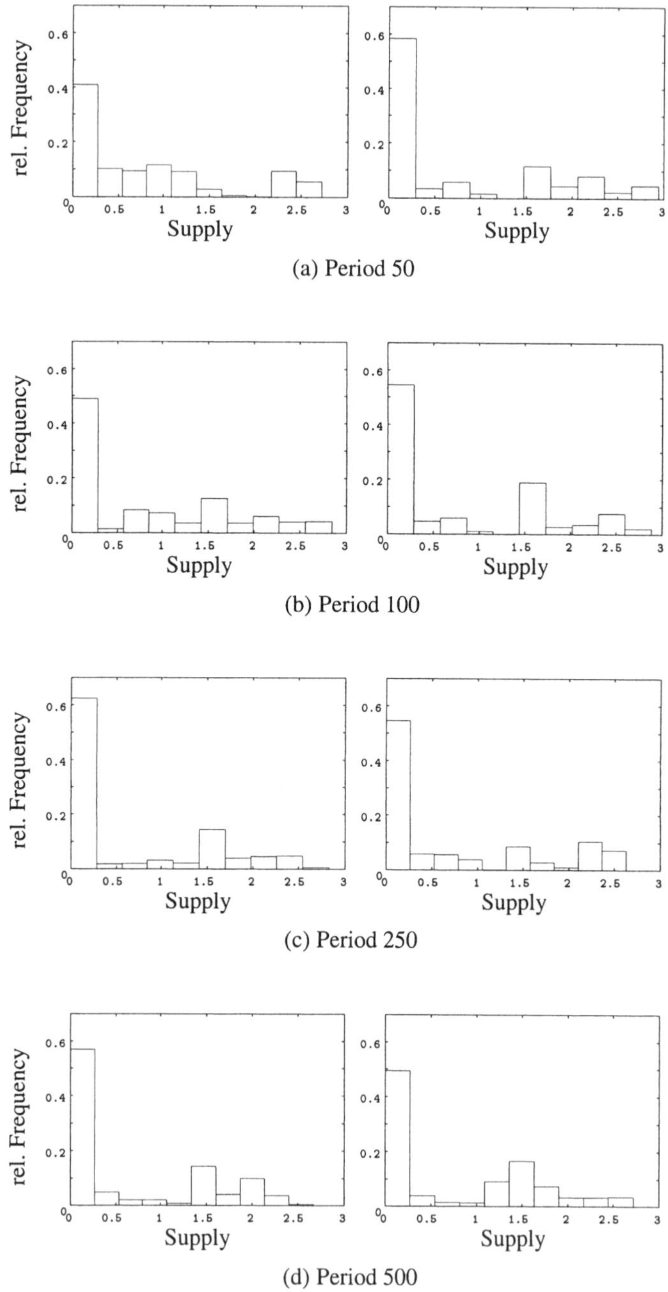

Fig. 7.3. Distribution of Strategies in the Canonical GA (left Row) and in the Modified GA (right Row)

The frequency of the oscillations will be analyzed using the tool of the sample spectrum.[10] The sample spectrum will help to uncover possible periodicities in the simulation results. Figure 7.4 confirms the presumption that the frequency of the oscillations is much higher in the canonical than in the modified GA.[11] For the

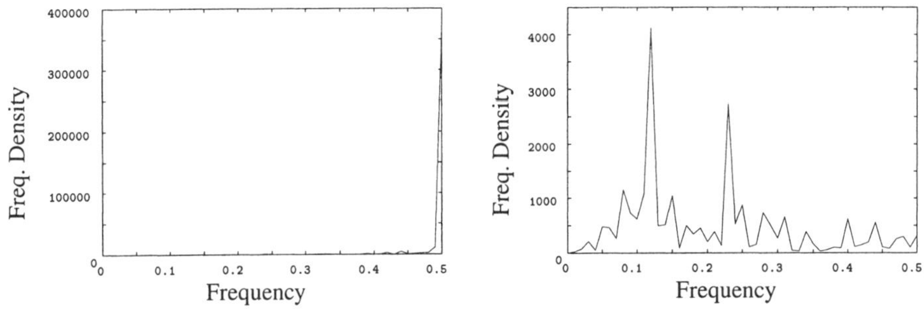

(a) Canonical GA (b) Modified GA

Fig. 7.4. Sample Spectrum

canonical GA (left subfigure), there are no considerable results of the spectral analysis. The maximum of the sample spectrum is located at a frequency of 0.5. This means, that there are no multi–period cycles in the result of the simulation. The result for the modified GA (right subfigure) is much richer: There are two strong peaks in the spectrum, namely at frequencies of 0.12 and 0.23. This means that the results of the modified GA lead to overlying regular cycles of length 8.33 and 4.35. This result means that the oscillations already apparent in Fig. 7.1 turn out to be somewhat regular macroeconomic cycles. This is an important result of the analysis: The modification of the canonical GA incorporating an intertemporal criterion of selection does, in the given economic case, lead to the arise of economic cycles. It is the aim of the rest of this chapter to find out the reasons in individual behavior causing these macro cycles.

---

[10] Simple building guidelines for sample spectra can be found in many textbooks on statistics and time series analysis like e.g. Hamilton (1994).

[11] The sample spectra displayed in Fig. 7.4 are computed using data of the last 450 periods of the simulations, i.e. the data of periods 51 to 500 in order to avoid possible disturbing effects of the initialization phase of the GAs.

Some Technical Considerations

The question is whether the occurrence of cycles can be traced back to the type of learning techniques that are used. It will be shown that the three genuine learning techniques of the GA, learning by imitation, communication, and experiment, have very dissimilar influences on the macro results of the model and thus on the cycles.

In order to get a better idea of the origins of the observed cycles, a detailed look on the economic problem is helpful.

The firms in the model try to maximize their one–period–profit. According to (7.3), this profit $\pi_{i,t}$ depends, among others, on the equilibrium price p_t. The equilibrium price, in turn, crucially depends on aggregate supply in period t. (7.6) gives the critical level of aggregate supply, i.e. the particular level of supply leading to an equilibrium price of zero:

$$S_{p_t=0} = n \cdot \frac{a}{b}. \tag{7.19}$$

Consequently, it can be written, that

$$p_t = \begin{cases} a - \frac{b}{n}\sum_{i=1}^{n} S_{i,t} & \text{for } \sum_{i=1}^{n} S_{i,t} < S_{p_t=0} \\ 0 & \text{for } \sum_{i=1}^{n} S_{i,t} \geq S_{p_t=0} \end{cases}. \tag{7.20}$$

From the point of view of a single firm n, equilibrium price (7.20) can also be formulated as

$$p_t = \begin{cases} a - \frac{b}{n}\sum_{i=1}^{n-1} S_{i,t} - \frac{b}{n} S_{n,t} & \text{for } \sum_{i=1}^{n} S_{i,t} < S_{p_t=0} \\ 0 & \text{for } \sum_{i=1}^{n} S_{i,t} \geq S_{p_t=0} \end{cases}. \tag{7.21}$$

From (7.21) and the particular form (7.2) of the cost function, the individual profit function of firm n can be written as

$$\pi_{n,t} = \begin{cases} \text{a) } 0 & \text{for } S_{n,t} = 0 \\ \text{b) } \left(a - \frac{b}{n}\sum_{i=1}^{n-1} S_{i,t} - \beta\right) S_{n,t} - \frac{b}{n} S_{n,t}^2 - \alpha & \text{for } S_{n,t} > 0 \text{ and } \sum_{i=1}^{n} S_{i,t} < S_{p_t=0} \\ \text{c) } -\alpha - \beta S_{n,t} & \text{for } S_{n,t} > 0 \text{ and } \sum_{i=1}^{n} S_{i,t} \geq S_{p_t=0} \end{cases} \tag{7.22}$$

First, from (7.22), it becomes obvious that the problem is a problem of state dependent fitness: The one period success of firm n does not only depend on its own supply strategy $S_{n,t}$, but also on the strategies of all other firms i.

The particularly interesting case is case b) of equation (7.22). This is the case where firm n is economically active and, at the same time, aggregate supply is below its critical level $S_{p_t=0}$. Partial differentiation of this equation shows that there is an optimal supply strategy for firm n. The profit maximizing supply[12] for n is

[12] A close look at part b) of equation (7.22) shows that the function is an inverted parabola of second degree in $S_{n,t}$, such that an optimum is automatically a maximum. This means that further analysis, e.g. the computation of second order derivations, is not necessary.

$$S_{n,t}^{\star} = \frac{1}{2}\left(n\frac{a-\beta}{b} - \sum_{i=1}^{n-1} S_{i,t}\right) \tag{7.23}$$

This result is the general case. Substituting the respective quantities for $\sum_{i=1}^{n-1} S_{i,t}$, (7.23) becomes (7.8) or (7.10), respectively. In other words: (7.23) gives the quantity of supply which — given the quantities $S_{1,t}$ to $S_{n-1,t}$ — is the Nash strategy of firm n. In the simulations, though, the capacities of the firm are restricted, such that no single firm is able to produce this optimal quantity. In the simulations, it is true that

$$D_i^{\max} < S_n^{\star} \quad \forall i. \tag{7.24}$$

Because the profit function (7.22, part b) is a monotonic function, there is a corner solution which lies in the relevant interval at the upper border of each firm's capacity. On the other hand, there is a second corner optimum to the profit function (7.22), which is the trivial production quantity of zero. For this alternative, the profit is zero and thus higher than anywhere in the closer neighborhood of this point. This finding trivially follows from the fact that, following (7.22, part b), a quantity of $S_{n,t} = 0$ results in a 'profit' of $\pi_{n,t} = -\alpha < 0$.

What is important for the following analysis is the fact that in the set of possible production quantities there are two different local optima of the profit function, which are both located at the corners of the domain of this function. From an economic point of view this means that it is always relatively good to produce one of the extreme quantities: Everything a firm can produce with its given capacity, or nothing at all.

Further Simulations

In order to find the causes of the cycles observed, more simulations will be run. The models are based on the concept of the intertemporal criterion of selection. Different to the modified GA employed up to now, some of the following algorithms do not include all three genetic operators.

The first simulation will be restricted to the use of selection/reproduction only, thus reflecting learning by pure imitation. The result of an exemplary run of the simulation is shown in Fig. 7.5.

The most striking observation is the high degree of oscillations of the aggregate supply over time. In many periods, the supply is high enough to bring the market price down to zero. For the economic parameters given above, the minimum aggregate supply leading to a price of zero, $S_{p_t=0}$, is

$$S_{p_t=0} = 500. \tag{7.25}$$

For an easier orientation, this quantity is marked in Fig. 7.5. All quantities of 500 or more lead to an equilibrium price of zero. It can be seen from the figure, that this critical quantity is exceeded in many periods. This can be easily explained as resulting from the special structure of the given economic problem in connection with the

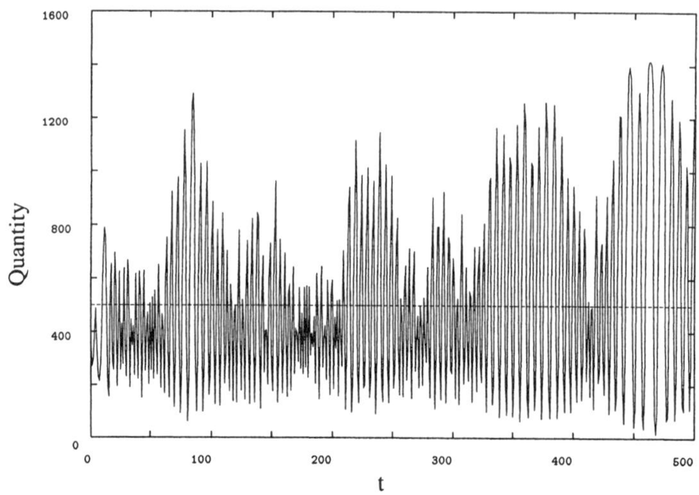

Fig. 7.5. Learning by Imitation

applied learning technique. As long as only a few firms choose a comparably high quantity of supply, they are relatively successful. But, due to imitation, supposedly good strategies are adopted by other firms. This leads to a much higher aggregate supply and thus to a lower price and to much lower profits. When aggregate supply exceeds the critical level of $S_{p_t=0} = 500$, at the latest, profits become negative. Negative profits, are worse than profits of zero. This means that in situations with many active firms, those firms are better off that do not produce at all. Now that economically inactive firms perform better than active suppliers, many firms will adopt the strategy of doing nothing. This, in turn, leads to a falling aggregate supply, the active firms left on the market are more successful again, they will be imitated, aggregate supply rises again, the price falls again, and so on. Cutting a long story short, the cycles can be interpreted as the result of imitation leading to waves of individual changes of strategies from being economically active to being economically inactive and vice versa.

As GA learning in its basic form does not allow for more than one period strategies, the learning of anti–cyclical or other forms of long run strategies can not be achieved by the model presented here.

The amplitude of oscillations can be decreased by additionally introducing the possibility of learning by experiment, i.e. by mutation.[13] Figure 7.6 shows the result of an exemplary run of the simulation of a GA with selection/reproduction, muta-

[13] This statement is only true for a 'normal' range of mutation probabilities μ of about $\frac{1}{1000} \leq \mu \leq \frac{1}{100}$. For lower probabilities, mutation happens too seldomly to change the algorithm permanently, for higher probabilities, mutation turns the algorithm into something like a random walk.

tion, and the intertemporal criterion of selection. The figure uses the same scale as Fig. 7.5, which makes it possible to compare the results of the simulations directly.

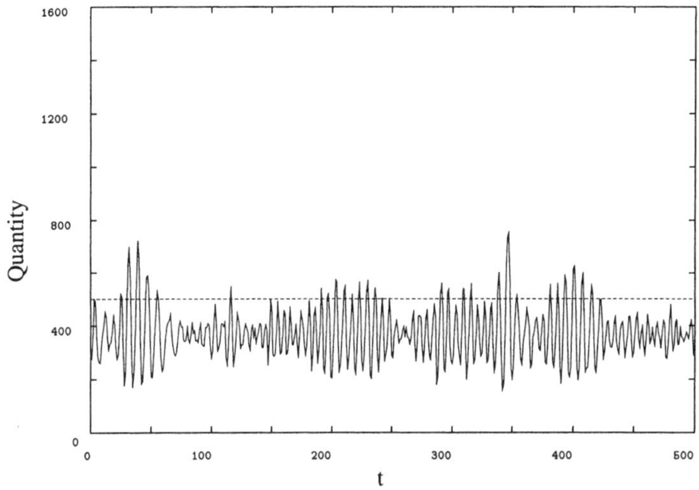

Fig. 7.6. Learning by Imitation and Experiment

The resulting oscillations are significantly reduced. As a consequence, the critical quantity $S_{p_t=0}$ is exceeded not as often as in the simulation for imitation only. Learning by experiment weakens the effect of imitation. Of course, agents still imitate. But many of the agents do not directly use the adopted strategy at the market. Instead, for most agents this strategy is only the base for further experiments. As the adopted strategies are most likely to be one of the two extreme strategies of zero or the maximum capacity, i.e. strategies located on the corners of the domain, experiments can only result in less extreme strategies, i.e. interior points of the domain. This means that in this case, different from the usual effect of mutation, mutation stabilizes macroeconomic dynamics.

Even stronger than the effect of learning by experiment is the impact of communication. Figure 7.7 shows the results of a simulation incorporating selection/reproduction and crossover, i.e. learning by imitation and by communication.

Again, the figure uses the same scale as Fig. 7.5 and 7.6. It is obvious that learning by communication decreases the degree of the oscillations even more than learning by experiments.[14] The effect of communication can be explained analogously to the effect of experiments: Communication modifies the extreme strategies adopted by the agents. Such a modification can only produce new strategies from the interior

[14] Of course, the value of the technical parameter of the crossover probability plays an important role. The value used in the simulations is $\chi = 0.5$. Many other simulations based on different values of χ showed that even for large variations of χ no significantly different results occurred.

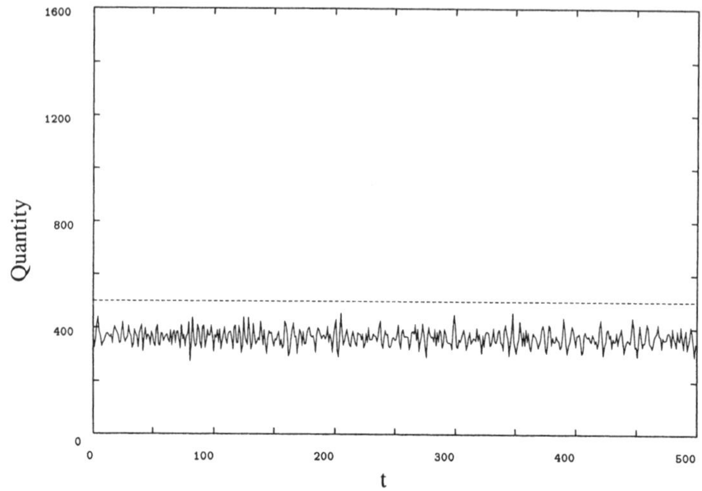

Fig. 7.7. Learning by Imitation and Communication

of the domain, i.e. strategies less extreme than full usage of a firm's capacity or no production at all. As communication in form of the one point crossover operator is a special form of computing a certain kind of average, learning by communication works even stronger than learning by experiments.

7.5 Summary

This chapter shows that the connection of a simple economic problem and a slight modification of the definition of economic success can result in the occurrence of macroeconomic cycles. Moreover, it can be shown that these macroeconomic cycles are caused by movements on the microeconomic level, which are determined by the certain form of learning technique the individuals use.

The cycles arising in the model are caused by two interacting phenomena. The first is the special structure of the underlying economic problem. The problem in focus has two locally optimal individual solutions. Which one of these is the global optimum depends on the global state of the economy. Depending on what happens on the aggregate level, sometimes the first and sometimes the second local optimum becomes globally optimal. The second cause of the cycles is the learning technique employed. Imitation plays the most important part. Due to the economic problem, the globally optimum strategy is always the locally optimum one which is used by the minority of the agents. As soon as the majority recognizes the true position of the optimum and adopts the presumably optimal strategy, the location of the optimum switches to the strategy most of the agents have just left. Thus, in a way, the economic story told in this chapter is the story of the turner and the hare: As soon as the turner believes to have reached the optimum at last, the optimum is already gone.

8 Algorithms with Real Valued Coding

8.1 Introduction

This chapter is dedicated to an economic problem with a much more complex structure than all the problems focused before. It is the problem of consumer choice of private households. In the model, a population of households has to divide their income between the consumptions of three different consumption goods. The final goal of their decision is to achieve optimal utility.

Technically, this means that now an algorithm is needed that allows for the simultaneous optimization of three independent variables and which can handle constrained optimization problems. This type of problems can be solved with the help of algorithms using real valued instead of binary coding of variables. Real valued coding is based on the work of Rechenberg and Schwefel on 'Evolution Strategies' and dates back to the 1970s.[1]

8.2 The Economic Model: Consumer Choice

8.2.1 The General Structure of the Model

Let there be a number of n agents (households) facing the standard textbook problem of consumer choice, i.e. selecting a bundle of consumption goods which, under the restriction of a limited budget, maximizes utility.

Agents are assumed to have identical utility functions, which do not change over time t. Utility is derived from consuming a bundle of m different goods indexed k. For convenience, the utility function is assumed to be of Cobb–Douglas type.

$$u_{i,t} = A\prod_{k=1}^{m} q_{i,k,t}^{\alpha_k}; \quad A > 0;\ \alpha_k > 0 \forall k = 1,\dots,m. \tag{8.1}$$

$q_{i,k,t}$ gives the quantity of good k agent i consumes in period t. A and α_k, $k = 1,\dots,m$ are parameters of the model.

[1] The historically first work on this topic is (Rechenberg, 1970), published as Rechenberg (1973). Some more very good material on real valued coding is given in Bäck et al. (1991) and in Michalewicz (1996, Chap. 8). An extensive comparison of Evolution Strategies and Genetic Algorithms can be found in Hoffmeister and Bäck (1991).

The budget M is assumed to be the same for every agent i in every period t, so the budget constraint is given by

$$M \geq \sum_{k=1}^{m} p_{k,t}\, q_{i,k,t}\,. \tag{8.2}$$

$p_{k,t}$ represents the market price for good k in t.

Thus, every agent i aims to solve the constrained maximization problem

$$\max_{q_{i,k,t}} u_{i,t} \quad \forall k = 1, \dots, m \tag{8.3}$$

$$\text{s.t.} \quad M \geq \sum_{k=1}^{m} p_{k,t}\, q_{i,k,t} \tag{8.4}$$

$$q_{i,k,t} \geq 0 \quad \forall k = 1, \dots, m \tag{8.5}$$

Equation (8.5) gives the usual non–negativity constraints.

Different from the standard textbook model, prices will not generally be held fixed, but will be subject to a stylized Walrasian mechanism. For each good k, in every period t, the price will be determined as the equilibrium price resulting from the interaction of aggregate demand for good k in t and aggregate supply of the good.

Aggregate demand for good k in t, $Q_{k,t}$ is simply the sum of individual demand for k in t:

$$Q_{k,t} = \sum_{i=1}^{n} q_{i,k,t}\,. \tag{8.6}$$

Aggregate supply will be modeled by a time invariant standard supply function for each good k, so that the equilibrium price $p^{\star}_{k,t}$ results as

$$p^{\star}_{k,t} = B_k + m_k \sum_{i=1}^{n} q_{i,k,t}\,. \tag{8.7}$$

8.2.2 The Basic Model

The basic model is a model of fixed prices. This means that in equation (8.7) $m_k = 0$, yielding

$$p^{\star}_{k,t} = B_k\,. \tag{8.8}$$

Note, that this case does not represent an 'economic' problem in the sense of agents' fitness being state dependent. Each agent's utility only depends on her own actions, but in no way on the actions of any other agent.

For fixed prices the solution to the problem of consumer choice can easily be derived.

By standard calculus, the solution can be determined as

$$q^{\star}_{i,k,t} = \frac{\alpha_k}{\sum_{k=1}^{m} \alpha_k} \frac{M}{B_k}; \quad \forall k; \forall i; \forall t. \tag{8.9}$$

This result yields two crucial characteristics common to every optimal bundle of consumption goods. The first characteristic is efficiency: The whole budget is being spent. In an optimal situation, (8.2) becomes binding:

$$M = \sum_{k=1}^{m} p_{k,t}\, q_{i,k,t}\,. \tag{8.10}$$

The second crucial characteristic of the optimal consumer choice is the fact, that marginal utility per Dollar is the same for every pair of goods k, l,

$$\frac{\partial u_{i,t}(\cdot)/\partial q_{k,i,t}}{p_{k,t}} = \frac{\partial u_{i,t}(\cdot)/\partial q_{l,i,t}}{p_{l,t}} \quad \forall k, l \in \{1, \ldots, m\}\,. \tag{8.11}$$

Both of these well known standard results will become of greater importance in the second part of the chapter.

8.2.3 The Enhanced Model

In the enhanced case, prices are no longer fixed, i.e. $m_k \neq 0$ in (8.7). As a consequence, the problem of consumer choice becomes a problem of state dependent fitness: Now, aggregate demand has an influence on the market price and the market price has an influence on every single agent's economic success.

With the introduction of flexible prices the problem becomes analytically unsolvable. This means that for flexible prices, a general explicit numerical solution analogous to (8.9) for the fixed price case cannot be computed. Nevertheless, at least for uniform populations, the characteristics (8.10) for efficiency and (8.11) for optimality still apply.

The question if boundedly rational agents are able to achieve relatively good solutions to the enhanced problem can be put in another way: As will be pointed out in greater detail later on (Sect. 8.5.1), there are two main influences on an agent's utility: The direct effect of her quantity decision and the indirect effect caused by all agents' demand influencing the price of the goods. In a world of bounded rationality, this indirect effect can be interpreted as a kind of external effect no agent accounts of.[2] Then, it is a question of *how bounded* the rationality of agents really is: If they recognize the external effect, their utility will be greater than if they ignore it. This means that, at least in this model, accounting for the external effect is a sign of rationality.[3]

---

[2] To be more precise, this is a monetary external effect. Though the characterization of external effects is standard in modern economic literature, it seems interesting and important to still refer to the original work of Buchanan and Stubblebine (1962).

[3] Note, that this concept is similar to the concept of 'externalities' used in modern endogenous growth theory (Romer, 1986; Lucas, 1988; Barro, 1990). There, so called externalities appear which are recognized by the allmighty social planer but not by the 'normal' individuals populating the economy.

8.3 The Genetic Algorithm

8.3.1 The Basics

A genetic algorithm aiming to model the above setting in an agent based manner must above all be capable of coping with two problems: a) The maximization problem in focus involves the optimization of more than just one independent variable, and b) the maximization problem in focus has to be solved subject to a constraint.

Both of the problems have been solved in natural sciences before,[4] but up to now there is no economic model making use of these results.

In this chapter, a hybrid algorithm will be employed, making use of principles from two worlds, from the world of genetic algorithms (GAs, see e.g. Goldberg, 1989) and from the world of evolution strategies (ESs, see e.g. Bäck et al., 1991). From GAs, the well known operators of crossover and selection/reproduction are used. In economics, they have been broadly interpreted as forms of social learning by communication and interpretation as well as the functioning of the market (Riechmann, 1999). From evolution strategies, the operator of mutation is used, being interpreted as a form of isolated individual learning by experiment. Moreover, the variables in focus will not be coded as bit strings, but as real valued numbers, which is also a feature of evolution strategies.

8.3.2 Coding

To make things clearer, an agent i will be fully described by her economic plans, i.e. the vector of demanded quantities for each good k in period t, $q_{i,k,t}$. In the simulations, there will only be three different goods available to the agents. Thus, an agent is characterized by a vector $q_{i,t}$,

$$q_{i,t} \in \mathbb{R}^3 . \tag{8.12}$$

An example would be

$$q_{10,5} = (11.2; 3.7; 17.0) \tag{8.13}$$

meaning that agent number 10 plans to consume 11.2 units of the first, 3.7 units of the second and 17 units of the third good in period 5.

This type of coding is different from the coding scheme used up to this point. Now, genetic individuals are no longer represented by a binary bit string, but by a vector of real numbers. This means, that the algorithm is not a genetic algorithm any more, because many authors use the type of coding as the distinction between genetic algorithms and other forms of evolutionary algorithms. Algorithms based on real valued coding are often counted as 'evolution strategies' rather than genetic algorithms. In this book, nevertheless, the phrase 'genetic algorithm' will be used for this type of algorithm, too. This position might be defended by the remark, that Goldberg (1991) shows close similarities in the behavior of real valued and binary coded algorithms.

---

[4] A summary of results can be found in Michalewicz (1996).

8.3.3 Standard Operators

Due to the change in the representation of the agents, the genetic operators have to be changed, too. As these operators are used as metaphors for learning techniques, the changes must take place in a way that preserves sensible behavioral interpretations of the operators.

The 'double operator' of selection and reproduction, often being interpreted as learning by imitation connected with the role of the market, needs no changes at all. Agents are selected from their population and reproduced into the next one with a probability equal to their relative fitness. Fitness, in this case, equals individual utility. This means, that in this chapter, the standard roulette wheel selection operator (Goldberg, 1989) will be used, not one of the selection operators stemming from the tradition of evolution strategies.

Recombination in the form of crossover is usually seen as a metaphor for learning by communication. The change of this operator is quite straightforward. In a real valued rather than a binary representation, agents' economic strategies can be separated into clearly defined economic substrategies. A substrategy in the current model is the consumption quantity of a single good. This means that in the above example (8.13) the agent has three substrategies: 11.2 for good one, 3.7 for good two, and 17 for good three. Crossover now works as usual, recombinating two agents' substrategies. The agents involved in crossover are chosen from their population, a crossover point is selected, the vectors of substrategies are cut at the crossover point, the resulting parts are interchanged and put together again, yielding two new strategies. Figure 8.1 shows an example.

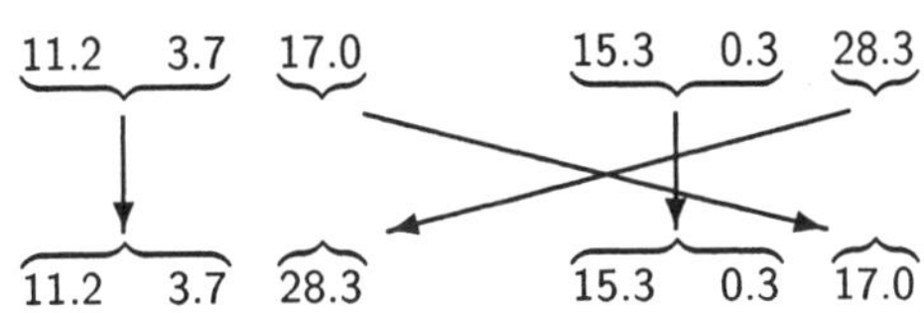

Fig. 8.1. Crossover (Example)

In the world of real valued coding of agents' strategies, the interpretation of crossover as a form of learning by exchanging substrategies becomes even clearer than in the world of binary coding.

The third standard operator, mutation, has to be changed, too. Mutation, often being interpreted as learning by experiment, has to undergo the most severe changes. Real valued coding certainly does not allow for simple bit flipping. Instead, the mutation operator from the tradition of evolution strategies can be used. In this tradition, a substrategy $q_{i,k,t}$ is mutated by adding a term v_k to it, where v_k is normally distributed with mean 0 and a finite variance σ^2, resulting in the new substrategy

$\tilde{q}_{i,k,t}$.[5]

$$\tilde{q}_{i,k,t} = q_{i,k,t} + \nu_k \quad \forall k \in \{1,\ldots,m\}; \quad \nu_k \sim N\left(0,\sigma^2\right) \tag{8.14}$$

By endogenizing the mutation variance σ^2, this operator could easily be extended in order to represent some kind of meta learning (see Chap. 6.3), but for the clarity of the economic argument this will not be done.

8.3.4 Enhanced Operators

In addition to the standard operators, two more 'enhanced' operators shall be employed. The first one is the well known election operator (Arifovic, 1994). Election requires two (or more) agents to meet, jointly work out new strategies, evaluate these strategies and then finally decide which strategy to use in reality. Though election, especially in its basic form, is not undisputed in its economic meaning, it is known to result in stable states of the learning process, which most of the time even represent optimal solutions to the underlying economic problem. Thus — economically meaningful or not — election represents a good benchmark for the test of the performance of other learning operators.

The second enhanced operator is something more than just an operator, it requires a slight change in the construction and implementation of the agents. For the operator of *preselection*, agents will be equipped with some memory. And although this memory is very limited, it will be shown to help improving agents' learning performance. Precisely, agents will be given the ability to remember one certain strategy together with the level of utility they once gained from employing this strategy. The specific strategy an agent remembers is her all time best strategy, i.e. the strategy that has brought her the highest utility during the whole learning process. In preselection an agent chooses from two possible strategies: the strategy she used in the last period (the fitness of which she can remember) and her all time best strategy. She decides by the fitness. The strategy with the higher fitness is chosen as the strategy the following learning processes of the current period (i.e. communication and experiment) are based on.

Note, that for non state dependent problems, like the fixed price problem of consumer choice, the preselection algorithm essentially works like an intra agent operator of elitist selection for the basic strategy in each period. In the simple fixed price model, an agent's fitness or utility is independent of what the others do, i.e.

$$u_i\left(q_{i,t}|S_t\right) = u_i\left(q_{i,t}\right) \quad \forall S_t \in S'. \tag{8.15}$$

S_t is the population in period t, S' is the set of all different populations.

In problems of state dependent fitness, in contrast, all actions of all the other agents in the population have an influence on an agent's fitness. This means, that for $m_k \neq 0$ in (8.7), the strategy an agent thinks of as her all time best one, might —

[5] In order to make sure the adherence to the non–negativity constraints (8.7), the pure mutation operator has to be accompanied by some mechanism guaranteeing that $\tilde{q}_{i,k,t} \geq 0$.

PREGA — Preselection Algorithm

while not STOP

- $t := t+1$
- Select Population $\overline{m}_t$ from $\overline{m}_{t-1}$
- **Preselection** on $\overline{m}_t$:
  - for Each Agent $i \in \overline{m}_t$
    - Preselection:
      $q_{i,t} := \text{argmax}_{u(\cdot)} \left\{ q_{i,t-1}; \mu_i \right\}$
    - Memorize Current Strategy:
      $\mu_i := \left\{ q_{i,t}; u\left(q_{i,t} | \overline{m}_t\right) \right\}$
- Crossover on $\overline{m}_t$
- Mutation on $\overline{m}_t$
- Evaluation on $\overline{m}_t$

Algorithm 8.1: Main Loop of Preselection Algorithm

due to the current population — not be as good as she thinks. A strategy that once performed brilliantly may work very poorly in the context of a different population. This is a fact that the agents in this model are assumed to ignore. Agents use the rule of preselection, because they simply do not know that they may be mistaken.

8.3.5 Coping with the Constraints

The problem in focus is a problem of constrained optimization. Agents not only have to maximize utility but also have to be careful not to exceed their budget. In the simulations, the budget constraint will not be *directly* accounted for. This means that there is no good the consumed quantity of which serves as some kind of residual. This means that agents *do not* do something like determine the quantity of the last good as all they can afford to buy by the rest of their budget like

$$q_{i,m,t} = \frac{1}{p_{m,t}} \left(M - \sum_{k=1}^{m-1} p_{k,t} q_{i,k,t} \right) . \tag{8.16}$$

Instead, agents freely decide on the quantity of all three goods, at first hand independent of the budget constraint. This also means, that in the fixed price cases, at the time of making their consumer plans, agents do not even know the prices of the goods, which makes their decision problem even harder.

The compliance to the budget constraint is secured by using a *penalty function*, which is a standard tool in evolutionary optimization.[6] Using a penalty function means to decrease an agent's fitness if she breaks the budget constraint. In economic terms, this looks like an extension to the utility function, which may be rather unusual to most theoretical economists.

In the simulations the following fitness function was used in order to transform utility $u_{i,t}$ into fitness $R_{i,t}$:[7]

$$R_{q_{i,t}} = \begin{cases} U(q_{i,t}) + M - \sum_{k=1}^{3} p_{k,t} q_{i,k,t} & \text{for} \quad \sum_{k=1}^{3} p_{k,t} q_{i,k,t} > M \\ U(q_{i,t}) & \text{for} \quad \sum_{k=1}^{3} p_{k,t} q_{i,k,t} \leq M \end{cases} . \tag{8.17}$$

Using fitness function (8.17) means, that an agent *can* break the constraints, but that she should *learn* not to do so.

8.4 Simulations and Results

For the model described above, simulations were run using three different algorithms, a) the canonical algorithm, using selection/reproduction, crossover and mutation, b) the election algorithm, using selection/reproduction and election, and c) the preselection algorithm, using selection/reproduction, preselection, crossover and mutation. The simulations were run for three different parameter sets which only differ with respect to the elasticity of supply.

All three sets thus share the values for $A = 1$ and for the budget M, $M = 100$, for B_k, $B_1 = B_2 = B_3 = 1$, and for α_k, $\alpha_1 = 0.2$, $\alpha_2 = 0.3$, and $\alpha_3 = 0.5$. The only difference is that for the first set ('FIXPRICE'), $m_1 = m_2 = m_3 = 0$, yielding $p_1 = p_2 = p_3 = B_k = 1$. Thus, FIXPRICE represents the fixed price case, or, put in different words, a case of infinitely high elasticity of supply.[8] The second set ('HIGHELASTICITY') uses $m_1 = m_2 = m_3 = 0.0001$, thus represent-

[6] See e.g. Michalewicz (1996, pp. 321).

[7] Negative fitness values can arise, so that before entering the selection operator, fitness has to be subject to one of the standard positive transfer mechanisms (Goldberg, 1989; Mitchell, 1996).

[8] The definition of 'elasticity of supply' differs between various textbooks of microeconomic theory. This chapter makes use of the definition by Henderson and Quandt (1986), who define the price elasticity of supply as the ratio of relative change in the quantity of supply (nominator) to the relative change of the price (denominator).
For this chapter this means that the elasticity of supply for good k, ε_k, is given by

ing a state of high elasticity of supply. The third set ('LOWELASTICITY') uses $m_1 = m_2 = m_3 = 0.1$ which leads to a state of low elasticity of supply.

Simulations were run for populations of $n = 500$ agents and for $t_{\max} = 500$ periods.

8.4.1 Fixed Prices

For the fixed price case, at least for the case of uniform behavior, optimal outcome can be determined analytically. If all agents within a population behave the same, the best strategy according to (8.9), given parameter set FIXPRICE is

$$q^{\star}_{1,k,t} = 20, \quad q^{\star}_{2,k,t} = 30, \quad q^{\star}_{3,k,t} = 50 \quad \forall \quad k,t\,. \tag{8.18}$$

This result represents both, efficiency and optimality. This means that for the results given in (8.18) the budget is fully spent (i.e. the budget residual is zero) and every agent's utility is as high as possible due to the budget.

The quality of the learning algorithms can be judged by comparing the results learned to the theoretical results given by (8.18). More than this, it seems appropriate to check if, and if so, how good, the budget constraint is met. In order to do this, the average budget residual ρ_t will be used, which is defined as the average amount of money not spent on consumption throughout the population, i.e.

$$\rho_t = \frac{1}{n}\sum_{i=1}^{n}\left(M - \sum_{k=1}^{3} p_{i,k,t}q_{i,k,t}\right)\,. \tag{8.19}$$

Representative simulation results for the three respective algorithms are given in the following Figs. 8.2 to 8.4. Each figure consists of two subfigures which give a plot of the population average of the quantities of good one to three (on the left) and a plot of the average budget residual (on the right).

It is easy to see that for all three algorithms, the quantities tend to converge towards the theoretically optimal quantities. The election algorithm seems to perform best whereas the canonical algorithm performs worst. This impression is supported by the results concerning the budget residual. Election converges to a residual equal to zero, preselection tends to oscillate around zero, whereas the canonical algorithm results in relatively large positive residuals. This means that each of the three learning methods is able not to violate the budget constraint, but only learning with election and learning with preselection enables the agents not to waste a part of their income.

$\varepsilon_k = \frac{\partial Q_k / Q_k}{\partial p_k / p_k}$.
This definition implies that the change in the quantity is a result of a change in market price. This chapter, though, will argue the other way round: A change in price is the reaction on a change in aggregate demand, i.e. a change in quantity.

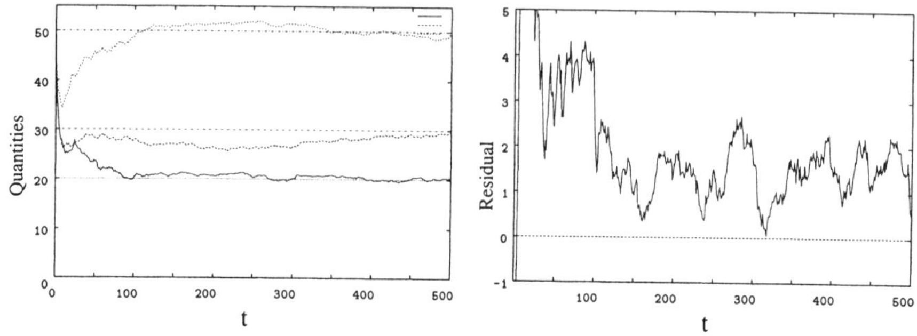

(a) Quantities: — q_1, ··· q_2, - - q_3 (b) Budget Residual

Fig. 8.2. Canonical Algorithm

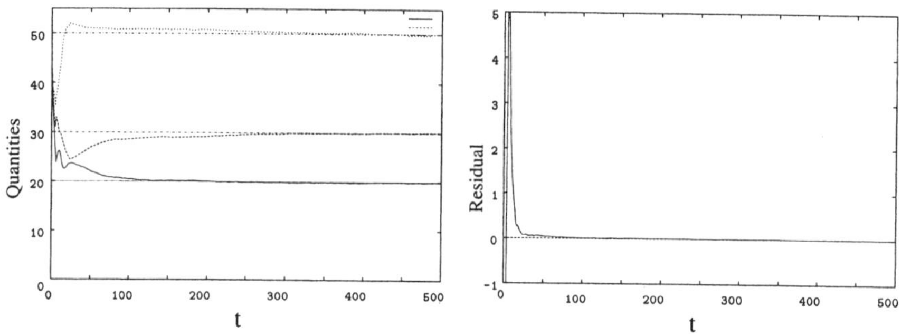

(a) Quantities: — q_1, ··· q_2, - - q_3 (b) Budget Residual

Fig. 8.3. Election Algorithm

8.4.2 Flexible Prices, High Elasticity

For the case of flexible prices, it becomes impossible to determine an explicit solution analytically even for the case of homogeneous behavior. In fact, the flexible price variant of the model is a kind of multi person Cournot game of the demand side. In order to judge the quality of the simulation results, two measures are introduced. The first one is the average budget residual defined in equation (8.19). The second one is the difference between the marginal utility per Dollar for each pair of the three goods. Although it is impossible to solve the problem explicitly, the fact remains that in an optimal solution of the consumer choice problem marginal utility per Dollar has to be equal for every possible pair of goods. Thus, a perfect solution

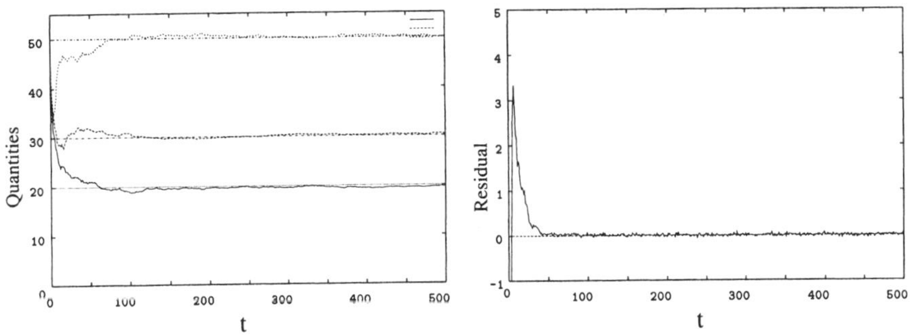

(a) Quantities: — q_1, ··· q_2, - - q_3

(b) Budget Residual

Fig. 8.4. Preselection Algorithm

should have two characteristics: a) Marginal utility per Dollar is the same for each of the three goods, and b) the average budget residual is zero.

The plots of representative simulations for the three algorithms and the HIGH-ELASTICITY case (Figs. 8.5 to 8.7) consist of three subfigures each. The first subfigure gives the population average of the quantities of each good. This subfigure only serves as an illustration. It shows the quantities learned. But now, in the case of flexible prices, it does not offer any means for judging the results. The second subfigure gives the average budget residual ρ_t. The third subfigure is a plot of the marginal utility per Dollar for each of the three goods.

A closer look at the figures confirms the results of the FIXPRICE case. The election algorithm performs best. Marginal utilities per Dollar seem to converge completely while the budget residual vanishes. The preselection algorithm generates slightly worse results. While the budget residual fluctuates around zero, marginal utilities per Dollar become similar but not equal. The canonical algorithm performs worst. Marginal utilities per Dollar become similar, but the budget is never fully spent.

8.4.3 Flexible Prices, Low Elasticity

The third case in focus, flexible prices with a low elasticity of supply, causes quite different results, as can be seen from Figs. 8.8 to 8.10. It can be seen that the canonical algorithm does not reach a sensible outcome. The budget constraint is never met while marginal utilities per Dollar never get close to each other. In the LOWELASTICITY case, a sensible consumer choice cannot be learned by use of the simple canonical algorithm learning rules.

Even worse is the result for the election algorithm. In every simulation run for this case, with only one explicitly shown in this chapter, the model collapsed. Election leads to totally unrealistic cases of violations of the budget constraint while

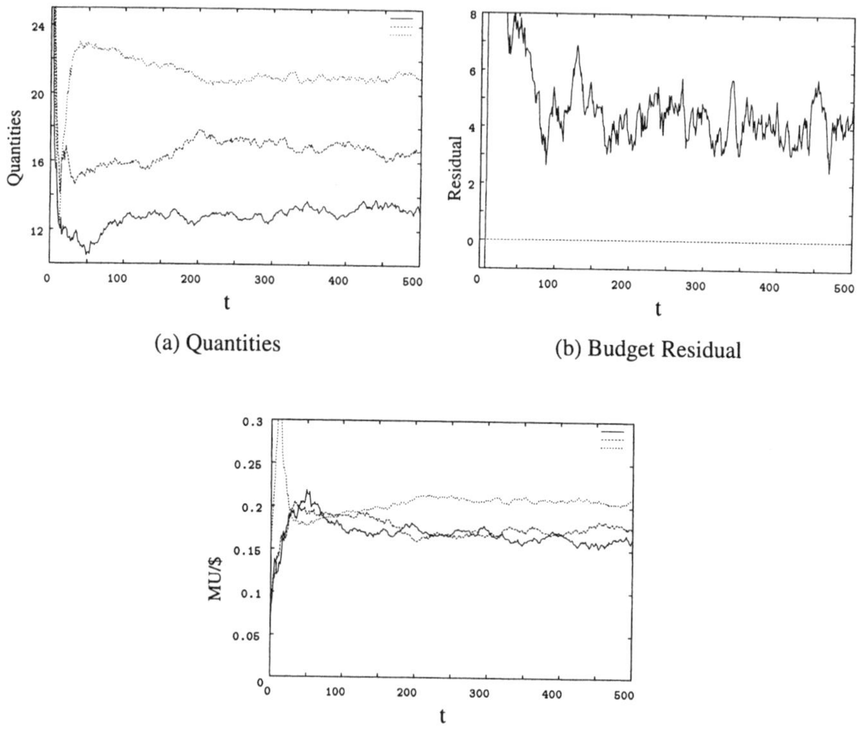

(a) Quantities

(b) Budget Residual

(c) Marginal Utility per Dollar

Fig. 8.5. Canonical Algorithm – High Elasticity of Supply: — q_1, ··· q_2, - - q_3

marginal utilities per Dollar do not converge at all. For the case of flexible prices and a low elasticity of supply, election is far from leading to any kind of sensible consumer choice.

The only sensible results are achieved by the preselection algorithm, which causes the marginal utilities per Dollar to become at least slightly similar to each other while the budget constraint is not violated too severely.

8.4.4 Summary of Results

The results of the analysis are essentially won from two sources: The plots of the simulations shown above and some statistics, which are based on one run of each simulation only. The statistics can be found in Appendix 8.6.

Concerning the budget constraint it can be found, that it seems to be relatively easy to learn not to violate it. For the FIXPRICE case as well as for HIGHELASTICITY, the canonical algorithm results in states which are significantly positive, while

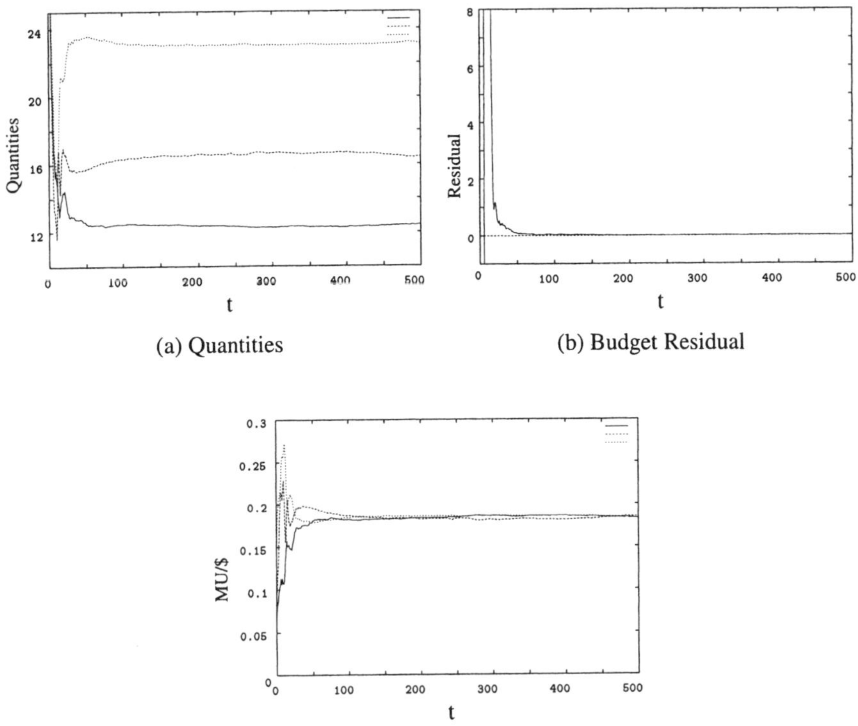

(a) Quantities

(b) Budget Residual

(c) Marginal Utility per Dollar

Fig. 8.6. Election Algorithm – High Elasticity of Supply: — q_1, ··· q_2, - - q_3

election is significantly very close to zero and preselection is even significantly equal to zero.

For the choice of the correct quantity or the best marginal utility per Dollar, for FIXPRICE and HIGHELASTICITY, the results from the plots do not look too bad, but from the statistics it can be found, that significances are quite poor. From the three different algorithms, the canonical one shows the highest degree of fluctuations (i.e. the highest variance) and consequently the highest (though still very poor) significance of reaching the optimal result, while election produces nearly no fluctuations at all, resulting in the least significance of an optimal outcome.

For LOWELASTICITY, only the preselection algorithm leads to sensible results at all.

All in all, it seems as if the preselection algorithm performs best over all types of economic situations. This means that a little memory to the past notably improves learning abilities.

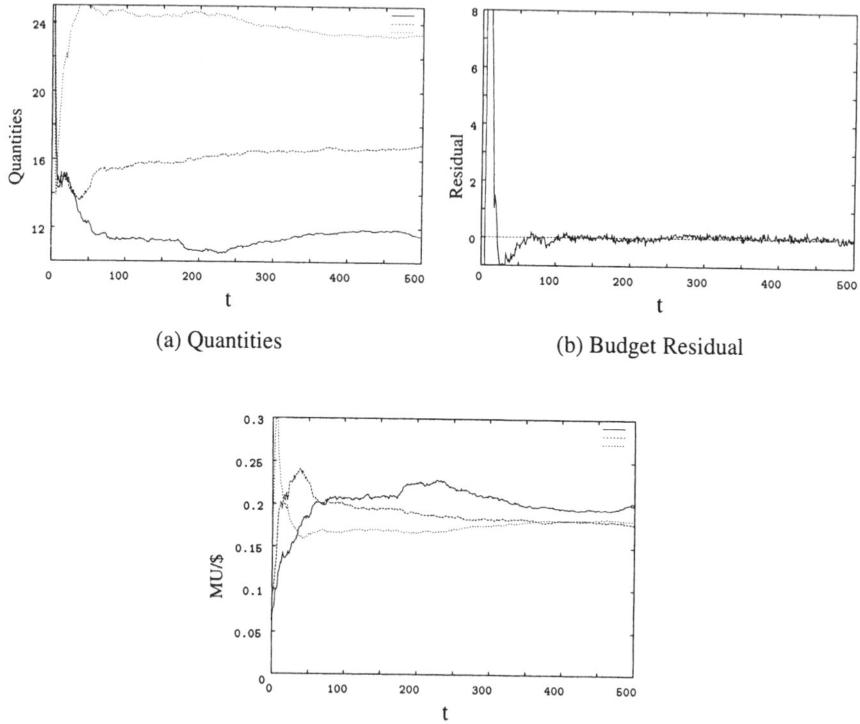

(a) Quantities

(b) Budget Residual

(c) Marginal Utility per Dollar

Fig. 8.7. Preselection Algorithm – High Elasticity of Supply: — q_1, ··· q_2, - - q_3

8.5 Conclusions

8.5.1 The Influence of State Dependency

As a conclusion to be drawn from the simulation results it can be found that it seems to be much harder to learn a sensible consumer choice in a situation with low elasticity of supply than in situation with high (or even infinitely high) elasticity.

The reason for this is the following. In each turn of the algorithm (in each market period) the resulting market prices and by that, the utility gained, reveal some information to each agent. This information is information about the quality of her last period consumption plan. Ceteris paribus, the plan was a good plan if utility is high and so the plan should not be changed too much for the next period. If, on the contrary, utility was not very high, the plan was obviously a bad one and thus should be changed. Unfortunately, this argument is only a ceteris paribus argument. The information revealed actually consists of two parts which cannot be distinguished.

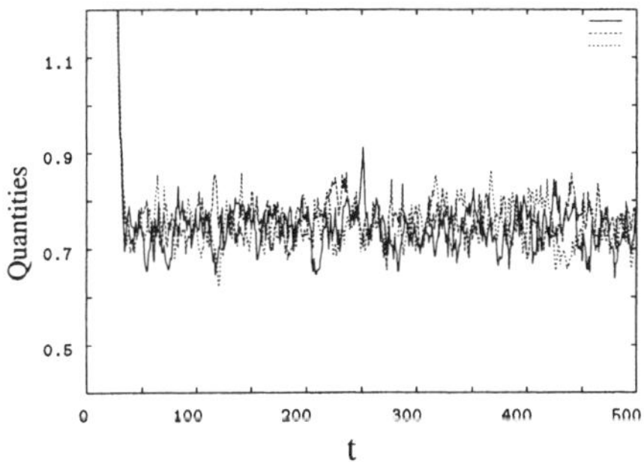

(a) Quantities

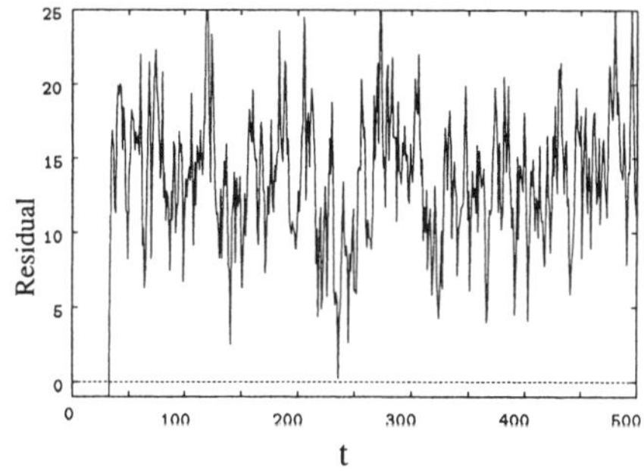

(b) Budget Residual

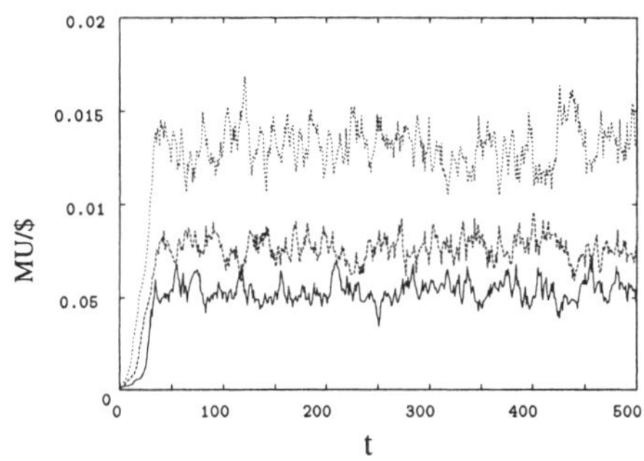

(c) Marginal Utility per Dollar

Fig. 8.8. Canonical Algorithm – Low Elasticity of Supply: — q_1, ··· q_2, - - q_3

Surely the information is information about the quality of the agent's plan. But it is only information about the quality of the agent's plan in the context of the plans of all other agents in the population. This means that from period to period the quality of an agent's plan can be changed either by a change in the plan itself or by a change in the plans of the rest of the population. While there certainly is a *direct* impact of the agent on her economic success, there is also an indirect impact caused by the rest of the population. This indirect impact is the *state dependency* of agents' fitness.

State dependency can be found to cause noise in the part of the information most valuable for the agent, i.e. the information about the quality of her plan. The stronger the state dependency, the stronger is the noise, the less valuable is the information to the agent, and thus the more complicated is the consumption decision. Thus, it should be shown that less elasticity of supply means more state dependency in the problem of consumer choice in order to give a reason why less elasticity seems to complicate the problem.

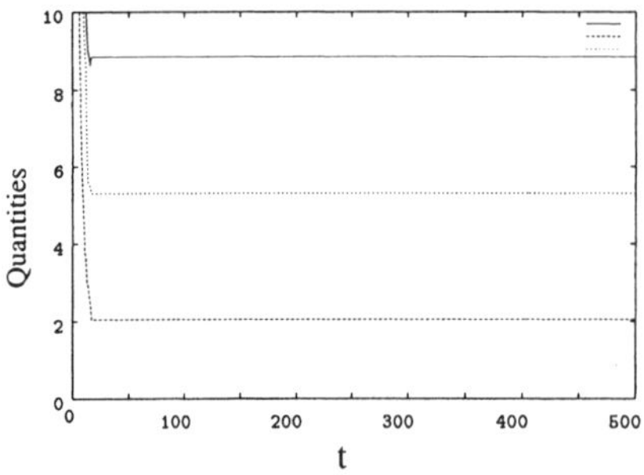

(a) Quantities

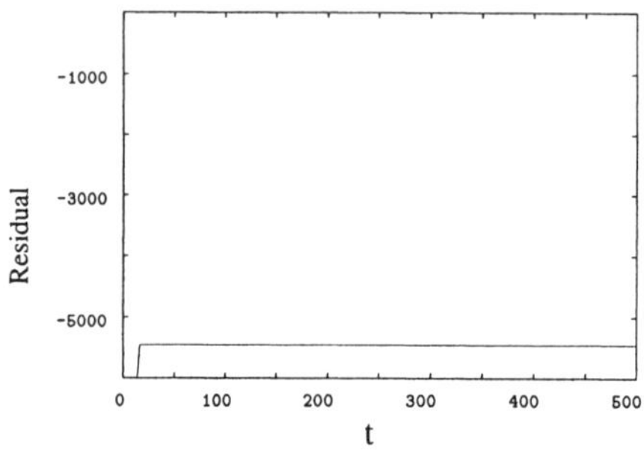

(b) Budget Residual

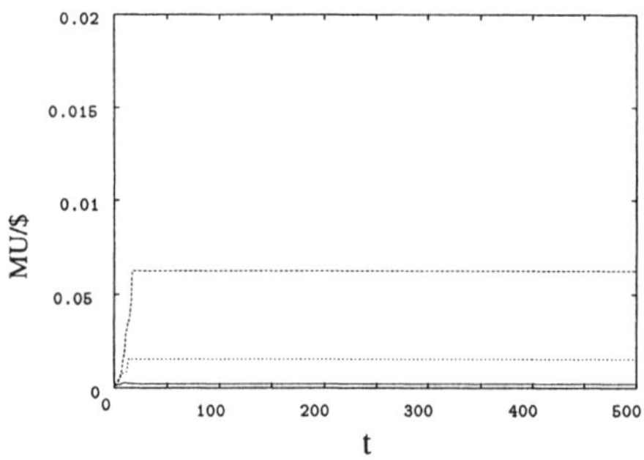

(c) Marginal Utility per Dollar

Fig. 8.9. Election Algorithm – Low Elasticity of Supply: — q_1, ··· q_2, - - q_3

It can be shown that the gradient m_k of the respective supply function (8.7) is a measure of state dependency. A sketch of the argument runs as follows: The utility function[9] (8.1) can be rewritten as integrating the budget constraint (8.2)[10], using $q_{i,m}$ as a numeraire, yielding

$$V_i = V\left(q_{i,1}, q_{i,2}, \cdots, q_{i,m-1}, M, p_1, p_2, \cdots, p_m\right). \tag{8.20}$$

A change in utility can be written as

$$\mathrm{d}\,V_i = \underbrace{\sum_{k=1}^{m-1} \frac{\partial V_i}{\partial q_{i,k}} \,\mathrm{d}\,q_{i,k}}_{\text{direct effect}} + \frac{\partial V_i}{\partial M}\,\mathrm{d}\,M + \underbrace{\sum_{k=1}^{m} \frac{\partial V_i}{\partial p_k}\,\mathrm{d}\,p_k}_{\text{indirect effect}}. \tag{8.21}$$

[9] For notational convenience, the period index t is omitted.

[10] An important prerequisite for this is the constraint being an equation. As most of the simulations do in fact result in a situation where the budget is fully spent, for (8.2), equality is being assumed.

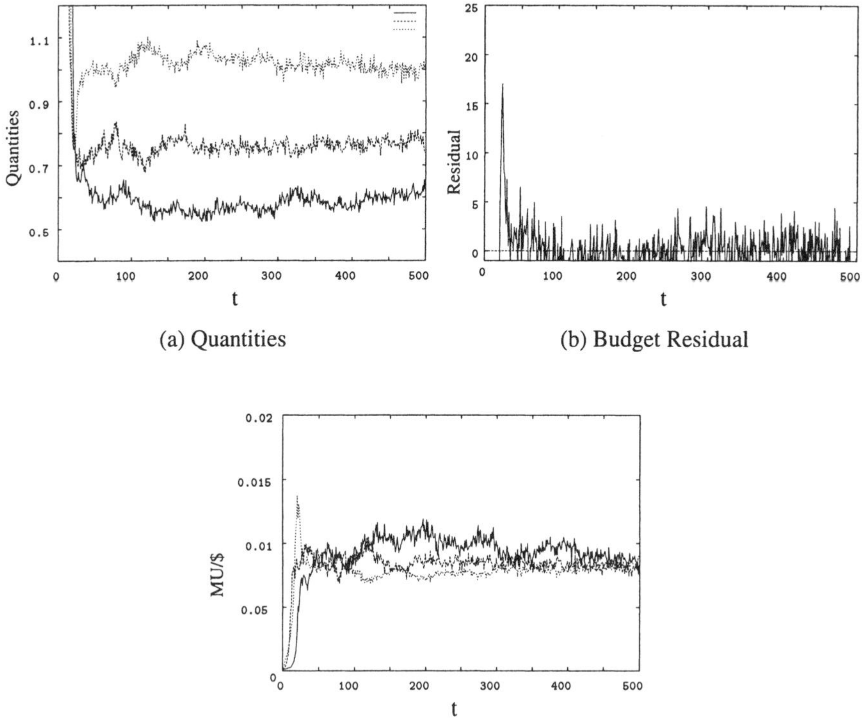

(a) Quantities (b) Budget Residual

(c) Marginal Utility per Dollar

Fig. 8.10. Preselection Algorithm – Low Elasticity of Supply: — q_1, ··· q_2, - - q_3

Let us assume the budget M to be constant (this assumptions fits with the simulations carried out), so that $\mathrm{d}M = 0$. Consequently, (8.21) becomes a bit simpler, resulting in

$$\mathrm{d}\,V_i = \underbrace{\sum_{k=1}^{m-1} \frac{\partial V_i}{\partial q_{i,k}}\,\mathrm{d}\,q_{i,k}}_{\text{direct effect}} + \underbrace{\sum_{k=1}^{m} \frac{\partial V_i}{\partial p_k}\,\mathrm{d}\,p_k}_{\text{indirect effect}}\,. \tag{8.22}$$

From this, it can be recognized that a change in an agent's utility can be caused by two effects, by the direct effect of the agent changing her quantities, and by the indirect effect of a change in prices.

The interesting aspect is the change of the prices. From (8.7) it can be deduced that a change in the price of good k is

$$\mathrm{d}\,p_k = \sum_{j=1}^{n} \frac{\partial p_k}{\partial q_{j,k}}\,\mathrm{d}\,q_{j,k} = m_k \sum_{j=1}^{n} \mathrm{d}\,q_{j,k}\,. \tag{8.23}$$

It can thus be seen that a change in the price of a good is caused by a change in the demand for this good by one or more of the agents.

A change in utility becomes

$$\mathrm{d}\,V_i = \underbrace{\sum_{k=1}^{m-1} \frac{\partial V_i}{\partial q_{i,k}}\,\mathrm{d}\,q_{i,k}}_{\text{direct effect}} + \underbrace{\sum_{k=1}^{m} \left(\frac{\partial V_i}{\partial p_k} m_k \sum_{j=1}^{n} \mathrm{d}\,q_{j,k} \right)}_{\text{indirect effect}} . \tag{8.24}$$

Abbreviating the change of aggregate demand for good k, $\sum_{j=1}^{n} dq_{j,k}$ as dQ_k, (8.24) can be simplified:

$$\mathrm{d}\,V_i = \underbrace{\sum_{k=1}^{m-1} \frac{\partial V_i}{\partial q_{i,k}}\,\mathrm{d}\,q_{i,k}}_{\text{direct effect}} + \underbrace{\sum_{k=1}^{m} \left(m_k \frac{\partial V_i}{\partial p_k}\,\mathrm{d}\,Q_k \right)}_{\text{indirect effect}} . \tag{8.25}$$

Focusing on the indirect effect, it is now easy to see that for each market k, it is the parameter m_k that decides on the impact of the indirect effect on an agent's utility.

If, for example, $m_k = 0$, there is no indirect effect at all. Only the agent herself has an influence on her utility. In other words: For $m_k = 0$, there is no state dependency. Notice, that this case is the case of fixed prices, which leads to relatively good results for all three types of algorithms.

If, on the contrary, m_k is very high, there is also a large influence of all other agents on each agent's utility. This is the case of high state dependency. This case is equal to the case of flexible prices and low elasticity of supply. In this case, due to the high degree of state dependency, the noise in the information caused is strong and consequently the results of the learning process are relatively bad.

Summarizing, the higher m (i.e. the lower elasticity of supply), the higher is the impact of state dependency on the change of each agent's utility. This makes it harder for an agent to recognize the impact of her own consumer plan on her economic success which in turn makes it harder to learn a sensible solution to the consumer choice problem.

8.5.2 The Influence of Different Learning Schemes

Election and the Concept of Potential Fitness

The algorithm using the election operator seems to perform very good in the FIX-PRICE and in the HIGHELASTICITY cases, whereas in the LOWELASTICITY case performance is extremely poor. In order to find out the reasons for this behavior, it is appropriate to recall the central working principle of election. During election, two agents meet and jointly try to find a new strategy. They do this, among others, by calculating the potential fitness for the newly created strategies, which should help to find out which strategy is the best one. The calculation of potential fitness requires the knowledge about all the influences on future economic success of the new strategies. As it is impossible to know about all of these influences, election assumes the influences to remain unchanged from one period to the next.

This means that the concept of potential fitness is basically a concept of 'ceteris paribus' fitness: An agent calculates the potential fitness of her strategy assuming all the other agents will not change their behavior. This means that agent i, while finding potential fitness, assumes that $\mathrm{d}\,q_{j,k} = 0 \,\forall\, i = \{1,\ldots n\}\,,\; i \neq j$. In other words, most of the indirect influence on actual fitness is neglected. This, of cause, is absolutely correct for situations without state dependency, like the FIXPRICE case, and this is still quite good for low degrees of state dependency like in the HIGHELASTICITY case. But, the more important the indirect effect, the more severe becomes the difference between actual fitness and potential fitness. In situations with high state dependency, e.g. in the LOWELASTICITY case, this may lead to systematically wrong strategy choices, as can be seen from the simulation results in Fig. 8.9.

Preselection

In contrast to election, preselection is not the end of the learning process in a period, but the beginning. Whereas in the process of election, the strategy resulting from the election process is the one to be applied in the market, the strategy resulting from preselection is subject to learning by communication (crossover) and experiment (mutation), before it is used at the market. This means that in situations with only little state dependency, preselection – like election – has the advantage of choosing between two strategies (the all time best strategy and the strategy used last period), but the 'pure' result of the preselection process can be slightly changed during the following two learning steps, which may be a disadvantage. But, these following two learning steps become the great advantage of preselection in situations with high degrees of state dependency. Different from election, preselection learning does not get stuck in strategies that are successful only due to potential but not to actual fitness, but it can still change the preselected strategy.

8.6 Summary

The chapter employs three different learning algorithms in order to find out, if boundedly rational agents can learn to choose the optimal consumption bundle. In the model, the problem is complicated by allowing for flexible prices and allowing for violations of the budget constraint.

It can be found that it is relatively easy to learn not to break the budget constraint, but that it seems to be quite complicated to find the optimal consumption bundle. Simulation results show that the problem becomes even worse if the elasticity of supply decreases. It is shown that a decrease in the elasticity of supply means an increase in the degree of state dependency. For some types of algorithm, state dependency works like an external effect: Agents do not include it into their private computation of future strategies, thus being badly mistaken in each future period of time.

Can boundedly rational agents learn the optimal consumer choice? — They can, if the problem is not too complicated. And they do even better if they have some memory of the past.

Appendix: Statistical Results

The following tables show data from one randomly chosen simulation each. All simulations were run for 1 000 periods with a population size of n=500. The data contains information about rounds 501 to 1 000 to eliminate possible startup effects of the algorithms.

FIXPRICE

The t–values are test statistics of an approximate Gauss tests[11] for $q_1 = 20$, $q_2 = 30$, $q_3 = 50$ and $\rho = 0$, respectively.

		Canonical	Election	Preselection
q_1	Mean	20.2484	20.0492	20.2077
	Var.	0.515554	0.000617538	0.0153379
	t	7.73661	44.2923	37.4965
q_2	Mean	30.8866	30.0306	29.9948
	Var.	1.36406	0.00149178	0.00520296
	t	16.9738	17.7022	-1.62135
q_3	Mean	47.4426	49.9195	49.7968
	Var.	1.33563	0.00358468	0.00447201
	t	-49.481	-30.0562	-67.9504
ρ	Mean	1.4224	0.000674724	0.000770113
	Var.	0.453434	3.88333 E(-7)	0.000613616
	t	47.2334	24.2108	0.69517

[11] This is a t–test for large populations.

HIGHELASTICITY

The t–value is a test statistic of an approximate Gauss test for $\rho = 0$, the values t_{12}, t_{13}, and t_{23} are test statistics of approximate Gauss test for $MU_1/\$ = MU_2/\$$, $MU_1/\$ = MU_3/\$$ and $MU_2/\$ = MU_3/\$$, respectively.

		Canonical	Election	Preselection
$MU_1/\$$	Mean	0.178931	0.185862	0.189568
	Var.	0.0000532438	8.59688 E(-7)	7.43989 E(-6)
$MU_2/\$$	Mean	0.178914	0.183026	0.181765
	Var.	0.0000914054	2.21833 E(-7)	3.54032 E(-6)
$MU_3/\$$	Mean	0.196372	0.184637	0.183881
	Var.	0.0000684217	2.27176 E(-7)	6.94431 E(-7)
t_{12}		0.0316065	60.9781	52.6552
t_{13}		-35.3568	26.2744	44.5869
t_{23}		-30.8784	-53.7592	-22.9925
ρ	Mean	4.1415	0.0108742	-0.0000875281
	Var.	0.63692	0.0000392457	0.00494539
	t	116.038	38.8137	-0.0278312

LOWELASTICITY

		Canonical	Election	Preselection
$MU_1/\$$	Mean	0.00531371	0.000225087	0.00901293
	Var.	3.19915 E(-7)	0	2.0274 E(-7)
$MU_2/\$$	Mean	0.00768015	0.00624466	0.00837344
	Var.	6.2859 E(-7)	0	9.85724 E(-8)
$MU_3/\$$	Mean	0.0131581	0.00156332	0.0080648
	Var.	1.04098 E(-6)	0	4.02153 E(-8)
t_{12}		-54.3326		26.0501
t_{13}		-150.36		43.0121
t_{23}		-94.7983		18.5254
ρ	Mean	13.3108	-5453.53	-0.538288
	Var.	26.2627	0	4.07375
	t	58.0792		-5.96352

9. A Multi Population Algorithm

9.1 Introduction

Like all the chapters in the third part of this book, this one, too, has an economic and a technical topic.

The technical topic is the modeling of economic problems with a GA based on more than one genetic population. A further example of this type of a multi population algorithm can be found in Birchenhall (1995), who describes the coevolution of two different types of economic agents, each type represented by a population of its own. Another example of a multi population GA is Arifovic (1995). The model in this chapter will be similar to the one by Arifovic (1995), but add some economic extensions. The economic topic of this chapter is an overlapping generations (OLG) model of a monetary economy. The model is based on the early work by Samuelson (1958) and Diamond (1965). From the model by Diamond, the idea of seignorage effects is adopted. The model in focus has often been used as a model of economic learning, including various different types of learning models and learning techniques. The reason for this is the fact that the model even in its simplest form, i.e. assuming rational expectations and homogeneity of the agents involved, leads to multiple equilibria. This means that the outcome of the model is indeterminate. Besides two possible stationary (macroeconomic) outcomes, with the help of some slight modification, even cyclical results are achievable (see Grandmont 1985). Some of the articles dedicated to this problem are the ones by Lucas (1986) and Marcet and Sargent (1989), who focus statistical learning in the OLG model, and the one by Bullard and Duffy (1998), analyzing the effects of different types of GA learning for the same case.

In the following, first the OLG model with money will be simulated with the help of two variants of multi population GAs. It will be shown, that the decisive result of Arifovic (1995) is not robust against changes in the learning mechanism: As long as learning in the model is based on the election operator, simulations result in one of the two stationary equilibria. The introduction of meta learning changes this result. With meta learning, simulation lead to the arise of cyclical outcomes. Thus, it will be shown why the results of election and meta learning are different.

After this, the OLG model will be extended by a intragenerational credit market. It will be argued that this extension is necessary to provide a sensible economic interpretation of the model for the case of heterogeneous individual behavior. Extensive theoretical analysis of this extended model shows that the results of the basic model are not necessarily reproduced: In the OLG model with money, heterogeneity matters. Theoretical analysis shows that in case of heterogeneity, the economic outcome of the model is very unlikely to be the same outcome as in the basic model without intragenerational credit relations. In order to find out more about the similarity or dissimilarity of both variants of the OLG model, a special GA simulation is constructed, which confirms the theoretical results and shows that both models do in fact not behave the same.

9.2 The Economic Model: A Basic Overlapping Generations Model with Money

9.2.1 The General Structure of the Model

The model in focus is a standard overlapping generations model with fiat money. It is a two generations, two periods model. Every generation t consists of n agents. Agents live for two periods. The only good in the economy is a homogeneous, perishable good. Every agent is endowed with w^1 units of this good in the first period and with w^2 units in the second period of her life. In addition, there exists money, which is intrinsically valueless, i.e. it is fiat money. As the only good in the economy cannot be stored, money is the only means of transferring wealth from one period to the next.

All agents i of the same generation t (t is the period of the 'birth' of agents of generation t.) have identical preferences characterized by the utility function[1]

$$U_{i,t} = U\left(c_{i,t}^1, c_{i,t}^2\right) = c_{i,t}^1 \cdot c_{i,t}^2 . \tag{9.1}$$

$c_{i,t}^1$ gives the consumption of agent i of generation t when young, $c_{i,t}^2$ is the consumption of the same agent in her old age.

Savings can only be held in form of money. $m_{i,t}$ is the individual nominal money demand of agent i of generation t. p_{t+1} gives the price of the good in period $t+1$.

The usual intertemporal budget constraints are

$$c_{i,t}^1 = w_1 - m_{i,t}\frac{1}{p_t}, \tag{9.2}$$

$$c_{i,t}^2 = w^2 + m_{i,t}\frac{1}{p_{t+1}}. \tag{9.3}$$

9.2.2 Theoretical Results

General Results

From standard calculus (individual constrained maximization of lifetime utility), the optimal first period consumption results as

[1] This special utility function is often used in OLG models, among others in the textbook by McCandless and Wallace (1991). Moreover, it is the one used by Arifovic (1995).

$$c_{i,t}^{1,*} = \frac{1}{2}\left(w^1 + \frac{p_{t+1}}{p_t}w^2\right). \tag{9.4}$$

Abbreviating the inflation factor as π_{t+1},

$$\pi_{t+1} = \frac{p_{t+1}}{p_t}, \tag{9.5}$$

the individually optimal money demand can be computed as

$$m_{i,t}^* = \left(w^1 - c_{i,t}^{1,*}\right) p_t \tag{9.6}$$

$$= \frac{1}{2} p_t \left(w^1 - \pi_{t+1} w^2\right). \tag{9.7}$$

Money supply is performed by the government. The money supply per agent in period t is m_t^s. Moreover, government skims off seignorage by a constant real amount of d per agent. The development of money supply per agent is given by the difference equation

$$m_{t+1}^s = m_t^s + d\, p_{t+1}. \tag{9.8}$$

Money market equilibrium in every period can be described by $n m_t^s = \sum_{i=1}^n m_{i,t}\, \forall t$. This means that in equilibrium, seignorage per capita is given by

$$d = \frac{m_{i,t}^* - m_{i,t-1}^*}{p_t} \tag{9.9}$$

$$= \frac{1}{2}\left(w^1 - \pi_{t+1} w^2 - \frac{1}{\pi_t} w^1 + w^2\right). \tag{9.10}$$

From (9.10), a difference equation for the development of inflation factors can be deduced:

$$\pi_{t+1} = \frac{w^1}{w^2} + 1 - 2\frac{d}{w^2} - \frac{w^1}{w^2}\pi_t^{-1}. \tag{9.11}$$

Equation (9.11), which is the central equation of the basic OLG model, has two stationary solutions, i.e. solutions for $\pi_t = \pi = \text{const.}\, \forall t$:

$$\pi = \frac{1}{2}\left(\frac{w^1}{w^2} + 1 - 2\frac{d}{w^2}\right) \pm \sqrt{\frac{1}{4}\left(\frac{w^1}{w^2} + 1 - 2\frac{d}{w^2}\right)^2 - \frac{w^1}{w^2}}. \tag{9.12}$$

The fact that there is no unique solution to (9.11) means that a priori it is not clear which path of development the economy will follow. Even worse, apart from the two stationary solutions, there are additional, non stationary solutions to (9.11).[2] Thus, the first question to be answered is the question, if the model reaches a stationary

[2] A complicated article on the possibility of cyclical solutions to this model is Grandmont (1985).

outcome at all. If this is the case, the second question must be, which one of the two possibilities will be the true result of the model. These questions are the topic of a number of economic papers, the majority of which, though, concentrate on the second question only.

The two stationary solutions to (9.12) are often called 'high inflation solution' and 'low inflation solution', respectively. Arifovic (1995) and Bullard and Duffy (1998) present various types of GA learning simulations for the given model. Their simulations tend to reach the low inflation solution in every case (Arifovic) or at least in most cases (Bullard/Duffy). Models based on learning mechanisms other than GA learning (e.g. Lucas 1986, Marcet and Sargent 1989) come to different conclusions.

Thus, to put it short, the interesting feature of the model is the fact that there is more than one solution equally possible. The model offers a degree of freedom. Many authors try to determine one definite solution by filling this degree of freedom by introducing one or the other form of learning. What makes things even more interesting, is the fact that which type of definite solution is reached seems to depend on which form of learning is used in the model.

Learning of the Consumption Quantity

It is important to analyze the model under the assumption, that the agents do not (as in the mainstream analysis presented above) know the optimal solution, but that they have to 'learn' it. An important paper dedicated to this aspect of the problem is the one by Arifovic (1995). Arifovic uses the same model as presented above, but assumes that agents do not know the prices p_t and p_{t+1}. This of course means that agents are no longer capable of analytically determining optimal consumption $c_{i,t}^{1,*}$ (from (9.4)): Agents are boundedly rational. Arifovic (1995) faces the question if, under these circumstances, agents can find an optimal consumption quantity by learning.

In Arifovic's model, agents learn due to the rules of a genetic algorithm. In every period, every young agent in the respective period plans and realizes her consumption $c_{i,t}^1$. From the plan, individual savings automatically arise as the real value of the amount of goods not consumed. In connection with the individual endowment of the second period of life and depending on prices p_t and p_{t+1} the real value of every agent's second period consumption results. At the end of her two period long life, every agent can thus compute her life time utility $U_{i,t}$. Now, the agent can judge the quality of her life time consumption plan relative to the quality of the plans of the other members of her generation. This knowledge, i.e. the exact life time consumption plan and its relative quality, is — so to say on the deathbed — taught by the agent to her newly born grandchild. This grandchild, who is in the first period of her life, is now free to modify the consumption plan she inherited, which means she 'learns' a presumably better one by using the usual techniques of imitation, communication, and experiment. When the plan is made and put into practice, things repeat: The grandchild recognizes the quality of her plan and passes her knowledge on to her grandchild, who modifies the plan, etc.

By using this model, Arifovic finds the agents to always learn the consumption plan which determines the low inflation solution of (9.12).

Learning of the Inflation Factor

A very similar way to the one used by Arifovic (1995) is the following: Agents learn by using a GA. But agents do not directly learn the consumption plan, but they learn to form expectations about inflation. Technically speaking, a genetic individual does not code a consumption quantity, like in Arifovic (1995), but the expected inflation factor.[3]

Every agent i of every generation t forms expectations of the future development of prices, $\pi^e_{i,t+1}$. This means that for agent i, her optimal first period consumption looks like a function of her expected price. For agent i, (9.4) becomes

$$c^{1,*}_{i,t} = c\left(\pi^e_{i,t+1}\right) = \frac{1}{2}w^1 + \frac{1}{2}w^2\pi^e_{i,t+1}. \tag{9.13}$$

Due to her expectations $\pi^e_{i,t+1}$, every agent i computes her presumably optimal first period consumption $c^{1,*}_{i,t}$.[4] Again, by the first period consumer choice, every agent implicitly chooses her savings. Aggregate savings of all agents of one period gives money demand in the same period, which on the money market results in the true period t price p_t.

At this time, the next generation, $t+1$, appears on the scene. Here, too, the usual consumption/savings decision takes place. Here, too, an actual price is determined on the money market, now p_{t+1}. It is this price, finally, which, together with p_t, gives the value of inflation π_{t+1} and thus the *real* value of second period consumption of every member of generation t. Every agent has to wait until the end of her life to finally know about inflation π_{t+1}, the real value of her consumption in the second period of her life, $c^2_{i,t}$, the true value of her utility, and — finally — the true quality of her plans.[5] Again, the knowledge of the privately expected inflation factor and the quality of this expectation can be passed on to the grandchild, who uses this

[3] In contrast to a very similar procedure in Bullard and Duffy (1998), the expected inflation is coded as a *number*, and not as a set of rules describing different ways of predicting inflation.

[4] This of course means that agents are smarter or 'have more rationality' than the agents in Arifovic (1995), because they are assumed to be able to compute their optimal consumption plan from their utility function and their inflation expectations. In other words: In the given variant of the model, agents are assumed to be able to maximize utility (9.1) with respect to their intertemporal budget constraint (9.2) and (9.3). At least for the given case, the assumption might be defended by the remark that for the special utility function (9.1) used in this model, the optimization means no more than just smoothing consumption over time.

[5] The procedure described above can be essentially boiled down to three simple steps: 1. The inflation factor π_{t+1} is determined. 2. From this, the real value of second period consumption $c^2_{i,t}$ becomes known. 3. From this, truly achieved utility arises as $U_{i,t}\left(c^1_{i,t}, c^2_{i,t}\right)$.

inheritance as the basis of her learning process, make plans of her own, receives the quality of her plans, passes her knowledge on, etc.

Although this interpretation of the model differs from the one by Arifovic (1995), both models are very similar, especially from the mathematical point of view. Mathematically seen, the only difference between the two variants is the particular variable that is used for optimization. The objective is the same for both variants. In the variant by Arifovic, the first period consumption quantity is directly optimized. In the variant presented above, optimization works indirectly via inflation expectations. Although this indirect variant seems a bit more complicated, it has a slight technical advantage: The results of this variant are explicitly comparable to the results of Lucas (1986), Marcet and Sargent (1989) and other models, which all use the second, indirect variant.

9.3 The Genetic Algorithm

The genetic algorithm used to simulate the problem described above is a standard algorithm with binary coding. The economic strategy of an agent is fully characterized by her expectation of next period's price. Accordingly, a genetic individual represents this price expectation. The only difference between the GA used in this chapter and the GAs used before is the fact that now the GA is based on two populations. In each round of the algorithm, two genetic populations are active, representing the two generations living in every single period of the OLG model. As described above, in the model, the passing of economic experience takes place from the grandparent to the grandchild. The inheritance of strategies skips one generation. This process is reflected by the structure of the GA. Experiences are passed within both of the populations, but there is no exchange of information between the populations. This means that there are actually two GAs running in parallel, which are almost independent from each other but interconnected by the economic problem. The general process is described in Algorithm 9.1. Let us call the two populations population A and population B. Each population represents one of the populations alive in each period of time. Alternatingly one of the populations represents a young and an old generation. If, for example, in period t population A represents the young generation, then B stands for the old generation living at the same time. After the next step in time, at period $t+1$, A contains the now old agents while B represents the generation of the newly born young ones. The connection between the populations and thus between the two parallel algorithms is the fact that in each period t, the young generation generates the true price p_t which is needed in order to determine the utility (and thus, fitness) of the agents of generation $t-1$.

The technical details of the two population GA is described in Algorithm 9.1.

Two different variants of the two population GA are used, one using the election operator. Despite of its well known lack of economic sense, this operator is used for two reasons. First, because of its strong stability properties, election serves as a benchmark case, again. Second, taking a look at election helps to explain the results

2POP-GA — Two Population GA

$t := 0$

Creation of First Populations Pop. A und Pop. B

Random Determination of First Price p_{t-1}

Money Market Activity of Pop. B leads to p_t

Evaluation of Pop. A due to $\pi_t = \frac{p_t}{p_{t-1}}$

while Stopping Condition not Met

> $t := t+1$; $(p_{t-1} := p_t)$
>
> Genetic Operators on Pop. A
>
> Money Market Activity of Pop. A leads to p_t
>
> Evaluation of Pop. B due to $\pi_t = \frac{p_t}{p_{t-1}}$
>
> $t := t+1$; $(p_{t-1} := p_t)$
>
> Genetic Operators on Pop. B
>
> Money Market Activity of Pop. B leads to p_t
>
> Evaluation of Pop. A due to $\pi_t = \frac{p_t}{p_{t-1}}$

ENDE

Algorithm 9.1: Structure of the Two Population GA

of Arifovic (1995). The second GA variant used is a GA using the operator of meta mutation (see 6.3). It will be shown that this variant will lead to interesting results.

9.4 Simulations and Results

9.4.1 The Election GA

As the basic model introduced above is very similar to the model by Arifovic (1995) (the only difference is the choice of the free variable), the results of the simulations based on the election operator are not too surprising: All the results given in Arifovic (1995) can be reproduced.[6] The general result of these simulations is the fact that macroeconomic data tend to establish the low inflation outcome of the OLG model. An impression of the results can be gained from Fig. 9.1 showing the outcome of the first 50 periods of an exemplary run of the two population GA with election. The figure displays four different inflation factors: The average expected inflation

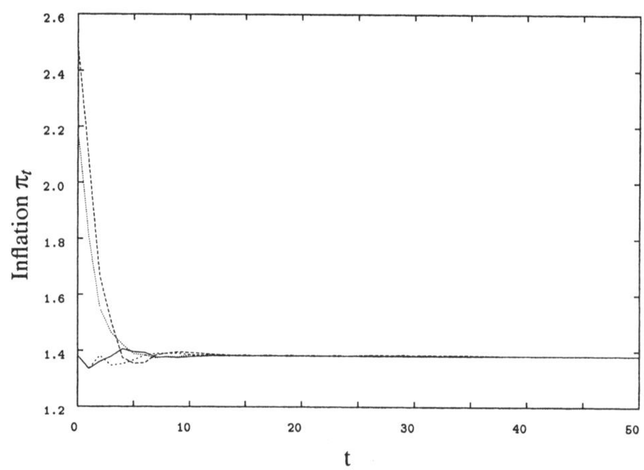

Fig. 9.1. True and Expected Inflation Factors in a Two Population Election GA

factor of the young population, the true inflation factor relevant for the young generation, and the same factors for the old generation in every period t. It can be seen that all four inflation rates converge very fast. The parameter set underlying the simulation leading to Fig. 9.1 is $w^1 = 150$, $w^2 = 30$, $d = 15$. This is the same set as parameter set 3 in Arifovic (1995, p. 231). The theoretically optimal low inflation solution for homogeneous behavior and the given parameter set is characterized by

[6] Particularly, refer to the results presented in Arifovic (1995, pp.231), which can all, without any exception be reproduced by simulations of the variant of the model presented above.

a stationary inflation factor of $\pi = 1.382$. This is exactly the inflation factor reached in the simulation. The most important characteristic of all simulations based on the election operator is the fact that always and independently of the starting conditions, an outcome is reached which is equal to the low inflation solution of the model for homogeneous behavior.

All in all, the election simulations confirm the experience made with election up to now. Again, election very quickly leads to an asymptotically stable state of uniform behavior.

9.4.2 Meta Mutation

The use of the operator of meta mutation instead of election leads to a totally different outcome. See Fig. 9.2 for an example. Meta learning does not produce any form of convergence. Neither the population mean inflation expectations not the resulting true inflation rates become close to each other. This means that the agents constantly form expectations which are totally wrong. Nevertheless, after some time of initialization, all four time series, expectations and true inflation factors, come to rest, i.e. cease to change over time.

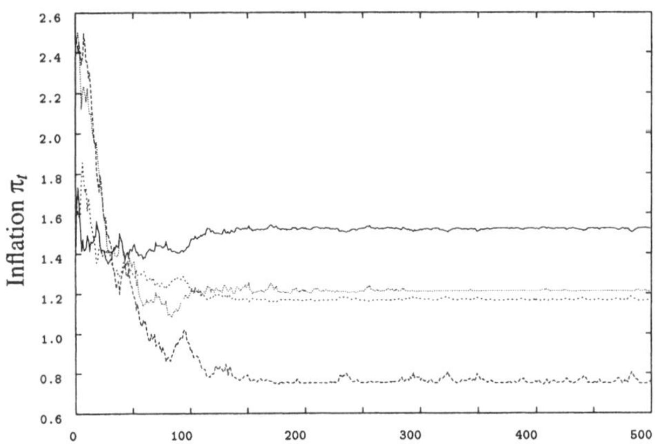

Fig. 9.2. True and Expected Inflation Factors in a Two Population Meta GA

If agents are constantly mistaken in their expectations and still do not change them, these wrong expectations must have something to them. More technically, it looks like the non converging outcome establishes a kind of local optimum to the economic problem. This local optimum is an optimum of a process of passing information from one generation to the second next one, while the conditions of the economic life of a generation is determined by the actions of the generation before. In other words: Every agent inherits her strategy from her grandmother, but the economic circumstances of her life from her mother.[7] The result of the simulations is a situation with an economic framework changing every period, but being the same every second one. The economy is characterized by a two period cycle in inflation factors and inflation expectations.

It can be shown that this phenomenon of cycles is not a technical artefact of the algorithm in use, but an outcome with a sensible economic explanation. The inflation expectation of an agent in period t depends on the relative quality of the expectation of her grandmother from generation $t-2$. The quality of grandma's expectation depended on true inflation π_{t-1}. Thus, the inflation expectation of every agent in generation t indirectly depends on the true inflation factor in $t-1$. Consequently, the vector of individual inflation expectations π_t^e can be seen as the result of a process of expectation formation $F(\cdot)$ mainly depending on the true inflation in the period before, π_{t-1}:

$$\pi_t^e = F(\pi_{t-1}) . \tag{9.14}$$

For the given case, the process of expectation formation $F(\cdot)$ is given by one round of the genetic algorithm. The inflation factor π_{t-1} mainly depends on the outcome of the money market in $t-1$,[8] which in turn is determined by the set of all individual expectations of generation $t-1$. This means that, with $G(\cdot)$ standing for the working of the money market, it can be written that

$$\pi_{t-1} = G\left(\pi_{t-1}^e\right) . \tag{9.15}$$

Every element of the vector π_{t-1}^e, i.e. every individual expectation of the young generation, is a reflex on the experiences of the grandmothers which themselves are mainly influenced by the inflation in $t-2$, π_{t-2}:

$$\pi_{t-1}^e = F(\pi_{t-2}) . \tag{9.16}$$

Defining function $Z(\cdot)$ as a compound function from $F(\cdot)$ (expectation formation) and $G(\cdot)$ (money market)

$$Z(\cdot) := F(G(\cdot)) \tag{9.17}$$

leads to

$$\pi_t^e = Z\left(\pi_{t-1}^e\right) . \tag{9.18}$$

(9.18) describes the general process of expectation formation over time in the OLG model with money. A stationary solution of this model in the sense of (9.12) is characterized by the additional condition $\pi_t^e = \pi_{t-1}^e \ \forall t$. More general,

[7] The reader might have already noticed that this is an economic model without men! (Nevertheless, the model can easily be extended to cover the behavior of both sexes.)

[8] Actually, the inflation factor depends on the result of *two* money markets, the one in $t-1$ and the one in $t-2$. To keep things simple, the money market in $t-2$ will be ignored, which leads to a clearer structure of the argument without touching the heart of the results.

$$\pi_t^e = \pi_{t-k}^e \tag{9.19}$$

describes a stationary cycle of period k. Following (9.14) to (9.16), such a solution at the same time demands that

$$\pi_t = \pi_{t-k} \,. \tag{9.20}$$

Cycles of the inflation expectations thus automatically imply cycles of the same period in true inflation factors, vice versa. Whether cyclical solutions are reached or not, depends on the exact type of expectation formation $F(\cdot)$ (and on the working principles of the money market $G(\cdot)$). The actual type of expectation formation is determined by the type of GA used for the simulations.

The outcome of the simulations of this chapter shows that GAs are capable of even modeling the arise of cyclical solutions to the OLG model. As the cycles are of period 2, the expectations found by the populations A and B remain unchanged over time. Consequently, there is also a cycle of period 2 in the true inflation factors.

9.5 An Overlapping Generations Model with Heterogeneous Agents

A closer look at the basic OLG model presented above reveals an interesting point: Agents are assumed to *learn* by means of a GA. It has been stated above that GA learning essentially means social learning, i.e. learning from one another. Thus, in order to present a satisfactory model of GA learning, agents must be heterogeneous. If agents in the model are heterogeneous, then they must hold different expectations of the inflation rate. This is the important point. If two heterogeneous agents come together in order to learn from each other and find out that they hold different believes about the development of future prices, they will establish a credit relationship. The agent believing in a relatively high inflation factor will give her real savings to the other agent who believes inflation not to become too severe and can thus promise to give the real savings back to the other agent in the next period.[9] The core extension to the basic OLG model with money presented here is the introduction of an intragenerational credit market.

It is the main purpose of this extension to the model to find out, if in the presence of heterogeneity the common practice of neglecting the possible existence of an intragenerational credit market can be justified. This can only be the case if the

[9] This idea is also mentioned by Bullard and Duffy (1998, p. 183):

> We explicitly rule out the possibility of a private consumption loan market, but the elimination of the consumption loan market does not prevent agents from achieving the optimal outcome.

In the following, it will be shown that actually not the *elimination* but the *introduction* of such an intragenerational credit market will prevent agents from achieving (presumably) optimal outcome, i.e. the respective outcome of the basic OLG model without such a market.

extended model leads to the same results as the basic one. Thus, in the following, it will be analyzed if this is the case.

In order to find out the importance and the role of heterogeneity in the given model, the extension to the basic model will first be analyzed analytically. The analysis will start with a closer look on the role of bounded rationality in this context. After that, the two important markets in the model, the intergenerational money market, and the intragenerational credit market will be discussed in detail. A more precise formulation of the working principles of the money market will help to obtain some precise analytical results. These results confirm the suspicion that the introduction of a credit market has in fact an important influence on the results of the model, severely changing its outcome. Finally, in order to achieve even more results, the extended model will be simulated with the help of a special kind of economic multi population GA.

9.5.1 The Extensions to the Basic Model

The extended model is based on the same utility function as the basic model, i.e.

$$U_{i,t} = c_{i,t}^1 \cdot c_{i,t}^2 . \tag{9.21}$$

Agents try to maximize their utility subject to the budget constraints stemming from the individual endowment w_1 and w_2. Again, every agent is endowed with the same amount of the good. $R_{i,t}^e$ is the reciprocal of the inflation factor $\pi_{i,t+1}^e = \frac{p_{i,t+1}^e}{p_{i,t}^e}$ expected by agent i of generation t. Thus, $R_{i,t}^e$ is the gross return the agent expects to achieve at the money market. As agent i believes this expectation to be the only true one, she believes that due to non arbitrage reasons, this will be the equilibrium factor of returns on the intragenerational credit market, too. Thus the expected budget restriction for agent i, with $s_{i,t}$ giving real saving, is

$$c_{i,t}^1 = w^1 - s_{i,t} \tag{9.22}$$

$$c_{i,t}^2 = w^2 + R_{i,t}^e s_{i,t} \tag{9.23}$$

Every agent can hold savings in two different forms. First, every agent can be active on this market as giver and taker of credits. She can borrow goods from others, thus being a demander on the intragenerational credit market. Borrowed goods will be written as $b_{i,t}$. An agent can also lend goods to others, thus being a supplier of intragenerational credits. The amount of goods lent to other is $l_{i,t}$.[10] Second, every agent can be active at the intergenerational money market. Young agents are always money demanders, they want to trade in money for their goods in order to transfer wealth into the next period. The real value of an agent's money demand is written as $g_{i,t}$. Moreover, some agents have to demand money in order to transfer the goods

[10] Of course, an agent's gross supply and gross demand on the intragenerational credit market could be aggregated. This is not done, in order to get a clearer idea of the working of the credit market.

into the next periods they accepted as a credit from other agents of her generation. This part of money demand is written as $h_{i,t}$. This means that total individual savings are defined as

$$s_{i,t} = l_{i,t} - b_{i,t} + g_{i,t} + h_{i,t}\,. \tag{9.24}$$

By assumption, $l_{i,t} \geq 0$, $b_{i,t} \geq 0$, and $g_{i,t} \geq 0$.

Standard calculus leads to the optimal first period consumption

$$c_{i,t}^{1,*} = \frac{1}{2}\left(w^1 + \frac{w^2}{R_{i,t}^e}\right)\,. \tag{9.25}$$

From this, optimal savings follow as

$$s_{i,t}^{*} = \frac{1}{2}\left(w^1 - \frac{w^2}{R_{i,t}^e}\right)\,. \tag{9.26}$$

Savings are positive as long as

$$R_{i,t}^e > \frac{w^2}{w^1}\,. \tag{9.27}$$

This is the reason why (9.27) will be used as an additional assumption.

Equation (9.26) can be formulated in a second way. Agent i, in her second period of life, wants to achieve an optimal value of saving given as $S_{i,t}^*$:

$$S_{i,t}^* = R_{i,t}^e s_{i,t}^* \tag{9.28}$$

$$= \frac{1}{2}\left(w^1 R_{i,t}^e - w^2\right)\,. \tag{9.29}$$

9.5.2 The Role of Bounded Rationality

Credit market returns R_t are assumed to arise from an auction, the particular form of which will be described below. Returns R_t depend on a great number of variables, most of which cannot be observed by the agents. Among other, some of the very important variables are the inflation expectations of every single agent. In addition, in some forms of auctions, even the precise sequence of market transactions plays a role in determining the market price. The agents in the model will be assumed to be boundedly rational in the sense of Simon (1957, 1981). Agents try to realize their consumer plan (9.25) with the optimal consumption $c_{i,t}^{1,*}$ constituting their aspiration level, i.e. the minimum level of utility they wish to achieve. Higher levels of $c_{i,t}^1$ than $c_{i,t}^{1,*}$ are desirable as long as this does not lead to a decrease in $s_{i,t}^1$. The same is true for increases in $s_{i,t}^1$ without a decrease of $c_{i,t}^1$.

Since the price of the only good in period t, p_t, does not arise before the actions in the credit market, agents in period t do not know p_t nor p_{t+1}, the price of the good in the next period. This means that expectations have to be formed concerning both prices. Thus, it will be assumed that agents form expectations of the inflation factor $\pi_{t+1} = \frac{p_{t+1}}{p_t}$.

Agents of the same generation form various different inflation expectations. This is the reason for the emergence of the intragenerational credit market. An agent expecting a relatively high interest rate on the money market will be willing to borrow goods from other agents in order to supply these goods on the money market as well.[11] In the next period, the goods are given back, possibly together with an additional interest return. The surplus from the money market activity must be divided between the partners in the intragenerational credit market in order to provide an incentive for both to participate in this market. An analogous argument is the one for agents expecting a relatively low interest rate on the money market and thus willing to supply goods in the intragenerational credit market. What arises from these different expectations within the same generation is an intragenerational credit market connecting these different expectations with the money market.

9.5.3 The Credit Market

Although there are various different forms of market structures,[12] the intragenerational credit market will be assumed to have a structure generating one price each period. This one price is valid for all participants in the market. The market form will be described in detail later on.

In order to find an equilibrium interest rate for the intragenerational credit market, credit supply and credit demand must be determined for every possible interest rate $R \in \left(R_{i,t}^{e,min}, R_{i,t}^{e,max}\right)$. $R_{i,t}^{e,min} = \min_i \left\{R_{i,t}^e\right\}$ stands for the minimum expected interest rate in the population, $R_{i,t}^{e,max} = \max_i \left\{R_{i,t}^e\right\}$ for the maximum one.

Credit Supply — Lending of Goods

Agent i will only give goods away in the credit market, if she expects to achieve higher returns from this market than in the money market. For the credit market supply of agent i, this means that

$$l_{i,t} \begin{cases} \geq 0 & \text{for } R > R_{i,t}^e \\ = 0 & \text{for } R \leq R_{i,t} \end{cases} . \tag{9.30}$$

The level of credit supply depends on planned savings s and by that on interest rates:

$$l_{i,t}(R) = \begin{cases} \frac{1}{2}\left(w^1 - \frac{1}{R}w^2\right) & \text{for } R > R_{i,t}^e \\ 0 & \text{for } R \leq R_{i,t}^e \end{cases} . \tag{9.31}$$

[11] On the money market of this model, goods are traded against money: The old generation's agents give money to the young ones who in turn give goods to the old.

[12] A survey on possible market structures is Wolfstetter (1996).

Individual credit supply is monotonically increasing in the interest rate R

$$\frac{\partial l_{i,t}(R)}{\partial R} = \begin{cases} \frac{1}{2}\frac{w^2}{R^2} & \text{for } R > R^e_{i,t} \\ 0 & \text{for } R \leq R^e_{i,t} \end{cases} . \tag{9.32}$$

Aggregate credit supply of generation t is the sum of all individual credit supply given R:

$$l_t(R) = \sum_{i=1}^{n} l_{i,t}(R) . \tag{9.33}$$

Because of (9.32), aggregate credit supply monotonically increases with R.

Credit Demand — Borrowing of Goods

Similar to the lending of goods, the borrowing of goods takes place. An agent i will only be willing to borrow goods from others, if she has to pay less interest R for this than she hopes to gain at the money market.

This means that

$$b_{i,t} \begin{cases} = 0 & \text{for } R > R^e_{i,t} \\ \geq 0 & \text{for } R \leq R^e_{i,t} \end{cases} . \tag{9.34}$$

The maximum amount agent i can borrow will be delimited by a credit restriction. Every agent i is only allowed to borrow an amount of the good she will be able to give back in the second period even in the worst case (the case of extremely wrong expectations). In this worst case, agent i still has one secure part of income in period two: w^2. Thus, the individual credit restriction reads

$$b_{i,t}R \leq w^2 . \tag{9.35}$$

Consequently, the individual credit demand is given as

$$b_{i,t}(R) = \begin{cases} \frac{w^2}{R} & \text{for } R < R^e_{i,t} \\ 0 & \text{for } R \geq R^e_{i,t} \end{cases} . \tag{9.36}$$

The individual credit demand decreases with the interest rate:

$$\frac{\partial b_{i,t}(R)}{\partial R} = \begin{cases} -\frac{w^2}{R^2} & \text{for } R < R^e_{i,t} \\ 0 & \text{for } R \geq R^e_{i,t} \end{cases} . \tag{9.37}$$

Again, the generation wide aggregate demand results as the sum of individual demands.

$$b_t = \sum_{i=0}^{n} b_{i,t}(R) . \tag{9.38}$$

b_t is monotonically falling with R.

Equilibrium

It must be found out if on the market characterized by equations (9.30) to (9.31) and (9.36) to (9.38) an equilibrium occurs. For this purpose, let us assume the agents i to be sorted descendingly by their expectations, i.e.

$$R^e_{i,t} \geq R^e_{i+1,t} \; \forall \, i \in \{1, \dots, n-1\} \, . \tag{9.39}$$

It follows that

$$R^{e,min}_{i,t} := \min_i \left\{ R^e_{i,t} \right\}^n_{i=1} = R^e_{n,t} \tag{9.40}$$

and

$$R^{e,max}_{i,t} := \max_i \left\{ R^e_{i,t} \right\}^n_{i=1} = R^e_{1,t} \, . \tag{9.41}$$

An equilibrium in the credit market in the relevant interval of interest rates $R^{e,min}_{i,t} \leq R \leq R^{e,max}_{i,t}$ exists if and only if at monotonically increasing credit supply and monotonically decreasing credit demand the excess demand is positive at $R = R^{e,min}_{i,t}$ and negative at $R = R^{e,max}_{i,t}$:

$$l_t\left(R^{e,min}_{i,t}\right) - b_t\left(R^{e,min}_{i,t}\right) > 0 \tag{9.42}$$

$$\wedge \quad l_t\left(R^{e,max}_{i,t}\right) - b_t\left(R^{e,max}_{i,t}\right) < 0 \, . \tag{9.43}$$

It follows from (9.32), (9.33), (9.37) and (9.38) that the necessary conditions are met by the demand and supply functions.

Additionally, it can be easily shown, that (9.42) and (9.43) are valid, too. At the interest of $R^{e,min}_{i,t} = R^e_{n,t}$, the credit supply is zero while the credit demand is positive:

$$l_t\left(R^{e,min}_{i,t}\right) = 0 \, . \tag{9.44}$$

$$b_t\left(R^{e,min}_{i,t}\right) = \sum_{i=1}^{n-1} b_{i,t}\left(R^{e,min}_{i,t}\right) + 0 \tag{9.45}$$

$$= (n-1)\frac{w^2}{R^{e,min}_{i,t}} > 0 \, . \tag{9.46}$$

This means that (9.42) is true. Moreover,

$$l_t\left(R^{e,max}_{i,t}\right) = l_{1,t}\left(R^{e,max}_{i,t}\right) + \sum_{i=2}^{n} l_{i,t} \tag{9.47}$$

$$= 0 + (n-1)\frac{1}{2}\left(w^1 - \frac{1}{R^{e,max}_{i,t}} w^2\right) > 0 \, . \tag{9.48}$$

$$b_t\left(R^{e,max}_{i,t}\right) = 0 \, . \tag{9.49}$$

Thus, (9.43) is met as well. Consequently, in the relevant interval of interest rate there is one unique interest rate leading to an equilibrium in the credit market.[13] Moreover, because of the given slopes of the demand and supply functions, the equilibrium is Walras stable.

Summarizing, the credit market is the part of the model, where every agent determines her credit demand $b_{i,t}$ or the amount to be received in the second period $B_{i,t} = b_{i,t} R_{w,t}$, respectively, as well as her credit supply $l_{i,t}$ or the second period value $L_{i,t} = l_{i,t} R_{w,t}$, respectively.

9.5.4 The Money Market

Demand

After the intragenerational credit relations have been established in the credit market, the demand for money $m_{i,t}$ is determined. This happens during a two step process. In the first step, every agent i checks if her optimal level of savings (9.29) is reached already by her actions in the credit market. If this is not the case, in the second step, the rest of the savings has to be achieved via the money market.

The second period value of real money holdings $g_{i,t}$ is $G_{i,t} = g_{i,t} \frac{p_t}{p_{t+1}}$. But, as neither p_t nor p_{t+1} is known by the agent, she has to rely on her expectations $\pi^e_{i,t+1}$ or the reciprocal $R^e_{i,t}$ for the computation of the desired amount of savings in form of money. This means that agent i expects a second period return of her real money holdings of $G^e_{i,t}$ units of the good:

$$G^e_{i,t} = R^e_{i,t} g_{i,t} \, . \tag{9.50}$$

Consequently, agent i will demand as much money $g_{i,t}$ as she needs to reach at least planned second period payoff of her savings, $S^*_{i,t}$ as given by (9.29).

$$\begin{aligned} g_{i,t} &= \max \left\{ \frac{1}{R^e_{i,t}} \left(S^*_{i,t} - L_{i,t} + B_{i,t} \right) ; \, 0 \right\} \\ &= \max \left\{ s\left(R^e_{i,t} \right) - \frac{1}{R^e_{i,t}} \left(L_{i,t} - B_{i,t} \right) ; \, 0 \right\} . \end{aligned}$$

In addition, agent i possibly needs even more money, because she might have to transfer the amount of goods into the next period she took as a credit in the intragenerational credit market. The real second period value of these goods is

$$H_{i,t} = \max \left\{ B_{i,t} - L_{i,t} ; \, 0 \right\} . \tag{9.51}$$

[13] To be more exact, if supply and demand functions are only monotonic instead of strictly monotonic, there might exist a continuum of equilibria, which nevertheless all lead to the same, unique equilibrium interest rate. For details on this point, see below: Sect. 9.5.8, pp. 162.

This amount, $H_{i,t}$, must be transferred via the money market, too. In order to determine the present value of $H_{i,t}$, $h_{i,t}$, the true inflation factor π_{t+1} or its reciprocal R_t must be known to the agent. As this is not the case, the agent again has to rely on her private expectations $R^e_{i,t}$ in order to compute $h_{i,t}$:

$$h_{i,t} = \max\left\{\frac{1}{R^e_{i,t}}\left(B_{i,t} - L_{i,t}\right);\, 0\right\}. \tag{9.52}$$

Total money demand of agent t is the sum of $g_{i,t}$ and $h_{i,t}$. This is the exact composition of real money demand $m_{i,t}/p_t$:[14]

$$\frac{m_{i,t}}{p_t} = g_{i,t} + h_{i,t}\,. \tag{9.53}$$

Generation wide money demand m^d_t results as the sum of all individual money demands minus the real value of governmental seignorage nd:

$$\frac{m^d_t}{p_t} = \sum_{i=1}^{n}\left(g_{i,t} + h_{i,t}\right) - nd\,. \tag{9.54}$$

Supply

While money demand arises from the young generation, money demand is given by the old agents. The agents of the old generation have traded goods against money in their youth and now wish to pass the money on to the new young ones and get some goods in return.

Every old agent owns money worth the value of her savings minus real governmental seignorage d, the nominal value of which is $d\,p_t$. This gives an aggregate money demand of

$$m^s_{t-1} = \sum_{i=1}^{n}\left(g_{i,t-1} + h_{i,t-1}\right)p_{t-1} + nd\,p_t\,. \tag{9.55}$$

Equilibrium

In the money market, the equilibrium price p_t is determined:

$$m^d_t \stackrel{!}{=} m^s_{t-1} \tag{9.56}$$

$$\Leftrightarrow \quad \left[\sum_{i=1}^{n}\left(g_{i,t} + h_{i,t}\right) - nd\right]p_t = \sum_{i=1}^{n}\left(g_{i,t-1} + h_{i,t-1}\right)p_{t-1} \tag{9.57}$$

$$\Leftrightarrow \quad p_t = \frac{\sum_{i=1}^{n}\left(g_{i,t-1} + h_{i,t-1}\right)}{\sum_{i=1}^{n}\left(g_{i,t} + h_{i,t}\right) - nd}\,p_{t-1}\,. \tag{9.58}$$

[14] $m_{i,t}$ is a *nominal* variable. Naively spoken, $m_{i,t}$ gives the number of Dollar bills needed for the savings.

From the results of three successive periods, one inflation factor emerges:

$$\pi_{t+1} = \frac{p_{t+1}}{p_t} \tag{9.59}$$

$$= \frac{\sum_{i=1}^n (g_{i,t}+h_{i,t})}{\sum_{i=1}^n (g_{i,t+1}+h_{i,t+1})-nd} \cdot \frac{\sum_{i=1}^n (g_{i,t}+h_{i,t})-nd}{\sum_{i=1}^n (g_{i,t-1}+h_{i,t-1})} \cdot \frac{p_t}{p_{t-1}} \tag{9.60}$$

$$= \frac{\sum_{i=1}^n (g_{i,t}+h_{i,t})}{\sum_{i=1}^n (g_{i,t+1}+h_{i,t+1})-nd} \cdot \frac{\sum_{i=1}^n (g_{i,t}+h_{i,t})-nd}{\sum_{i=1}^n (g_{i,t-1}+h_{i,t-1})} \cdot \pi_t \,. \tag{9.61}$$

Equation (9.61) gives the development of true inflation as a difference equation. Although this equation has a relatively simple mathematical structure, is contains very complex economic processes. An explicit solution to (9.61) cannot be computed without the knowledge of all individual plans of credit supply and credit demand of every agent of three successive generations. This, of course, needs the knowledge about the way each of these agents forms her expectations. In order to obtain this knowledge at least for the model builder, the mechanism of expectations formation will be given by an economic GA.

9.5.5 The Proceeding of the Model

The model of the economy as well as the GAs described below proceeds due to certain discrete steps. In detail, these steps are the following:

1. Every agent of generation t forms expectations concerning the inflation $\pi^e_{i,t+1}$ or the interest rate $R^e_{i,t}$, respectively.
2. Every agent plans her savings $s_{i,t}$ (9.26) or $S_{i,t}$ (9.29), respectively.
3. The intragenerational credit market opens. Every agent tries to build up her desired level of savings as advantageous as possible. Thus, $l_{i,t}$ (9.32) and $b_{i,t}$ (9.36) emerge.
4. The money market opens. Here, the transfer of credits $h_{i,t}$ (9.52) takes place. Moreover, the rest of desired savings $g_{i,t}$ (9.51) is realized.
   Now, the true value of first period consumption emerges:
   $$c^1_{i,t} = w^1 - l_{i,t} + b_{i,t} - g_{i,t} - h_{i,t} \,. \tag{9.62}$$
5. Interaction of generations t and generation $t-1$ on the money market leads to the true price p_t (9.58).
6. The next generation, generation $t+1$ undergoes steps 1 to 5. On the new money market, p_{t+1} and consequently π_{t+1} and R_t arise.
7. The interest rate R_t reveals the true value of savings of every agent of generation t and thus the value of second period consumption
   $$c^{2,a}_{i,t} = w^2 + L_{i,t} - B_{i,t} + R_t\,(g_{i,t}+h_{i,t}) \,. \tag{9.63}$$

   Now, at last, the utility (9.21) of every agent and consequently the quality of every agent's inflation expectations is given.

9.5.6 A Walrasian Credit Market

Up to now, the definition of the model is very general. In order to achieve more detailed results, the form of the credit market has to be defined more precisely. Thus, the credit market will be assumed to be a Walrasian market. This means, among others, that on the market, one price emerges, bringing demand and supply into equilibrium. This equilibrium price is $R_{w,t}$. It is the general price valid for all agents active on the market.[15]

Credit Suppliers

All agents i with $R_i < R_{w,t}$ are credit suppliers. Their credit supply at the Walrasian equilibrium interest rate $R_{w,t}$ can be computed from (9.31) as

$$l_{i,t} = \frac{1}{2}\left(w^1 - \frac{1}{R_{w,t}}w^2\right). \tag{9.64}$$

Credit suppliers expect a second period payoff of

$$L_{i,t} = R_{w,t}l_{i,t} = \frac{1}{2}\left(R_{w,t}w^1 - w^2\right). \tag{9.65}$$

Because of $R_i < R_{w,t}$, credit demand of these agents is zero:

$$b_{i,t} = B_{i,t} = 0. \tag{9.66}$$

Following (9.51), the money demand for the purpose of saving $g_{i,t}$ is

$$\begin{aligned} g_{i,t} &= \max\left\{\frac{1}{2}\left(w^1 - \frac{1}{R^e_{i,t}}w^2\right) - \frac{1}{R^e_{i,t}}\frac{1}{2}\left(R_{w,t}w^1 - w^2\right);\, 0\right\} && (9.67)\\ &= \max\left\{\frac{1}{2}w^1\left(1 - \frac{R_{w,t}}{R^e_{i,t}}\right);\, 0\right\} && (9.68)\\ &= 0. && (9.69)\end{aligned}$$

Money demand for the purpose of transferring credits, $h_{i,t}$, follows from (9.51) as

$$\begin{aligned} h_{i,t} &= \max\left\{-\frac{1}{R^e_{i,t}}L_{i,t};\, 0\right\} && (9.70)\\ &= \max\left\{-\frac{1}{2}\frac{1}{R^e_{i,t}}\left(R_{w,t}w^1 - w^2\right);\, 0\right\}. && (9.71)\end{aligned}$$

[15] The general validity of the Walrasian equilibrium price is important to the model. The 'law of one price' constituted by this market form is the most important difference between this model and models with matching markets.

According to (9.27), $R_{w,t} > \frac{w^2}{w^1}$, and consequently

$$h_{i,t} = 0\,. \tag{9.72}$$

This result can be understood intuitively: All agents i expecting a lower interest rate in the money market than in the credit market will save in form of giving credits only, i.e. $b_{i,t} = 0$. This means that they do not take goods as credits and consequently that they do not have to transfer any goods from credits taken into the next period — $h_{i,t} = 0$. Moreover, as no further savings are necessary, money demand for the purpose of saving is zero as well, $g_{i,t} = 0$.

First period consumption of every credit supplier can be derived from(9.22) and (9.24) to

$$c^1_{i,t} = w^1 - l_{i,t} \tag{9.73}$$

$$= \frac{1}{2}\left(w^1 + \frac{1}{R_{w,t}}w^2\right)\,. \tag{9.74}$$

Planned and realized second period consumption is

$$c^2_{i,t} = c^{2,a}_{i,t} = w^2 + L_{i,t} - B_{i,t} + G_{i,t} + H_{i,t} \tag{9.75}$$

$$= \frac{1}{2}\left(R_{w,t}w^1 + w^2\right)\,. \tag{9.76}$$

From (9.74) and (9.76), it can be seen that the consumption in both periods and consequently utility is *independent of the individual expectations* $R^e_{i,t}$. This result can easily be explained. All credit suppliers are active in the credit market only. For this market, there exists an equilibrium price: $R_{w,t}$. Individual expectations are only important for the process of determining this price. The amount of payoffs, then, only depends on the equilibrium price $R_{w,t}$.

Credit Demanders

For a more precise analysis of the credit market, the specific form of the credit demand function must be known. All agents i with $R^e_{i,t} > R_{w,t}$ are credit demanders. At the Walrasian equilibrium interest rate $R_{w,t}$ they do not offer any credits:

$$l_{i,t} = L_{i,t} = 0\,. \tag{9.77}$$

This means that they have to carry out all their desired savings directly via the money market.

Credit demand, accounting for the credit restriction, results from (9.35) to

$$b_{i,t} = \frac{1}{R_{w,t}}w^2\,, \tag{9.78}$$

$$B_{i,t} = w^2\,. \tag{9.79}$$

This amount of goods has to be transferred to the next period via the money market:

$$B_{i,t} = H_{i,t}\,. \tag{9.80}$$

Agent i expects the interest rate in the money market to become $R^e_{i,t} > R_{w,t}$. Consequently, she has to trade in $h_{i,t}$ money:

$$h_{i,t} = \frac{1}{R^e_{i,t}} w^2\,. \tag{9.81}$$

Agent i expects to gain a surplus from the credit market to the extend of $b_{i,t} - h_{i,t}$:

$$b_{i,t} - h_{i,t} = \frac{w^2}{R_{w,t}} - \frac{w_2}{R^e_{i,t}} = \frac{R^e_{i,t} - R_{w,t}}{R^e_{i,t} R_{w,t}} w^2\,. \tag{9.82}$$

The amount of money held for the purpose of direct savings is

$$g_{i,t} = s_{i,t}\left(R^e_{i,t}\right) \tag{9.83}$$

$$= \frac{1}{2}\left(w^1 - \frac{1}{R^e_{i,t}} w^2\right)\,. \tag{9.84}$$

This means that the first period consumption of a credit demander is given by[16]

$$c^1_{i,t} = w^1 + b_{i,t} - g_{i,t} - h_{i,t} \tag{9.85}$$

$$= \frac{1}{2}\left(w^1 + \frac{1}{R^e_{i,t}} w^2\right) + \frac{R^e_{i,t} - R_{w,t}}{R^e_{i,t} R_{w,t}} w^2\,. \tag{9.86}$$

After R_t has emerged in the money market, the true payoff from the money market is

$$G^a_{i,t} = g_{i,t} R_t \tag{9.87}$$

and

$$H^a_{i,t} = h_{i,t} R_t\,. \tag{9.88}$$

Consequently, true second period consumption $c^{2,a}_{i,t}$ is

$$c^{2,a}_{i,t} = w^2 - B_{i,t} + G^a_{i,t} + H^a_{i,t} \tag{9.89}$$

$$= R_t\left(g_{i,t} + h_{i,t}\right) \tag{9.90}$$

$$= \frac{1}{2}\left(R_t w^1 + \frac{R_t}{R^e_{i,t}} w^2\right)\,. \tag{9.91}$$

[16] Equation (9.85) contains the implicit assumption that the expected surplus from credits is used for first period consumption already.

True first period consumption equals planned first period consumption: $c_{i,t}^{1,a} = c_{i,t}^{1}$. Thus, true consumption and consequently utility *depends on individual expectations* $R_{i,t}^{e}$. The direction of this dependence can be found out by a simple derivation:

$$U_{i,t} = c_{i,t}^{1,a} \cdot c_{i,t}^{2,a}. \tag{9.92}$$

and thus

$$\frac{\partial U_{i,t}}{\partial R_{i,t}^{e}} = \frac{\partial c_{i,t}^{1,a}}{\partial R_{i,t}^{e}} c_{i,t}^{2,a} + \frac{\partial c_{i,t}^{2,a}}{\partial R_{i,t}^{e}} c_{i,t}^{1,a}. \tag{9.93}$$

Because of

$$\frac{\partial c_{i,t}^{1,a}}{\partial R_{i,t}^{e}} = -\frac{1}{2}\frac{w^2}{R_{i,t}^{e\ 2}} + \frac{w^2}{R_{i,t}^{e\ 2}} \tag{9.94}$$

$$= \frac{1}{2}\frac{w^2}{R_{i,t}^{e\ 2}} \tag{9.95}$$

and

$$\frac{\partial c_{i,t}^{2,a}}{\partial R_{i,t}^{e}} = -\frac{1}{2}\frac{w^2}{R_{i,t}^{e\ 2}} \tag{9.96}$$

it follows that

$$\frac{\partial U_{i,t}}{\partial R_{i,t}^{e}} = -\frac{1}{2}\left(w^2\right)^2 \frac{R_t}{R_{i,t}^{e\ 2}} \frac{R_{i,t}^{e} - R_{w,t}}{R_{i,t}^{e} R_{w,t}}. \tag{9.97}$$

Due to the assumption that $R_{i,t}^{e} > R_{w,t}$ (agent i is a credit demander), the sign of $\frac{\partial U_{i,t}}{\partial R_{i,t}^{e}}$ can be deduced:

$$\frac{\partial U_{i,t}}{\partial R_{i,t}^{e}} < 0. \tag{9.98}$$

This means that true utility of a credit taker is the higher, the closer her expectations are to the Walrasian equilibrium interest rate.

The curvature of $U_{i,t}$ follows from the second derivative

$$\frac{\partial^2 U_{i,t}}{\partial \left(R_{i,t}^{e}\right)^2} = \left(w^2\right)^2 \frac{R_t}{R_{i,t}^{e}} \left(\frac{1}{R_{w,t}} - \frac{3}{2}\frac{1}{R_{i,t}^{e}}\right). \tag{9.99}$$

At first hand, the sign of (9.99) is indeterminate. A null of the function (9.99) and thus a point of inflection of $U_{i,t}$ can be found at

$$\frac{\partial^2 U_{i,t}}{\partial \left(R^e_{i,t}\right)^2} = \left(w^2\right)^2 \frac{R_t}{R^e_{i,t}} \left(\frac{1}{R_{w,t}} - \frac{3}{2}\frac{1}{R^e_{i,t}}\right) = 0 \tag{9.100}$$

$$\Leftrightarrow \quad R^e_{i,t} = \frac{3}{2} R_{w,t} \tag{9.101}$$

and thus at the right of $R_{w,t}$.

In the neighborhood of $R_{w,t}$,

$$\lim_{R^e_{i,t} \downarrow R_{w,t}} \frac{\partial^2 U_{i,t}}{\partial \left(R^e_{i,t}\right)^2} = -\frac{1}{2}\left(w^2\right)^2 \frac{R_t}{R_{w,t}{}^4} > 0. \tag{9.102}$$

The utility function in $R^e_{i,t}$ of credit demanders has a right curvature near $R_{w,t}$, but switches to a left curvature from $R^e_{i,t} = \frac{3}{2} R_{w,t}$ on.

Suppliers and Demanders

At the point $R^e_{i,t} = R_{w,t}$, the function $U_{i,t}\left(R^e_{i,t}\right)$ describing utility dependent of individual interest rate expectations, is not continuous.

The left limit derives from the utility of credit suppliers at this point.

$$U^A := \lim_{R^e_{i,t} \uparrow R_{w,t}} U_{i,t}\left(R^e_{i,t}\right) = \frac{1}{4}\left[R_{w,t}\left(w^1\right)^2 + 2w^1w^2 + \frac{1}{R_{w,t}}\left(w^2\right)^2\right]. \tag{9.103}$$

The 'right' limit at $R^e_{i,t} = R_{w,t}$ is

$$U^N := \lim_{R^e_{i,t} \downarrow R_{w,t}} U_{i,t}\left(R^e_{i,t}\right) = \frac{1}{4} R_t \left[\left(w^1\right)^2 + \frac{2}{R_{w,t}} w^1 w^2 + \frac{1}{R_{w,t}{}^2}\left(w^2\right)^2\right]. \tag{9.104}$$

There are no general, but only casewise results concerning the difference between U^A and U^N.

$$U^A - U^N =$$
$$\frac{1}{4}\left[\left(R_{w,t} - R_t\right)\left(w^1\right)^2 + 2\left(1 - \frac{R_t}{R_{w,t}}\right) w^1 w^2 + \frac{1}{R_{w,t}}\left(1 - \frac{R_t}{R_{w,t}}\right)\left(w^2\right)^2\right]. \tag{9.105}$$

There are three different cases:

a) $R_t > R_{w,t} \quad \Rightarrow \quad U^A < U^N$.
b) $R_t = R_{w,t} \quad \Rightarrow \quad U^A = U^N$.
c) $R_t < R_{w,t} \quad \Rightarrow \quad U^A > U^N$.

This means that there are three possible forms of the function $U_{i,t}\left(R^e_{i,t}\right)$, as shown in Fig. 9.3. The figure shows curves *a* to *c* belonging to cases a) to c) described above.

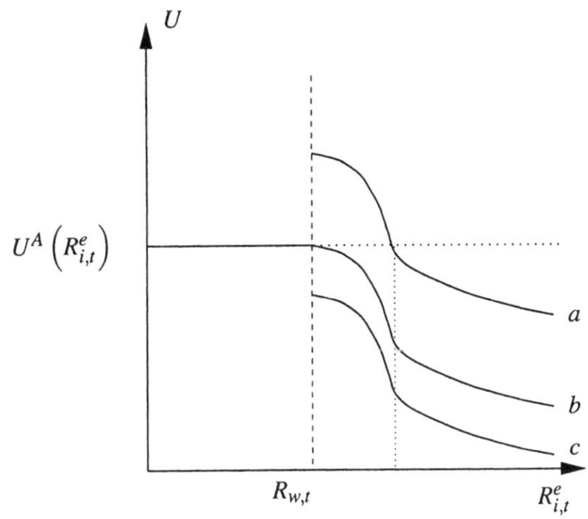

Fig. 9.3. Utility Depending on Expected Interest Rate

Case a) is the only case with a unique optimum. This means that only in case a) there exists a unique optimal kind of behavior which can be learned. Only in this case, a stationary solution like the solution to the basic model without an intragenerational credit market exists at all. But even in this case, for a technique like GA learning, it is very hard to *learn* the optimum strategy, because just at the optimum, the utility function (technically spoken: the fitness function) is non continuous.[17]

9.5.7 Theoretical Conclusions: Stability Properties of the Expectations Equilibrium Revisited

In the basic OLG model with money and in the extended model, one point is of particular interest: It is the point where all agents expect an interest rate of $R^e_{i,t}$ which is exactly the same as the one truly emerging from the money market, R_t. This is the point of correct expectations, which in the basic model is the characteristic of the dynamic equilibrium states.

The theoretical analysis of the extended model leaves some doubts if for the extended case, such a state will be reached at all. Moreover, even if such a state were reached, it is still not sure if such a state would not be left again, i.e. if such a state in the extended model is asymptotically stable. Thus, the stability properties will be analyzed more closely.

The equilibrium in focus is characterized by a vector of uniform individual interest rate expectations, with expectations being correct in the sense that the expected interest rate is exactly the same as the one emerging ex post. Thus, the vector of

[17] Fitness functions like the one given as (9.92) are known to be 'GA hard' and can lead to wrong, i.e. non optimal outcomes of GAs. See Goldberg (1987) and Jones and Forrest (1995).

correct expectations is given by

$$R^e_{i,t} = R_t \; \forall i \in \{1, \ldots, n\} . \tag{9.106}$$

At this point of correct expectations both models, the basic and the extended one, behave the same: In the case of uniform expectations, the intragenerational credit market does not open, thus leading the structure of the extended model back to the structure of the basic one.

In order to analyze the further behavior of the model, the development of the inflation π_t or the interest rate R_t must be known. This development is described in (9.61) for the inflation and can easily be transformed into an equation for the interest rate:

$$R_t = \frac{\sum_{i=1}^n (g_{i,t+1} + h_{i,t+1}) - nd}{\sum_{i=1}^n (g_{i,t} + h_{i,t})} \cdot \frac{\sum_{i=1}^n (g_{i,t-1} + h_{i,t-1})}{\sum_{i=1}^n (g_{i,t-1} + h_{i,t-1})} \cdot R_{t-1} . \tag{9.107}$$

Formally, (9.107) is a simple first order difference equation. The development of R_t essentially depends on $g_{i,t-1}$, $g_{i,t}$, $g_{i,t+1}$, $h_{i,t-1}$, $h_{i,t}$, and $h_{i,t+1}$, and thus on the interest rates expected by three generations. As long as there are no further observations or assumptions concerning these expectations, (9.107) cannot be analytically solved nor iterated. Thus, it cannot be generally determined if the point (9.106) will be reached.[18]

Assuming individual expectations to emerge from a process of GA learning still does not help to solve (9.107). In order to get some more precise results, nevertheless, some simulations are conducted based on a very special variant of an economic GA.

9.5.8 The Genetic Algorithm

General Structure

The given problem, the problem of dynamic consumption/savings choice for heterogeneous agents and an intragenerational credit market, can be implemented by a genetic algorithm. This GA is mainly the same as the GA for the basic OLG model without a credit market. Again, the algorithm is a two population GA with genetic individuals encoding individual inflation expectations. Thus, the structure of the GA is the one displayed in Algorithm 9.1, the exact run is a replication of the seven steps discussed in Sect. 9.5.5.

The only difference between the basic and the extended GA model is the credit market, which is implemented in form of a Walrasian auction. This, the computer based implementation of a Walrasian auction with only a finite number of participant, is non trivial.

[18] For converging learning mechanisms like the one presented by Lucas (1986) it *can* be shown that (9.107) is reached. In this model, though, the effects of heterogeneity are neglected.

A Walrasian Auction with a Finite Number of Participants

In order to compute a Walrasian equilibrium interest rate in a simulated credit market, for every possible interest rate $R \in \left(R^e_{n,t}, R^e_{1,t}\right)$, the credit supply and the credit demand must be computed.[19]

From the discussion of the preceding sections, it is known that within the relevant interval of interest rates, credit supply is monotonically increasing while credit demand is monotonically decreasing in the interest rate. This means that in the simulations, the Walrasian equilibrium interest rate can be determined by recursive approximation. Algorithm 9.2 shows the exact procedure.

GetEqPrice(p_1, p_n **)** — Walrasian Auction

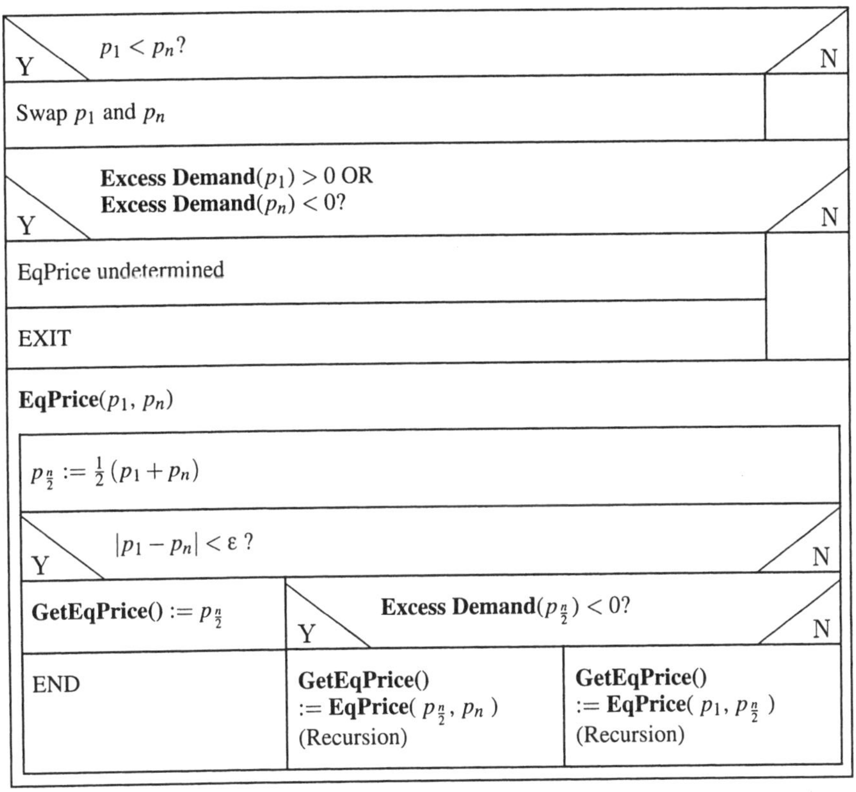

Algorithm 9.2: Determination of the Walrasian Equilibrium Price

[19] The assumption of agents being sorted descendingly by their expectations is still valid.

As a consequence of the fact that there is only a finite number of participants on the market, sometimes the resulting equilibrium quantity is not unique. This is a consequence of the fact that the generation wide aggregate credit supply function (9.33) is not continuous. Instead there are up to $n-1$ steps. Every individual credit supply function (9.31) has an ordinate intercept of $R^e_{i,t}$. Adding up all the individual credit supply functions gives a generation wide aggregate credit supply function with a step at each $R = R^e_{i,t}$, $i \in \{1, \cdots, n\}$. This is illustrated for a stylized market with two credit suppliers in Fig. 9.4.

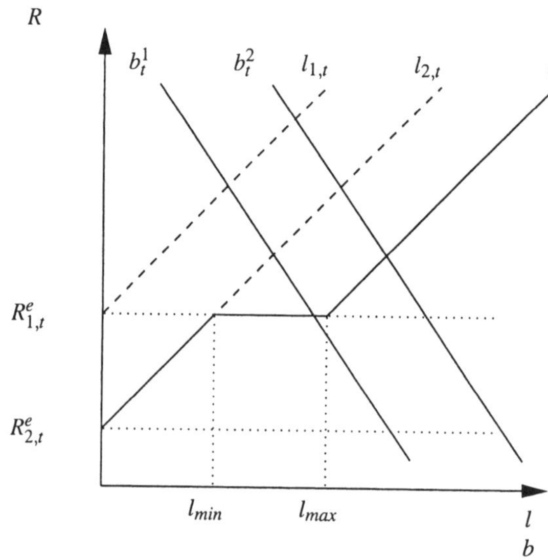

Fig. 9.4. Stylized Credit Market with Two Suppliers

In Fig. 9.4, the aggregate credit supply function has a step at $R = R^e_{1,t}$. If the supply function is crossed by the demand function at this point, there is a unique equilibrium price $R^e_{1,t}$ but no unique equilibrium quantity. The equilibrium quantity is located in the interval between l_{min} and l_{max}. The problem is of course non existent, if the interception of demand and supply does not fall together with a step of the aggregate supply function. In the simulations, it is assumed that in the non unique case, the quantity turns out to be l_{min}.

9.5.9 Results

Not surprisingly, all simulations based on the GA for the extended model lead to a breakdown of the system in form of computational or economic exceptions. The computational exception reached is the state of divisions by zero, which reflects the occurrence of (in the limit) infinitely high inflation factors. Thus, the first set of experiments based on the GA lead to the conclusion, that at least for the simulations, stationary solutions to the problem *never* occur. This result can be seen as a hint that the results of the basic OLG model with money is not robust against an extension by an intragenerational credit market.

If a stationary state of the economy is not reached, it can nevertheless be asked if such a state, once occurring, would be asymptotically stable, i.e. not left by the economy any more. In order to answer this question a special GA was constructed. The algorithm itself is the same as the one used before, with one exception: Genetic individuals are not initialized randomly, but with a certain value, i.e. the value reflecting the correct expectations. This special GA, so to say, starts in the stationary state of the economy. The main aim is to find out, if these simulations, starting from the fix point, stay there forever, or if this fix point is left. The GA in focus uses the operator of election. This means that the GA used is the GA variant known for its strong stability properties. If the fix point is asymptotically stable, it should not be left by the election GA.

The results of the simulations are negative: There was not a single run of the simulations where the fix point was not left by the economy. Although, due to the inductive nature of the analysis, this is no proof that the extended OLG model does not posses a stable state, these results give a strong evidence that this might be the case.

Thus, the core result of the analysis is the finding that in presence of heterogeneity, in OLG models, the existence or occurrence of intragenerational credit relations must not be ignored. Including such an intragenerational credit market leads to totally different outcomes of the model. In this case, too, heterogeneity matters.

9.6 Summary

The chapter discussed a model much more complicated in its structure than all the models discussed before. Consequently, the GA used is more complicated than the GAs used before: It is a two population GA, simultaneously dealing with two genetic populations in every period.

For the analysis carried out, there is an important finding for the basic OLG model with money: Most papers facing this model concentrate on the stationary solutions. For GA learning models in this context, this seems to be justified by the results of Arifovic (1995), showing that GA simulations of the basic OLG model always result in one of the stationary outcomes. This chapter, though, shows that there are variants of economic GAs that result in other, cyclical solutions. The quality of results of GA simulations, again, crucially depend on which specific GA variant is used.

As a consequence of heterogeneity of the agents in social learning models, an extended model was constructed, including an intragenerational credit market. Theoretical analysis shows that this extension of the model dramatically changes the theoretical results. All fix points of the basic model disappear. Simulations show that the model itself breaks down. The usual justification for ignoring heterogeneity and its effects in this type of models is the assumption that the explicit introduction of heterogeneity would not change the core results of the model. The analysis in this chapter shows that this argument is wrong.

10. Final Remarks

The main goal of this book is to show how genetic algorithms can be used in economic modeling. It should have been proved that the question 'Can genetic algorithms be sensibly used in order to model and analyze economic problems?' must be answered 'Yes'.

As stated in the introduction, the abandonment of perfect rationality in economic model automatically leads to the necessity of the integration of learning processes into economic models.

An introduction into the structure of genetic algorithms points out that GAs are in fact rather simple computational tools, which at the same time have the advantage of carrying very intuitive interpretations as learning mechanisms.

More rigorous theoretical analysis of GAs as Markov processes, as evolutionary games, and as processes of compound individual and social learning reveal some deeper characteristics of GAs used as models of economic learning processes: GA learning in its most basic form and in connection with the market in the long run leads to states which can be shown to be near optimal and evolutionarily stable. Long run results are independent of the starting conditions of the process.

Is is shown that the concept of GA learning can be successfully applied to a number of economic problems. Doing so, it can be found that changes to the specific learning process and the GA reflecting it can lead to sometimes dramatic changes of the outcome of the models. All of these changes can be clearly explained by the changes in the behavior of the agents involved. This means that with the help of GA learning models, even macroeconomic results can be traced back to their microeconomic sources. Specific learning processes analyzed include meta learning, the change to long run measures of economic success and the introduction of individual memory.

The importance of agent based models for theoretical economic research, though, reaches far beyond the limits of this book. More topics can be faced, more models can be constructed, which are no longer limited by the needs of mathematical tractability. Using agent based models means complementing classical deductive research methods by a new branch of inductive tools, thus opening new fields of research and possible discovery.

In the near future, closer connections of GA models with models from other branches of economic theory will appear. Close relationships can be found between

GA learning models and game theory, topology and even geographical economics. Consequently, this book is only a starting point of much more work still to be done.

Bibliography

Alchian, A. A. (1950). Uncertainty, evolution, and economic theory. *Journal of Political Economy*, 58:211–221.

Amman, H. M., Kendrick, D. A., and Rust, J., editors (1996). *Handbook of Computational Economics*, volume 1. Elsevier, Amsterdam.

Andreoni, J. and Miller, J. H. (1995). Auctions with artificial adaptive agents. *Games and Economic Behavior*, 10:39–64.

Arifovic, J. (1994). Genetic algorithm learning and the cobweb–model. *Journal of Economic Dynamics and Control*, 18:3–28.

Arifovic, J. (1995). Genetic algorithms and inflationary economies. *Journal of Monetary Economics*, 36:219–243.

Arthur, W. B. (1989). Competing technologies, increasing returns, and lock–in by historical events. *The Economic Journal*, 99:116–131.

Arthur, W. B. (1991). Designing economic agents that act like human agents. *American Economic Review, Papers and Proceedings*, 81:353–359.

Arthur, W. B. (1993). On designing economic agents that behave like human agents. *Journal of Evolutionary Economics*, 3:1–22.

Arthur, W. B. (1995). *Increasing Returns and Path Dependence in the Economy*. University of Michigan Press, Ann Arbor.

Arthur, W. B., Ermoliev, Y. M., and M., K. Y. (1987). Path–dependent processes and the emergence of macro–structure. *European Journal of Operational Research*, 30:294–303.

Axelrod, R. (1987). The evolution of strategies in the iterated prisoner's dilemma. In Davis, L., editor, *Genetic Algorithms and Simulated Annealing*, pages 32–41. Pitman, London.

Azariadis, C. (1993). *Intertemporal Macroeconomics*. Blackwell, Oxford, UK.

Bäck, T. (1992a). The interaction of mutation rate, selection, and self–adaption within a genetic algorithm. In Männer, R. and Manderick, B., editors, *Parallel Problem Solving from Nature 2*. Elsevier Science, Amsterdam.

Bäck, T. (1992b). Self–adaption in genetic algorithms. In *Proceedings of the First European Conference on Artificial Life*, Cambridge, MA, London. MIT Press.

Bäck, T., Hoffmeister, F., and Schwefel, H.-P. (1991). A survey of evolution strategies. In Belew, R. K. and Booker, L. B., editors, *Proceedings of the 4th International Conference on Genetic Algorithms*, pages 2–9, San Mateo, CA. Morgan Kaufmann.

Bäck, T. and Schütz, M. (1996). Intelligent mutation rate control in canonical genetic algorithms. In Ras, W. and Michalewicz, M., editors, *Foundation of Intelligent Systems 9th International Symposium, ISMIS 96*, pages 158–167, Berlin, Heidelberg, New York. Springer.

Barro, R. J. (1990). Government spending in a simple model of endogenous growth. *Journal of Political Economy*, 98:S103–S125.

Beasley, D., Bull, D. R., and Martin, R. R. (1993a). An overview of genetic algorithms: Part 1, Fundamentals. *University Computing*, 15:58–69.

Beasley, D., Bull, D. R., and Martin, R. R. (1993b). An overview of genetic algorithms: Part 2, Research topics. *University Computing*, 15:170–181.

Birchenhall, C. (1995). Modular technical change and genetic algorithms. *Computational Economics*, 8:233–253.

Birchenhall, C., Kastrinos, N., and Metcalfe, S. (1997). Genetic algorithms in evolutionary modelling. *Journal of Evolutionary Economics*, 7:375–393.

Blanchard, O. J. and Fischer, S. (1990). *Lectures on Macroeconomics*. MIT Press, Cambridge, MA, London.

Blume, L. E. and Easley, D. (1993). Economic natural selection. *Economics Letters*, 42:281–289.

Bona, J. L. and Santos, M. S. (1997). On the role of computation in economic theory. *Journal of Economic Theory*, 72:241–281.

Buchanan, J. M. and Stubblebine, W. C. (1962). Externality. *Economica*, 29:371–384.

Bullard, J. and Duffy, J. (1998). A model of learning and emulation with artificial adaptive agents. *Journal of Economic Dynamics and Control*, 22:179–207.

Chao, L. L. (1974). *Statistics. Methods and Analyses*. McGraw–Hill, New York, 2 edition.

David, P. A. (1985). Clio and the economics of QWERTY. *American Economic Review*, 75:332–337.

Davis, L. (1991). *Handbook of Genetic Algorithms*. Van Nostrand Reinhold, New York.

Davis, T. E. and Principe, J. C. (1993). A markov chain framework for the simple genetic algorithm. *Evolutionary Computation*, 1:269–288.

Dawid, H. (1994). A Markov chain analysis of genetic algorithms with a state dependent fitness function. *Complex Systems*, 8:407–417.

Dawid, H. (1999). *Adaptive Learning by Genetic Algorithms*. Springer, Berlin, Heidelberg, New York, 2 edition.

Diamond, P. A. (1965). National debt in a neoclassical growth model. *American Economic Review*, 55:1126–1150.

Feller, W. (1968). *An Introduction to Probability Theory and its Applications*, volume 1. John Wiley & Sons, New York, 3 edition.

Franke, R. (1997). Behavioural heterogeneity and genetic algorithm learning in the cobweb model. Discussion Paper 9, IKSF — Fachbereich 7 — Wirtschaftswissenschaft. Universität Bremen.

Franke, R. (1998). Coevolution and stable adjustments in the cobweb model. *Journal of Evolutionary Economics*, 8:383–406.

Friedman, D. (1998). On economic applications of evolutionary game theory. *Journal of Evolutionary Economics*, 8:15–43.

Fudenberg, D. and Levine, D. K. (1998a). Learning in games. *European Economic Review*, 42:631–639.

Fudenberg, D. and Levine, D. K. (1998b). *The Theory of Learning in Games*. MIT Press Series on Economic Learning and Social Evolution. MIT Press, Cambridge, MA.

Fudenberg, D. and Tirole, J. (1991). *Game Theory*. MIT Press.

Goldberg, D. E. (1987). Simple genetic algorithms and the minimal, deceptive problem. In Davis, L., editor, *Genetic Algorithms and Simulated Annealing*, pages 74–88. Morgan Kaufmann, San Mateo.

Goldberg, D. E. (1989). *Genetic Algorithms in Search, Optimization, and Machine Learning*. Addison–Wesley, Reading, Massachusetts.

Goldberg, D. E. (1991). Real–coded genetic algorithms, virtual alphabets, and blocking. *Complex Systems*, 5:139–167.

Goldberg, D. E. and Deb, K. (1991). A comparative analysis of selection schemes used in genetic algorithms. In Rawlins, G. J. E., editor, *Foundations of Genetic Algorithms*, pages 69–93, San Mateo, CA. Morgan Kaufmann.

Goldberg, D. E. and Segrest, P. (1987). Finite markov chain analysis of genetic algorithms. In Grefenstette, J. J., editor, *Proceedings of the Second International Conference on Genetic Algorithms*, pages 1–13.

Goodman, R. (1988). *Introduction to Stochastic Models*. Benjamin/Cummings, Menloe Park, California.

Grandmont, J.-M. (1985). On endogenous competitive business cycles. *Econometrica*, 53:995–1045.

Hamilton, J. D. (1994). *Time Series Analysis*. Princeton University Press, Princeton, New Jersey.

Hayek, F. A. v. (1969). *Freiburger Studien*, chapter 15, Der Wettbewerb als Entdeckungsverfahren, pages 249–265. J. C. B. Mohr (Paul Siebeck), Tübingen.

Hayek, F. A. v. (1978). *New Studies in Philosophy, Politics, Economics and the History of Ideas*, chapter 12, Competition as a Discovery Process, pages 179–190. Routledge & Kegan Paul, London.

Haykin, S. (1999). *Neural Networks. A Comprehensive Foundation*. Prentice–Hall, London, UK, 2 edition.

Heinemann, M. (1998). Adaptive learning of rational expectations using neural networks. forthcoming, Journal of Economic Dynamics and Control.

Heiner, R. A. (1988). Imperfect decisions and routinized production: Implications for evolutionary modelling and inertial technical change. In Dosi, G., Freeman, C., Nelson, R., Silverberg, G., and Soete, L., editors, *Technical Change and Economic Theory*, chapter 7, pages 148–169. Pinter Publishers, London, New York.

Henderson, J. M. and Quandt, R. E. (1986). *Microeconomic Theory. A Mathematical Approach*. McGraw–Hill, New York, 3 edition.

Hirshleifer, J. and Martinez Coll, J. C. (1992). Selection, mutation, and the preservation of diversity in evolutionary games. Papers on Economics & Evolution 9103, European Study Group for Evolutionary Economics.

Hofbauer, J. and Sigmund, K. (1988). *The Theory of Evolution and Dynamical Systems*. Cambridge University Press, Cambridge, UK.

Hofbauer, J. and Sigmund, K. (1998). *Evolutionary Games and Population Dynamics*. Cambridge University Press, Cambridge, UK.

Hoffmeister, F. and Bäck, T. (1991). Genetic algorithms and evolution strategies — similarities and differences. Papers on Economics & Evolution 9103, European Study Group for Evolutionary Economics.

Holland, J. H. (1975). *Adaptation in Natural and Artificial Systems*. University of Michigan Press, Ann Arbor.

Holland, J. H. (1992). *Adaptation in Natural and Artificial Systems*. MIT Press, Cambridge, MA, London, 2 edition.

Holland, J. H. (1996). The rationality of adaptive agents. In Arrow, K. J., Colombatto, E., Perlman, M., and Schmidt, C., editors, *The Rational Foundations of Economic Behaviour*, chapter 12, pages 281–297. MacMillan, London.

Holland, J. H. and Miller, J. (1991). Artificial adaptive agents in economic theory. *American Economic Review, Papers and Proceedings*, 81:365–370.

Isaacson, D. L. and Madsen, R. W. (1976). *Markov Chains, Theory and Applications*. John Wiley & Sons, New York.

Jones, T. and Forrest, S. (1995). Genetic algorithms and heuristic search. Discussion Paper, Santa Fe Institute, Santa Fe, New Mexico.

Judd, K. L. (1997). Computational economics and economic theory: Substitutes or complements. *Journal of Economic Dynamics and Control*, 21:907–942.

Judd, K. L. (1998). *Numerical Methods in Economics*. MIT Press, Cambridge, MA, London.

Kimble, G. A. (1973). *Encyclopedia Americana*, volume 17, chapter Learning, pages 116–122. Americana Corporation, New York.

Kirman, A. P. (1992). Whom or what does the representative individual represent? *Jornal of Economic Perspectives*, 6(2):117–136.

Koza, J. R. (1992). *Genetic Programming. On the Programming of Computers by Means of Natural Selection*. MIT Press, Cambridge, MA, London.

Koza, J. R. (1994). *Genetic Programming II. Automatic Discovery of Reusable Programs*. MIT Press, Cambridge, MA, London.

Kydland, F. E. and Prescott, E. C. (1996). The computational experiment: An econometric tool. *Journal of Economic Perspectives*, 10(1):69–85.

Lane, D. A. (1993a). Artificial worlds and economics, Part I. *Journal of Evolutionary Economics*, 3:89–107.

Lane, D. A. (1993b). Artificial worlds and economics, Part II. *Journal of Evolutionary Economics*, 3:177–197.

Lucas, R. E. (1988). On the mechanics of economic development. *Journal of Monetary Economics*, 22:3–42.

Lucas, R. E. J. (1986). Adaptive behavior and economic theory. *Journal of Business*, 59:S401–S426.

Magnusson, L. and Ottosson, J., editors (1997). *Evolutionary Economics and Path Dependence*. Edward Elgar, Cheltenham, UK, Brookfields, US.

Mailath, G. J. (1992). Introduction: Symposium on evolutionary game theory. *Journal of Economic Theory*, 57:259–277.

Marcet, A. and Sargent, T. J. (1989). Least–squares learning and the dynamics of hyperinflation. In Barnett, W. A., Geweke, J., and Shell, K., editors, *Economic Complexity: Chaos, Sunspots, Bubbles, and Nonlinearity*, chapter 7, pages 119–137. Cambridge University Press, Cambridge, UK.

Marimon, R., McGrattan, E., and Sargent, T. J. (1992). Money as a medium of exchange in an economy with artificially intelligent agents. *Journal of Economic Dynamics and Control*, 14:329–373.

Marks, R. E. (1992). Breeding hybrid strategies: Optimal behaviour for oligopolists. *Journal of Evolutionary Economics*, 2:17–38.

Maynard Smith, J. (1982). *Evolution and the Theory of Games*. Cambridge University Press, Cambridge, UK.

Maynard Smith, J. (1989). *Evolutionary Genetics*. Oxford University Press, Oxford, UK.

McCandless, G. T. and Wallace, N. (1991). *Introduction to Dynamic Macroeconomic Theory: An Overlapping Generations Approach*. Harvard University Press, Cambridge, MA, London.

Metcalfe, J. S. (1994). Competition, Fisher's proncìple and increasing returns in the selection process. *Journal of Evolutionary Economics*, 4:327–346.

Michalewicz, Z. (1996). *Genetic Algorithms + Data Structures = Evolution Programs*. Springer, Berlin, Heidelberg, New York, 3 edition.

Mitchell, M. (1996). *An Introduction to Genetic Algorithms*. MIT Press, Cambridge, MA, London.

Nelson, R. R. (1994). Routines. In Hodgson, G. M., Samuels, W. J., and Tool, M. R., editors, *The Elgar Companion to Institutional and Evolutionary Economics*, pages 249–253. Edward Elgar, Aldershot, UK.

Nelson, R. R. and Winter, S. G. (1982). *An Evolutionary Theory of Economic Change*. MIT Press, Cambridge, MA, London.

Nix, A. E. and Vose, M. D. (1992). Modeling genetic algorithms with Markov chains. *Annals of Mathematics and Artificial Intelligence*, 5:79–88.

Phlips, L. (1988). *The Economics of Imperfect Information*. Cambridge University Press, Cambridge, UK.

Plott, C. A. (2000). Makets as information gathering tools. *Southern Economic Journal*, 67:1–15.

Press, W. H., Teukolski, S. A., Vetterling, W. T., and Flannery, B. P. (1992). *Numerical Recipes in C. The Art of Scientific Computing*. Cambridge University Press, Cambridge, England, 2 edition.

Rasmussen, E. (1994). *Games and Information. An Introduction to Game Theory*. Blackwell, Oxford, UK, 2 edition.

Rechenberg, I. (1970). *Optimierung technischer Systeme nach Prinzipien der biologischen Evolution.* PhD thesis, Technische Universität Berlin.

Rechenberg, I. (1973). *Evolutionsstrategie: Optimierung technischer Systeme nach Prinzipien der biologischen Evolution.* Frommann–Holzboog, Stuttgart.

Riechmann, T. (1997). Learning and behavioral stability — An economic interpretation of genetic algorithms. Diskussionspapier 209, Universität Hannover, Fachbereich Wirtschaftswissenschaften.

Riechmann, T. (1998a). Genetic algorithms and economic evolution. Diskussionspapier 219, Universität Hannover, Fachbereich Wirtschaftswissenschaften.

Riechmann, T. (1998b). Learning how to learn. Towards an improved mutation operator within GA learning models. In *Computation in Economics, Finance and Engeneering: Economic Systems*, Cambridge, England. Society for Computational Economics.

Riechmann, T. (1999). Learning and behavioral stability — An economic interpretation of genetic algorithms. *Journal of Evolutionary Economics*, 9:225–242.

Riechmann, T. (2000). A model of boundedly rational consumer choice. An agent based approach. Diskussionspapier 232, Universität Hannover, Fachbereich Wirtschaftswissenschaften.

Rome, F. and Sangiovanni-Vincentelli, A. (1991). A theoretical framework for simulated annealing. *Algorithmica*, 6:302–345.

Romer, P. M. (1986). Increasing returns and long run growth. *Journal of Political Economy*, 94:1002–1037.

Romer, P. M. (1992). Two strategies for economic development: Using ideas and producing ideas. In *Proceedings of the World Bank Annual Conference on Development Economics 1992*, pages 63–91.

Rudolph, G. (1994). Convergence analysis of canonical genetic algorithms. *IEEE Transactions on Neural Networks*, 5:96–101.

Samuelson, L. (1997). *Evolutionary Games and Equilibrium Selection.* MIT Press Series on Economic Learning and Social Evolution. MIT Press, Cambridge, MA, London.

Samuelson, P. A. (1958). An exact consumption–loan model of interest with or without the social contrivance of money. *Journal of Political Economy*, 66:467–482.

Sangiovanni-Vincentelli, A. (1991). Editor's foreword. *Algorithmica*, 6:295–301.

Sargent, T. J. (1993). *Bounded Rationality in Macroeconomics.* Claredon Press, Oxford.

Selten, R. (1990). Bounded rationality. *Journal of Institutional and Theoretical Economics (JITE)*, 146:649–658.

Selten, R. (1998). Features of experimentally observed bounded rationality. *European Economic Review*, 42:413–436.

Simon, H. A. (1957). *Models of Man.* John Wiley & Sons, New York, London, Sidney.

Simon, H. A. (1981). *The Sciences of the Artificial.* MIT Press, Cambridge, MA, London, 2 edition.

Simon, H. A. (1987). Bounded rationality. In Eatwell, J., Milgate, M., and Newman, P., editors, *The New Palgrave. A Dictionary of Economics*, volume 3, pages 266–268. MacMillan, London.

Simon, H. A. (1994). Bounded rationality. In Eatwell, J. and Milgate, M., editors, *The New Palgrave. A Dictionary of Economics*, volume 1, pages 266–268. MacMillan, London.

Simon, H. A. (1997). *Empirically Grounded Economic Reason*, volume 3 of *Models of Bounded Rationality*. MIT Press, Cambridge, MA, London.

Stroustrup, B. (1994). *The Design and Evolution of C++*. Addison-Wesley, Cambridge, MA, London.

Stroustrup, B. (1997). *The C++ Programming Language*. Addison-Wesley, Cambridge, MA, London, 3 edition.

Tesfatsion, L. (1997). How economists can get alife. Discussion Paper, Iowa State University.

Tiez, R. (1990). On bounded rationality: Experimental work at the university of frankfurt/main. *Journal of Institutional and Theoretical Economics (JITE)*, 146:659–672.

Tisdell, C. A. (1996). *Bounded Rationality and Economic Evolution. A Contribution to Decision Making, Economics and Management*. Edward Elgar, Cheltenham, UK, Brookfields, US.

Weibull, J. W. (1995). *Evolutionary Game Theory*. MIT Press, Cambridge, MA, London.

Windrum, P. and Birchenhall, C. (1998). Is product life cycle theory a special case? Dominant designs and the emergence of market niches through coevolutionary–learning. *Structural Change and Economic Dynamics*, 9:109–134.

Witt, U. (1985). Coordination of individual economic activities as an evolving process of self–organization. *Economic Appliquée*, XXXVII:569–595.

Witt, U. (1993a). Evolutionary economics: Some principles. In Witt, U., editor, *Evolution in Markets and Institutions*, pages 1–16. Physica–Verlag, Heidelberg.

Witt, U. (1993b). Introduction. In Witt, U., editor, *Evolutionary Economics*, pages xiii–xxvii. Edward Elgar, Aldershot, England.

Wolfstetter, E. (1996). Auctions: An introduction. *Journal of Economic Surveys*, 10:367–420.

Index

Druck:	Strauss Offsetdruck, Mörlenbach
Verarbeitung:	Schäffer, Grünstadt